British Maritime Empire's Falmouth Connection

George E. Applewhite

Abstract

At the beginning of the nineteenth century, the Cornish port of Falmouth was an important base within an ever-expanding British empire. From here, people, letters, goods and information travelled back and forth from Cornwall to the rest of the world.

This thesis investigates the extent to which Falmouth was a significant part of Britain's maritime empire during the period 1800-1850, looking specifically at four areas of interest. First, it argues that Falmouth's Packet Service played a significant role in intelligence gathering during the Napoleonic Wars, victory in which led to major expansion of the British empire. Second, that the town developed Cornwall's mining expertise to the extent that it could be exported to new colonies, or become instrumental in spreading the influence of informal empire. Third, that the import of plant specimens from the colonies had a direct effect on class-based hierarchies of power in and around the town. And finally, that contact between the British and foreigners in and from the port led to renegotiations of identity based on race that were inextricably tied into colonialism.

The role of Cornwall in the dialogue between Britain and its colonies, and the importance of Falmouth as a port within the British empire, have previously been neglected in academic study, with attention given to larger metropolitan locations such as Liverpool and Southampton. This thesis continues work exploring imperialism within one specific locality, shifting in focus from the urban to the rural. In doing this, a diversity of written and archival sources are used to discuss how several elements of empire came together in one place. The work demonstrates that Falmouth was a site clearly affected by colonialism, and was to a certain extent influential within it due to its maritime significance.

Table of Contents

Abstract — 2

Introduction — 6
- A safe harbour — 6
- A maritime community — 9
- The Falmouth identity — 15
- Falmouth and the British empire — 23
- Approaches to history — 25
- A port of the first consequence — 30

Chapter 1: Sightings and secrecy: maintaining communications during the Napoleonic Wars — 34
- Tactics: keeping watch — 43
- Strategy: Deception, interception and the 'Secret Office' — 53
- Putting Falmouth on the map — 62

Chapter 2: Science, technology and trade: exporting Cornwall to the empire — 68
- Creating the legend of Cornish mining — 86
- From Cornwall to Latin America: informal empire — 95
- Cornish mining on the global stage — 108

Chapter 3: The empire garden: plant hunting and hierarchies of power — 115
- Living symbols of power — 131
- Upper class leisure and 'cottager' gardens — 137

Chapter 4: Bringing the empire home: identity and the Other — 151
- Encountering difference — 155
- The Orient in Falmouth — 158
- 'Britishness' and civilisation — 173
- Encounters from Falmouth — 185
- Local and global discourse — 199

Conclusion — 201
- A final sailing — 201
- A new era — 210
- Beyond Falmouth — 215

References — 218

Books	218
Journal articles	230
Websites	232
Archival Sources	238
Newspapers	239
Media	243
Miscellaneous	243

Introduction

A safe harbour

> The action began at twelve o'clock, by the leading ships of the columns breaking through the enemy's line, the Commander in Chief about the tenth ship from the van, the Second in Command about the 12th from the rear, leaving the van of the enemy unoccupied; the succeeding ships breaking through in all parts astern of their leaders, and engaging the enemy at the muzzles of their guns; the conflict was severe; the enemy's ships were fought with a gallantry highly honourable to their officers, but the attack on them was irresistible, and it pleased the Almighty Disposer of all Events, to grant His Majesty's arms a complete and glorious victory: about three p.m. many of the enemy's ships having struck their colours, their line gave way.[1]

Today, the events of October 21, 1805, are well known. The Battle of Trafalgar marked a key turning point in the Napoleonic Wars. Soon after the death of Admiral Lord Nelson, the news of the Admiralty's triumph and the tragic tale of his Lordship's death were recorded in a dispatch by his successor, Cuthbert Collingwood. In this, the era of sail, communicating this news to the general public was more complicated than it might have been in our modern age. The delivery of Collingwood's dispatches would later become a story almost as popular as accounts of the battle itself. Having written the words that would soon echo around Britain, Collingwood called for Lieutenant Lapenotiere of HMS *Pickle*, one of the smallest ships in the fleet, saying: 'Now take these dispatches to England; you will receive £500 and your Commander's commission.'[2] At 9.45 a.m. on 4 November, Lapenotiere finally arrived in Britain, landing at a busy port in the far south-west. The strong winds of previous days had dropped to what was recorded in the ship's log as 'Moderate breezes'.[3] The *Pickle*'s destination, the final point of departure for voyaging British ships, and the first sight of 'Sweet Home'[4] for those returning, was

---

[1] 'The London Gazette Extraordinary', *The Morning Chronicle*, 7 November 1805, p. 1.
[2] Peter Warwick, *Voices from the Battle of Trafalgar* (Cincinnati: David & Charles, 2006), p. 26.
[3] Warwick, p. 27.
[4] *A Panorama of Falmouth* (Falmouth: Cornish Magazine Office, 1827), p. 9.

not Southampton, Liverpool, or even Plymouth. The harbour dubbed 'the most valuable in the United Kingdom' was, in fact, the rural Cornish town of Falmouth.[5]

Falmouth, on the south coast of Cornwall, is a town far younger than many others in the region. Its origins as a town, and its name, date back only to the sixteenth and seventeenth centuries. During the reign of Henry VIII, the present-day settlement was a hamlet named Smithwick, or Smithick. The growth of Falmouth was linked to England's maritime relationship with the rest of the world, notably France and Spain. During the first half of the sixteenth-century, Anglo-French antagonism grew and fears of a French or Spanish attack on England mounted.[6] In 1537, a fleet of Spanish ships became engaged in combat with four French warships in the Carrick Roads – the waterway leading into Falmouth Harbour – highlighting the vulnerability of the Fal area to attack from the sea, and its inability to prevent or halt combat.[7] Having one of the deepest natural harbours in England, Falmouth had sufficient deep water for the anchorage of a fleet of warships and would therefore be a likely invasion point.[8] In response to this threat John Arundell, a Cornish landowner, proposed the erection of defences at the mouth of the harbour.[9] To defend the coastline from raids, a castle fortress was built at nearby Pendennis.[10]

On 5 October 1661, a Royal Charter was granted, marking the transition of the hamlet of Smithwick to the growing town of Falmouth by awarding the new town rights of self-government.[11] After the charter, the population of Falmouth grew and it became an area dominated by maritime industries, supplying provisions to ships and sailors, importing and exporting goods, and after 1689, hosting the Packet Service.[12] This was a branch of the General Post Office, responsible for transporting and

---

[5] Ibid.
[6] 'Defended Cornwall', *Historic Environment Service* <http://www.historic-cornwall.org.uk/flyingpast/images/PDF_downloads/DefendedCornwall.pdf> [accessed 16 July 2012] (p. 2)
[7] Richard Linzey, *Fortress Falmouth*, 2 vols (Swindon: English Heritage, 2000), II, p. 3.
[8] 'List Entry Summary', *Heritage Gateway*, <http://www.heritagegateway.org.uk/Gateway/Results_Single.aspx?uid=1270096&resourceID=5> [accessed 2 August 2012]
[9] Linzey, p. 3.
[10] Linzey, p. 3.
[11] Megan Westley, 'A Royal seal of approval: 350 years of Falmouth', *National Maritime Museum Cornwall* <http://www.nmmc.co.uk/index.php?/collections/curators_choice/a_royal_seal_of_approval_350_years_of_falmouth> [accessed 8 January 2014]
[12] James Whetter, *The History of Falmouth* (Redruth: Dyllansow Truran, 1981), p. 28.

delivering mail overseas. Prior to 1689 and war between Britain and France, any mail destined for Spain was transported overland through France, meaning that when hostilities broke out between the two nations an alternative route had to be created, this time involving passage by sea.[13] Falmouth was chosen as the base of the international mail service due to the natural design of its harbour, being deep enough to allow ships to depart even in low tide, and its relative safety and distance from the privateers that hounded ships in other ports such as Plymouth.[14] Thus, the first route for the Packet ships based in Falmouth was to Spain.[15] As time passed, the Packet Service expanded to meet demand, with many more routes added. By 1808, in the throes of the Napoleonic Wars, there were thirty-nine.[16]

Falmouth was a young town, manufactured and grown rapidly to serve the castle, rather than growing organically. Letters between James I and Sir Nicholas Hals, governor of Pendennis Castle, reveal that the growth of a more substantial settlement at Smithwick was engineered so that the resultant town could serve as a base for servicing ships and supplying troops in the event of an invasion.[17] Falmouth did not have a strong local identity in the same way that other, historic, towns and villages in Cornwall might have done. Its residents hadn't lived there as a community for generations, and as such the town as a whole would have been far less insular and more open to external influences, such as empire. Arthur Norway, the Victorian biographer of the Service, argued that the town's meagre size and lack of importance prior to the founding of the Packets was seen as an advantage by the General Post Office, as this corresponded to a lack of competing trade and 'absence of traditions'.[18] Built to boom – or bust – Falmouth depended on maritime trade and engaged fully with all that it entailed.

---

[13] Whetter, *The Rise of the Port of Falmouth*, p. 21.
[14] David Mudd, *The Falmouth Packets* (Bodmin: Bossiney Books, 1978), p. 5.
[15] M.E. Philbrick, 'Some Falmouth Packet Captains 1729-1832' in *History around the Fal: Part Two* (Exeter: Fal Local History Group/University of Exeter, 1983), pp. 56-82 (p. 56).
[16] Bob Dunstan, *The Book of Falmouth and Penryn* (Buckingham: Barracuda Books Limited, 1975), p. 69.
[17] S. Padfield Oliver, *Pendennis & St Mawes: An Historical Sketch of Two Cornish Castles* (Truro: W. Lake, 1875), p. 22.
[18] Arthur H. Norway, *History of the Post Office Packet Service, Between the Years 1793-1815* (London: Macmillan and Co., 1895), pp. 3-4.

A maritime community

It is natural, therefore, that as a young maritime town dominated by its immense harbour, Falmouth would find its commercial footing in the maritime industries. The Packet Service, which will be expanded upon in far more detail in Chapter One, directly and indirectly employed around 1,000 people within the town by the early nineteenth century, approximately a quarter of the overall population.[19] The activity of Packet vessels, and other trading ships, led to a number of secondary service industries, such as the supply of ships' stores, chandlery and victualling.[20] Shipyards in nearby Flushing – the village that was home to many of the Packet captains – built and repaired both Packet Service and naval vessels.[21]

Private shipping companies also chose to hire or place agents in Falmouth. The Dublin and London Steam Marine Company employed W and E.C. Carne as agents in the town, providing passage and freight services from there to London on its ships.[22] Commercial sailings such as these, in addition to the frequent arrivals and disembarkations of the Packet Service, would have made the harbour a busy and exceptionally noisy place, with a constant influx of people. Louis Simond, a French gentleman visiting in 1809, noted seeing a carriage 'overladen with passengers', and hearing a 'universal clatter of iron on the pavement'.[23] Mail coaches were in frequent passage, while those with less money might travel with Russell's Wagons, which were slower and less comfortable.[24]

The town also had its own naval bank,[25] classical and mathematical school, merchants' hospital for seamen, dispensary, and Custom House and Excise Office. The hospital was supported by those in the employ of the Packet Service, who paid –

---

[19] Whetter, *The History of Falmouth*, p. 21 and 36.
[20] Dunstan, p. 69.
[21] E Bennett, 'Shipbuilding on the Fal. The Early Years' in *History around the Fal: Part Two* (Exeter: Fal Local History Group/University of Exeter, 1983), pp. 23-26.
[22] 'Advertisements and Notices', *Royal Cornwall Gazette, Falmouth Packet & Plymouth Journal*, 3 January 1829.
[23] *Cornwall: the Travellers' Tales*, ed. by Todd Gray (Exeter: The Mint Press, 2000), I p. 82.
[24] Susan Gay, *Old Falmouth* (London: Headley Brothers, 1903), p. 143.
[25] Run by in 1819 by Messrs. Praed, Rogers, Tweedy and Willams. Truro, Cornwall Records Office, X394/13.

in 1815 – sixpence per month for its upkeep.[26] Numerous hotels and inns hosted passengers and ships' crews arriving in the port, among them the Greenbank Commercial and Packet Royal Hotel (still in operation as the Greenbank Hotel) and the Navy Tavern. Indeed, in 1815, there was a total of nineteen lodging houses and nine hotels or inns within Falmouth.[27] There was also a brewery, run by William Allen and known as Allen's Brewery, until his death in the 1840s.[28] Entertainment facilities included a theatre, assembly rooms, and bowling green.[29] In November 1826, the Public Subscription Rooms opened, 'for the general accommodation of gentlemen in the Army, Navy, and Strangers who may visit the town'.[30]

From this description, it becomes clear that Falmouth was a thriving town with commercial interests dictated by its maritime connections. Weight is added to this argument by the fact that during the parliamentary reform of 1832, the town gained representation (subsuming and thereby protecting its 'notoriously corrupt' neighbour Penryn) for the first time, returning two members, Liberal Sir Robert Rolfe and Conservative Lord Tullamore, for Penryn and Falmouth.[31] In contrast, a high number of 'rotten' Cornish boroughs – thirteen, in fact – were completely disenfranchised.[32] Falmouth's inclusion was driven by the Duke of Buckingham's drive to recognise 'large towns [...] which, from their commercial and trading situation, may appear to have become entitled to be represented in Parliament'.[33]

Another interesting indicator of the growing prosperity and commercial importance of Falmouth lies in the fact that the town once contained a thriving Jewish community. Historically, between 1290 and 1656, there were no openly Jewish groups in England, as the religion was condemned and practitioners of it were

---

[26] R Thomas, *A Falmouth Guide* (Falmouth: J. Lake, 1815), p. 56.
[27] Thomas, *A Falmouth Guide*, pp. 76-77.
[28] London, National Archives, PROB 11/1998/15.
[29] Thomas, *A Falmouth Guide*, p. 65.
[30] 'Chronological Table', *Royal Cornwall Gazette, Falmouth Packet & Plymouth Journal*, 20 January 1827.
[31] *By-Elections in British Politics 1832-1914*, ed. by TG Otte and Paul Readman (Woodbridge: The Boydell Press, 2013), p. 61.
[32] 'Imperial Parliament', *Royal Cornwall Gazette, Falmouth Packet & Plymouth Journal*, 9 June 1832.
[33] 'The Duke of Buckingham's Reform Bill', *Royal Cornwall Gazette, Falmouth Packet & Plymouth Journal*, 21 April 1832.

persecuted and even killed.[34] When Oliver Cromwell took over the governance of the country, Judaism was tolerated and synagogues and burial grounds constructed, encouraging a slow process of migration from places such as Holland, Germany and Poland.[35] By the mid-nineteenth century, there were between 35,000 and 40,000 Jews living in Britain, primarily residing in the capital and major ports.[36] This was due to the fact that Jewish communities traditionally settled where commerce was strong and where they were less likely to be excluded by their religion.[37] Falmouth was known as a town in which religions other to the Church of England were tolerated: the Quaker George Croker Fox's family, whose descendents will feature regularly in this thesis, settled in Falmouth in 1759 and prospered.[38]

From 1740, a Jewish community grew up within Falmouth, and by the nineteenth century the town had its own synagogue and Jewish cemetery.[39] The memoirs of Falmouth resident Israel Solomon, born there in 1803, note journeys made by his family to Lisbon for business,[40] demonstrating that the appeal of the town lay in its port and the associated trades that could be carried on in, around and through it. By 1842, there were around seventy or eighty Jews living in Falmouth.[41] This early population originally sustained itself by peddling goods such as cutlery, buckles and jewellery, orchestrated by Zender Falmouth, the first Jew to settle there. Zender encouraged a community to form by paying for peddlers' licenses for Jews and advancing a small stock of items on credit. They then returned to Falmouth each Friday to fulfil religious obligations and replenish their stock. By the early nineteenth century, however, many of Falmouth's Jews instead had their own shops in the town. These included pawnbrokers, silversmiths, watchmakers, coin and bullion agents, clothes dealers, china and glass dealers, and grocers.[42]

---

[34] 'Origins', *National Archives* <http://webarchive.nationalarchives.gov.uk/+/http://www.movinghere.org.uk/galleries/histories/jewish/origins/origins.htm> [accessed 23 May 2014].
[35] Ibid.
[36] Ibid.
[37] Ibid.
[38] Dunstan, p. 46.
[39] Dunstan, pp. 36-37.
[40] Israel Solomon, 'Records of My Family', *The Susser Archive* <http://www.jewishgen.org/jcr-uk/susser/israelsolomonstory.htm> [accessed 12 May 2014].
[41] Dunstan, p. 37.
[42] Godfrey Simmons and Keith Pearce, 'The People' in *The Lost Jews of Cornwall: From the Middle Ages to the Nineteenth Century*, ed. by Keith Pearce and Helen Fry (Bristol: Redcliffe Press, 2000), pp. 196-278 (pp. 211-215).

Todd Endelman views the growth of Jewish port communities such as this as a direct result of the expansion of the Royal Navy in the eighteenth century: creating the need for more maritime services and infrastructures, which in turn stimulated commercial activity.[43] Naval locations such as Portsmouth, Plymouth and Chatham had thriving Jewish communities at the turn of the nineteenth century.[44] In Falmouth, the effect was also created by the presence of the ever-expanding Packet Service. Here, the maritime meant money, and money led to the formation of a tolerant, business-savvy population.

In addition to the thriving Jewish population, there was – as previously noted – a large and active Quaker population in Falmouth. At the centre of this population was the extended Fox family, who were notable and prolific landowners and traders in and around the town. Originally from Wiltshire, a branch of the Fox family moved to Fowey in Cornwall in the early seventeenth century, becoming established as merchants. As Falmouth would later become, Fowey was then a prosperous and busy port with many opportunities for trade. By the mid-eighteenth century, the family business, led by George Croker Fox, had moved to the growing town of Falmouth, which was known for its tolerance of religious sects:[45] the Quakers had been in the town since 1670.[46] Within Falmouth, the Foxes had friends including local clergy of all denominations, the town apparently nurturing a welcoming and open attitude to religion.[47] In 1815, a guide to Falmouth noted multiple places of worship, including an 'independent chapel' built in 1790, a Baptist Chapel built in 1803, a Methodist Chapel dating to 1791, and a Unitarian Meeting from 1812.[48] There was also (as noted) a Jewish synagogue, Roman Catholic Church and, of course, an Anglican church. The Quaker Friends' Meeting House was located in Quay Street and had been built in 1805.[49] The Catholic Church catered not only for residents but also for travellers to the port from other countries. The earliest Catholic Church in the town

---

[43] Todd M. Endelman, *The Jews of Britain, 1656 to 2000* (California: University of California Press, 2002), p. 50.
[44] Ibid.
[45] Charles Fox, *Glendurgan: A Personal Memoir of a Garden in Cornwall* (Penzance: Alison Hodge, 2004), p. 13
[46] Thomas, *A Falmouth Guide*, p. 47.
[47] Ibid.
[48] Thomas, pp. 43-48.
[49] Ibid.

was a hut built by French fishermen for their use, with the later structure being funded by donations from the French royal family.[50] Such an extensive provision for religious minorities makes clear the town's unique demographic composition by the early nineteenth century: this was a religious population consisting of transient visitors to the town and permanent residents attracted by its overseas connections and tolerance.

The rise of Falmouth in terms of prosperity and commerce is again evidenced in the formation of a local newspaper in 1801.[51] Falmouth was a prime location for the introduction of a newspaper, as a great deal of information came into the town through its mail service, and many people conducted trade from the port. The Falmouth Packet ships were so vital to the news service that their moniker even appeared in the newspaper's original title, *The Cornwall Gazette and Falmouth Packet*. Commanders of the Packets worked under orders to gather intelligence of all kinds wherever they went, and reported this back through official forms, journals and letters,[52] and, undoubtedly, through word of mouth in the port. In 1802, the paper was able to boast readers as far away as Liverpool due to the speed at which it was able to print news.[53] The paper claimed that due to its location, it enjoyed 'a decided superiority over every other provincial print, [enabling] us frequently to anticipate even the daily papers of London.'[54] Though the initial newspaper enterprise failed due to the debts of its publisher, Thomas Flindell, from 1803 it was resurrected and printed in Truro as the *Royal Cornwall Gazette*, though the news sources, centred in Falmouth, remained the same.[55]

Clearly, the great amount of people and information that passed through the town made it a natural location for gathering news, and with so many businessmen in the vicinity – or with commercial interests in it – there would have been a real need for overseas intelligence. As early as 1755, news from a ship in Falmouth was being printed in the *General Evening Post*: in this instance, an account of an earthquake in

---

[50] Dunstan, p. 35.
[51] 'Flindell, Thomas (1767-1824)', in *Dictionary of Nineteenth-century Journalism in Great Britain and Ireland*, ed. by Laurel Brake and Marysa Demoor (Gent: Academia Press, 2009), p. 222.
[52] For instance, London, National Archives, ADM 1/4073.
[53] June Palmer, *Truro During the Napoleonic Wars* (London: Allan Bell & Co., 1992), p. 3.
[54] Ibid.
[55] 'Flindell, Thomas (1767-1824)', p. 222.

Lisbon which disrupted shipping.[56] The ship news that the *Royal Cornwall Gazette* printed on its formation was commercially important, and thus valuable, as it allowed the ships' owners, merchants and insurers to track their investments and remain aware of anything that might affect them, while also keeping the relatives of crew up to date.[57] Thus, the newspaper today stands as a strong indicator of Falmouth's early importance in overseas trade, being formed at a time when there were a relatively small number of provincial newspapers in existence, compared to the second half of the nineteenth century.[58] The *Manchester Guardian*, for instance, was formed in 1821, twenty years after the first Falmouth newspaper.[59] In addition to being a marker of importance, the publication will also serve as a highly valuable source of information throughout this thesis, its pages creating a detailed picture of life in Cornwall during the time of empire.

As a young and uniquely maritime location, Falmouth's local identity and civic consciousness were intrinsically linked to the sea. From 1823, the Packet Service was run by the Admiralty, while during the first decades of the nineteenth century, the Navy was also strongly present in the town due to the Napoleonic Wars. In 1794, at least two naval squadrons were based in Falmouth, while many others would have passed through.[60] One might expect that the town would therefore have felt this naval and governmental link in its identity. And yet, this was not entirely so. There seems to have been a persistent and problematic self-differentiation between the people of Falmouth and these official bodies. The town's residents enjoyed their position of power as an essential location for the mails, and as a safe haven for ships in wartime, and formed a local identity in which they were essentially a self-governing arm of officialdom. As this thesis will explain, the town was a vitally important part of the British empire, and this importance is demonstrated by its manifestation in the civic consciousness.

---

[56] Bob Clarke, *From Grub Street to Fleet Street : an illustrated history of English newspapers to 1899* (Aldershot: Ashgate, 2004), p. 202.
[57] Clarke, p. 203.
[58] The *Royal Cornwall Gazette* preceded the formation of newspapers in Wales, according to Linda Colley, *Britons: Forging the Nation 1707-1837* (London: Pimlico, 1992), p. 220.
[59] 'History of the Guardian', *The Guardian* <http://www.theguardian.com/gnm-archive/2002/jun/06/1> [accessed 29 August 2014].
[60] Richard McGrady, *Music and Musicians in Early Nineteenth-Century Cornwall: The world of Joseph Emidy – slave, violinist and composer* (Exeter: University of Exeter Press, 1991), p. 23.

The Falmouth identity

During the Napoleonic Wars, crew members within Falmouth's Packet Service were granted an officially separate identity, affording them exemption from impressment. This meant that because of the vital service provided by the Packets – which delivered military mail and dispatches overseas, while also serving as intelligence agents (a topic to be explored in depth later) – its crew were deemed more useful in its employ than they would be in the Navy. In maritime towns such as Falmouth, men aged 18 to 55 could be 'impressed'; forcibly recruited into military service by press-gangs.[61] Protection papers were issued to cover all Packet crew members and were signed by the Lords of the Admiralty, exempting men working 'in the service of the ship'.[62] Packet men taken as prisoners of war were also given priority when it came to exchanging prisoners with the French. In January 1799, Francis Freeling, Secretary of the General Post Office, wrote to the Lords of the Admiralty enclosing a list of sixty-one captured Packet crew and outlining his command from the Post Master General that 'the earliest Steps may be taken to effect their Exchange.'[63] Within this letter was an additional reminder to 'their Officers in the Impress Service' that they should permit the released prisoners to rejoin their ships without molestation.[64] At every turn, the importance of the Packet man as a member of Britain's wartime society was reinforced.

The power held by the wider population of Falmouth was no less evident when it came to the enforcement of the law and the will of the military and government. The town could serve as an extension of the law when needed, as a port for the landing of military prisoners and French prisoners of war. Two buildings in the town served as inland penitentiaries, while hulks in the harbour imprisoned particularly insubordinate offenders.[65] In 1794, it was reported in the *Oracle and Public Advertiser* that French prisoners in Falmouth were behaving in a more orderly

---

[61] 'Information Sheet No. 078: Impressment', *National Museum of the Royal Navy* <http://www.nmrn-portsmouth.org.uk/sites/default/files/Impressment.pdf> [accessed 12 October 2015].
[62] London, National Archives, ADM 1/4073
[63] London, National Archives, ADM 1/4073
[64] London, National Archives, ADM 1/4073
[65] Dunstan, p. 107.

manner due to the shooting of one of their number.[66] However, there is also evidence that the perception of power within Falmouthians worked against justice when it suited them.

In 1837, a Falmouth seaman by the name of William Woods stood trial with the prospect of seven years' transportation for stealing fish from a trawler.[67] He sought clemency due to his 15 years of unblemished service in the Royal Navy and as a Coastguard Officer, and his good behaviour while in Falmouth Prison. Tellingly, leniency was also sought on the grounds that Woods' original trial was unfair; with it argued that the jury was prejudiced against him because of his role as a Coastguard Officer in a town notorious for smuggling. He was supported in his case by one H Fitzgerald of the Coastguard Service, along with six naval captains. This appeal – which successfully saw Woods having his sentence reduced to one year's imprisonment – serves as a window on the simmering tension between Falmouth as a naval town and the residents' own less compliant proclivities. This was by no means an isolated incident: in 1812 the *West Briton* newspaper had reported that Joseph Platt, a Customs Officer, had been sent death threats signed by 'A Friend to the community, Falmouth', for interfering with the Packet crews' illegal trading.[68] Clearly, though serving as a location for government power, Falmouth offered citizens a parallel sense of authority in their own right.

It is precisely this power, held by Falmouth, and the importance of both the town and its inhabitants to the British empire, that moves this work away from being a study of Cornish identity and the imperial imaginary. Although it will touch upon the emigration of the Cornish overseas, and the presence of tourists in the town, it would be wrong to class Falmouthians as 'Cornish' in terms of identity: as discussed, the town had a unique self-identity. The imperial imaginary depended upon the portrayal of the Cornish as, in James Vernon's words, 'a race distinguished by their 'primitive' and intricate relationship to nature.'[69] In general terms, the people of Cornwall were thought to be marginal: dark and wild due to their Celtic blood, and in essence,

---

[66] 'News', *Oracle and Public Advertiser*, 21 March 1794.
[67] London, National Archives, HO 17/48/83.
[68] *Life in Cornwall in the Early Nineteenth Century* (Truro: D. Bradford Barton Ltd., 1970), p. 36.
[69] James Vernon, 'Border Crossings: Cornwall and the English (imagi)nation' in Imagining Nations, ed. by Geoffrey Cubitt (Manchester: Manchester University Press, 1998), pp. 153-172 (p. 160).

'English but not English', occupying an ambivalent separate sphere.[70] Vernon takes as an example the artists' 'colony' of Newlyn, which was formed in the 1880s when artists such as Stanhope Forbes and Lamorna Birch moved from elsewhere in the UK to Cornwall. To the incomers, Newlyn, in the far west of Cornwall, was at the time a romantically wild area, with the people seemingly hewn by nature to be 'fit habitants of such a region'.[71] This is clearly not the case when it comes to the settlement of Falmouth. Not only were its people engaged with, and at the forefront of, the emergence of the latest technology through the formation of the Royal Cornwall Polytechnic Society (to be discussed at length later), but due to the town's mail routes and frequent sailings they were in no way isolated from the rest of the UK, or indeed, the rest of the world. There was a clear, fast connection between the town and the UK, and it operated as a part of the country. Additionally, unlike Forbes' Newlyn school, where outsiders came in and seemingly 'colonised' the area,[72] Falmouth's people – such as its captains, agents, and Customs inspectors – had power and independence in their own right, with incomers generally being of equal or lesser standing. As such, the locale was an oddity in Cornwall: a separate being from the geographically isolated and racially inferior (as popularly viewed) Cornish masses.[73] Due to this distinction, this thesis – though naturally at times touching upon areas throughout Cornwall – will consider the town of Falmouth as a unique location, with a primary interest in analysing how its remarkable culture and functioning relate to the British empire. It can be viewed not as a colony of 'the savage within',[74] but as a busy administrative centre.

Evidently, while the people of Falmouth considered themselves independent from officialdom in some ways, the British empire as a whole did have a profound impact on civic consciousness. In fact, the unique cosmopolitan character of the port of Falmouth, and the separate local identity of its inhabitants, demonstrates the significant affect had by a phenomenon known as 'time-space compression'. Doreen Massey's 1994 work on 'A Global Sense of Place', though discussing globalisation and communications in the postmodern era, holds great relevance when considering

---

[70] Vernon, p. 153.
[71] Vernon, p. 160.
[72] Vernon, p. 160.
[73] Vernon, p. 157.
[74] Vernon, p. 156.

the British empire in the first half of the nineteenth century. Massey argues that as worldwide communications speed up, the idea of 'places' becomes more uncertain, and retaining a sense of local place more problematic.[75] She writes of 'time-space compression': referring to 'movement and communication across space, to the geographical stretching-out of social relations, and to our experience of all this'.[76] Today, this transcendence of spatial barriers might be seen through email communications, online video calling and Western streets lined with a wide range of what Massey calls 'cultural imports'. However, as she herself admits, this variety of time-space compression can be traced back to early British colonial times, when people travelled further for the first time and new imported and exported products were introduced to societies.[77]

If time-space compression relates to the stretching of geographical boundaries and movement and communication across space, the expansion of the British empire can be seen as a clear instance of this. The GPO Packet Service based in Falmouth provided a high-speed – for the time – international mail service that connected countries to Britain and made communication far easier than it had previously been. By the 1830s, Packet steamships were able to transport mail and passengers from Falmouth to Vigo, in north-west Spain, in just fifty-four hours.[78] The mail coach, keeping communications running around Britain, was 'the age's favourite vehicle', due to its speed.[79] With travel becoming faster, a fascination with time and the number of hours or days a journey took was created. Newspapers such as the *Royal Cornwall Gazette* reported the number of days a Packet ship sailing took as a matter of course: almost every sailing story contained this information. During the Napoleonic Wars, Europe was effectively closed off by blockades and a ban on commercial shipping, though Packet Service activity was allowed to continue, making its vessels the only generally available means of communicating overseas. Cultural imports were also in great demand during the early nineteenth-century. Falmouth, being an active and busy port with many visiting merchants, became a location where new and interesting products, such as Mediterranean fruits, liquor,

---

[75] Doreen Massey, *Space, Place and Gender* (Cambridge: Polity Press, 1994), pp. 146-147.
[76] Massey, p. 147.
[77] Ibid.
[78] Beck, p. 27.
[79] *Elegance and Decadence*. BBC4, 13 September 2011.

and silk, could be found first.[80] It was cultural imports such as this – not to mention the intellectual impact of close contact with the foreign – that distinguished Falmouth's sense of identity from the rest of Cornwall.

However, vastly improved communications networks did not mean that everyone within the empire was able or willing to use them. Most working class people wouldn't be able to afford passage on a Packet ship, which was costly. A steerage ticket to Barbados was thirty pounds,[81] with an average labourer earning only twenty pounds and sixteen shillings a year.[82] Mobility, and control over it, therefore reflects the power that some people have, and others do not.[83] The increased mobility of the East India Company, though initially beneficial to the Cornish copper industry, eventually left people dealing in tin at a disadvantage. By making more colonial connections, and creating new overseas trade links, the Company was able to insist on lower profit margins for the Cornish by threatening to take their business elsewhere.[84] To excluded groups in the nineteenth century, the British empire was simply an idea and a construction, and their local vicinity remained of paramount interest and importance. It is for this reason that this thesis will not focus solely on the empire as a global network. Many of the inhabitants of Falmouth would have been concerned only with their local area, and the effect that the empire had upon it.

There is much to be discerned about identity in nineteenth-century Falmouth from the material available to researchers, and in particular, it is important to note the absence of a meaningful presence of some social groups within the town's activities. The voices of women will be sadly outweighed by those of men in this thesis. Though the diaries of Caroline Fox have been consulted, she appears to have been a rare quantity in terms of historical visibility. Fox was an extremely well-educated woman living in a Quaker household in which the equality of the sexes was

---

[80] Daniel Lysons, *Magna Britannia: Cornwall* (London: T. Cadell and W. Davies, 1814), p. 101.
[81] R. Thomas, *A Falmouth Guide* (Falmouth: J. Lake, 1815), p. 70.
[82] 'Agricultural Repertory', *Royal Cornwall Gazette, Falmouth Packet & Plymouth Journal*, 28 January 1815.
[83] Massey, p. 149.
[84] *Papers respecting the negotiation with His Majesty's ministers for a renewal of the East-India Company's exclusive privileges for a further term after the 1st March 1814*, p. 89.

promoted.[85] Her portrayal of life in the port is lively and descriptive, and she was more involved in the daily interactions of her male peers than many other women of the time. In fact, it is Fox who provides some of the most fascinating insights into the 'male' scientific and cultural life of Falmouth. In most other historical records, there is a clearly dominant masculine voice, most likely due in part to the industrial and maritime sphere upon which I am focusing, and the restrictions on women's access to time-space compression. In this context, the feminine role seems generally to have been narrowed to that of a passive participant or watcher: they are almost exclusively present in James Williamson's records of life aboard Packet Service vessels as accompanying passengers only. Generally – taking one Miss Powell, 'a very pleasant and agreeable lady "of a certain age"' as an example – they accompanied wealthy men travelling to the colonies, either as wives or servants.[86] Miss Powell travelled in 1829 to serve her employer, Sir Peregrine Marshland, in Halifax. On other voyages, women are absent altogether: Williamson's account of an April 1830 journey to St Domingo, Mexico and Havana notes twenty-one male crew members and five male passengers aboard.[87] Most lone travellers were male, signifying how time-space compression was – as it continues to be – an exclusive and often isolating experience for those without mobility. In this sense, though Falmouth was a town with a greater than usual acceptance of religion and race, it was not remarkable in any way for its attitude toward the sexes. While women were certainly active within the town, their realm was generally separate. When it comes to discussions of the Royal Cornwall Polytechnic Society and Royal Horticultural Society of Cornwall, for instance, women are present in domestic spheres such as 'fancy work', watercolour painting, and indigenous plants,[88] but not in areas that relate to mobility within time-space compression, such as mining technology and

---

[85] Caroline Fox, *Memories of Old Friends: Being Extracts from the Journals and Letters of Caroline Fox*, ed. by Horace N. Pym (Philadelphia: J. B. Lippincott & Co., 1882), p. xviii.
[86] James Williamson, 'Journal of a Voyage from Falmouth to Halifax & Bermuda and back', *Maritime Views* <http://www.nmmc.co.uk/index.php?/packet_surgeons_journals/voyage_3/> [accessed 26 February 2014]
[87] James Williamson, 'Journal of a Voyage from Falmouth to St Domingo, Mexico & Havana & back', *Maritime Views* <http://www.nmmc.co.uk/index.php?/packet_surgeons_journals/voyage_6/> [accessed 1 March 2014]
[88] See, for instance, 'Cornwall Polytechnic Society', *Royal Cornwall Gazette, Falmouth Packet & Plymouth Journal*, 28 December 1833 and 'Royal Horticultural Society of Cornwall', *Royal Cornwall Gazette, Falmouth Packet & Plymouth Journal*, 30 September 1836.

exotic imports. Due to this, and a desire to restrict the focus of this work to Falmouth's links to empire, the thesis will naturally have a male bias.

Within Falmouth, therefore, some had the ability to travel to and from the British empire, while others instead interacted with the colonies and Europe through the people and products that came into their town. While the Packet Service and Falmouth Harbour provided the most definite link between Falmouth and the rest of the world, the town itself was, in many less striking ways, consistently engaging with colonialism through influential figures, trade, and visiting mariners. The town was unusual for the way in which it served as a contact zone for the empire, allowing for a wide interaction with the colonies and colonial peoples, even among those who were not in a position to travel. This thesis will argue that time-space compression had a marked impact on local surroundings, as it did on the town's civic consciousness and collective identity. Already, we have seen how the townspeople felt themselves to be separate and unique, with a sense of power offered by their geographically advantageous position. Without travelling away from the town, residents' lives were impacted upon by its connectivity. However, running alongside a concern with the local was the creation and promotion of a British national identity, which, like time-space compression, attempted to bind together the British at home and in colonies abroad, in order that they feel part of one whole.

The British empire was constituted, as Jane Carey and Jane Lydon argue, of 'networks of power, knowledge, opportunity and mobility'.[89] Through these transnational circulation networks flowed a constant traffic of people, ideas, goods, and cultures. The ever-changing and multitudinous discourses of empire were constructed through connections between colonial sites.[90] In this way, what Lester describes as 'the trans-global constitution of the network' led to a permeable imperial 'centre' that is perhaps better viewed as circuits connecting Britain and its

---

[89] Jane Carey and Jane Lydon, 'Introduction: Indigenous Networks' in *Indigenous Networks: Mobility, Connections and Exchange*, ed. by Jane Carey and Jane Lydon (New York: Routledge, 2014), pp. 1-26 (p. 1).
[90] David Lambert and Alan Lester, 'Introduction: Imperial Spaces, Imperial Subjects' in *Colonial Lives Across the British Empire: Imperial Careering in the Long Nineteenth Century*, ed. by David Lambert and Alan Lester (Cambridge: Cambridge University Press, 2006), pp. 1-31 (p. 9).

colonies.[91] Institutions such as the newspaper press provided a means of disseminating discourses of empire and creating a sense of global community, with regional or national publications, including Falmouth's *Royal Cornwall Gazette*, reporting news received from each other.[92] The Packet Service assisted in this by physically transporting newspapers from colonies to each other, or to Britain, free of charge.[93] The result was 'well-traversed circuits of information': 'communicative circuits'[94] of which Falmouth was a key part. Information wasn't purely shared, however. Discourses, such as those of technology or the emancipation of slaves, were created through these circuits of communication; ultimately creating the means for 'the diffusion of an appropriate form of civilisation around the world.'[95]

This thesis will consequently view Falmouth as one of many highly influential colonial spaces within a global community. The mutual constitution of colonial and British culture depended on sites such as this: maritime bases facilitating the passage of ships.[96] In turn, suggest David Lambert and Alan Lester, such constant contact led each site to develop its own, unique identity or character.[97] This reinforces the sense that participation within a global imperial community led to a reciprocal, two-way dialogue, rather than the site functioning as a simple, one-direction gateway. The character and identity of Falmouth was thus substantially marked by its links with the British empire. The main and overarching theoretical stance taken throughout this work will consequently be the consideration of Falmouth as a gateway to empire, through which people, goods and ideas flowed. The result of this was the creation of a unique cultural and intellectual sphere greatly affected by the growing phenomenon of time-space compression.

---

[91] Alan Lester, 'British Settler Discourse and the Circuits of Empire', *History Workshop Journal*, 54 (2002), 24-48 (p. 25).
[92] Lester, p. 31.
[93] Lester, p. 32.
[94] Ibid.
[95] Lester, p. 44.
[96] Lambert and Lester, p. 10.
[97] Lambert and Lester, p. 14.

Falmouth and the British empire

In recent years, a move has been made by some academics towards narrowing the focus on Britain to more specific areas, recognising individual locations and their role within the wider empire. This sense of a key port serving as a gateway is an idea formed in a small number of other publications. One text that successfully studies a single locality and its relation to empire is the work *Southampton: gateway to the British Empire*, published in 2007, edited by Miles Taylor.[98] In this work, Taylor and contributing writers seek to address what they perceive to be the neglect of Southampton's imperial history by exploring and mapping out the ways in which this location contributed to the empire.[99] Taylor argues that Southampton was once a 'gateway to and from the empire', as, arguably, was Falmouth, but despite the town's once-global reach, the book is written from the perspective of 'a local and regional case study', with contributors seeking to explore the extent to which daily life in provincial areas such as this were affected by imperialism.[100] This marks a departure from the focus of many works on colonialism, which often look out from Britain to the empire to discuss the effect this wider empire had on a colony or former colony. From the perspective of exploring Falmouth's imperial past, this is an interesting work to study for the way in which it approaches its subject – exploring the local in a global context – and for the method adopted in doing this. In an attempt to tell the story of Southampton from a local perspective, the histories of real and influential people and organisations, such as the Earl of Carnarvon, David Livingstone, and the Southampton School of Art, and specific moments in time, such as the Titanic disaster, are represented. This is an approach which will be evident in this thesis, as a local perspective is sought through the traces of characters such as Barclay and Caroline Fox, and numerous Packet Service employees, through events and moments in time such as the Napoleonic Wars and Cornish emigration, and through organisations such as the Royal Cornwall Polytechnic Society and the General Post Office (GPO).

---

[98] *Southampton: Gateway to the British Empire*, ed. by Miles Taylor (London: I. B. Tauris, 2007)
[99] Miles Taylor, 'Preface' in *Southampton: gateway to the British Empire*, pp. x-xii (p. xi).
[100] Ibid.

In an approach similar to that adopted by Taylor et al, the 2008 book *The empire in one city?*, edited by Sheryllyne Haggerty, Anthony Webster and Nicholas J. White, recognises the importance of Liverpool in the British empire, and urges a discussion of the local in relation to imperialism.[101] John M. MacKenzie, in his introduction to the work, states: 'It is clear that the mutual and interactive relationship between Britain, global power and its empire [...] can be fully understood only through a series of local histories.'[102] The editors' introduction observes that while other texts discussing Liverpool during the time of empire have been produced, none engages in questioning how the city related to the empire, or how the empire in turn impacted on the city and its identity.[103] This notion of reciprocity, and the effect that the local and global had on each other, becomes a key concept in the text. Liverpool was not only a 'gateway to empire', but also a product of it: the gateway 'to' empire being more of a revolving door through which ideas and influences could also come back into the city.[104] I would argue that a similar situation exists with regard to existing literature on the topic of Falmouth. Its history has been discussed, but rarely in academic circles and, within these circles, a study of imperialism and a reciprocal relationship between town and empire has not been carried out.

What marks this work on Falmouth as different is its comparatively rural, and geographically small, setting. Liverpool, Southampton and Glasgow were all cities or large towns, and existing research into the local and the empire has taken place within an urban context, while Falmouth has only ever expanded to the size of a busy rural town. The 1999 book *Imperial Cities*, edited by Felix Driver and David Gilbert and also produced with an introduction by MacKenzie, is specific in its focus only on urban locations.[105] By 2008, however, MacKenzie seems to recognise the importance of smaller locations in his hopes that Haggerty, Webster and White's work will encourage further research into the 'cities, towns and localities' of Britain.[106] It will be the argument of this thesis that a small, rural location, separated

---

[101] *The empire in one city?: Liverpool's Inconvenient Past*, ed. by Sheryllynne Haggerty, Anthony Webster and Nicholas J. White (Manchester: Manchester University Press, 2008)
[102] John M. MacKenzie, 'General Editor's Introduction' in *The empire in one city?*, p. ix.
[103] Sheryllyne Haggerty, Anthony Webster and Nicholas J. White, 'Introduction: The empire in one city?' in *The empire in one city?*, pp. 1-34 (p. 4).
[104] MacKenzie, 'Afterword' in *The empire in one city?*, p. 225.
[105] John M. MacKenzie, 'General Editor's Introduction' in *Imperial Cities*, p. xi.
[106] MacKenzie, 'General Editor's Introduction' in *The empire in one city?*, p. ix.

by distance from metropolitan centres such as London, could nevertheless function as a valued and valuable part of the British empire. Readers may wonder why Falmouth itself, which has already been described as a small, rural location with a somewhat fleeting interaction with empire, matters? This work will not simply provide a parochial history or protect and promote the legacy of this port, though that is certainly a worthwhile result. It is instead intended that it will function as a means of better understanding the wider British empire and imperial history through a concentrated lens.

Approaches to history

Within this thesis, context is of vital importance in examining the historical discourses of the period 1800-1850, not only in the study of literature but across a variety of other texts, from fields such as science, technology and art. The new historicist approach, which emerged in the 1980s, altered the way that history is now discussed, with its emphasis on original sources and the contemporary context of these sources. This method celebrates interdisciplinarity by combining many different traditional areas of study: an approach utilised in *Literature, Science and Exploration in the Romantic Era* by Fulford, Lee and Kitson, in which the topics of literature, science and colonialism are studied as one history, instead of three separate contexts.[107] Accordingly, within this thesis there will be a strong emphasis on the context surrounding events and works, as none can, will, or should, be viewed in isolation.

The importance of context when approaching historical study is also discernible in Carl Thompson's text *The Suffering Traveller and the Romantic Imagination*, which discusses travel in the Romantic period.[108] Another key approach in Thompson's text is the utilisation of anecdotal evidence, through the words of real people such as William Hazlitt, Mariana Starke, Lord Byron, and Robert Southey. Thompson also refers to popular culture within his work, rather than restricting himself to a specific

---

[107] Tim Fulford, Debbie Lee and Peter J. Kitson, *Literature, Science and Exploration in the Romantic Era* (Cambridge: Cambridge University Press, 2004)
[108] Carl Thomspon, *The Suffering Traveller and the Romantic Imagination* (Oxford: Clarendon Press, 2007)

canon of Romantic literature.[109] Gallagher and Greenblatt support the use of anecdotal evidence in research, arguing that in their own work, where 'real bodies and living voices' had long fallen silent, anecdote could be utilised as the trace closest to actual experience.[110]

Gallagher and Greenblatt, and indeed Thompson, place the literary text and the anecdote side by side, in a conjunction that the two former describe as 'powerful and compelling'.[111] They argue that both are texts, and also fictions in the way that they are made, but that the two are essentially different.[112] In this difference lies strength: combining two kinds of text – the anecdotal and the literary – provides a new perspective on events and what is termed 'the touch of the real'.[113] Referring to the anecdote and previously unheard voices when outlining the context of a canonical text, for instance, allows for a new view of a familiar history, which may differ from the accepted version of history.[114]

When seeking to provide a strong contextual background to research such as this, original source material from the time period must be a useful resource. A large and important part of the active researching of this project has been dedicated to archival research, utilising both local and national repositories. Ben Gidley, in his discussion of historical and archival research, identifies four main types of possible source material: primary, secondary, oral, and documentary.[115] While secondary sources such as existing academic publications and historical accounts will be useful in laying the contextual and theoretical foundations for this work, the majority of the research undertaken will involve the use of primary sources, 'actual records that have survived from the past', and documentary sources, 'written sources' which may include items such as letters, scrapbooks, and newspaper clippings.[116] The types of sources utilised in this research have included official and unofficial letters,

---

[109] Thompson, p. 13.
[110] Catherine Gallagher and Stephen Greenblatt, *Practicing New Historicism* (Chicago: University of Chicago Press, 2000), p. 30.
[111] Gallagher and Greenblatt, p. 31.
[112] Ibid.
[113] Ibid.
[114] Gallagher and Greenblatt, pp. 36-37.
[115] Ben Gidley, 'Doing historical and archival research' in *Researching Society and Culture*, ed. by Clive Seale, 2nd edn (London: Sage Publications, 2004), pp. 249-264 (p. 250).
[116] Ibid.

newspapers, illustrations, diaries and journals, maps, and forms. Primary and documentary sources such as these are the best resource for this work as it falls into Gidley's category of research where archival sources provide 'the only means of access'.[117] In researching the history of a specific locality such as Falmouth, local archives are naturally of great value. Work on the project has included visits to the Cornwall Records Office and the Courtney Library, both in Truro, the Cornish Studies Library in Redruth, Bartlett Library in Falmouth, and Morrab Library in Penzance. Records relating to the GPO Packet Service and the Admiralty in Falmouth have been consulted at the National Archives in Kew.

One difficulty which must be taken into account by those carrying out work with archives is the possible bias or political motivation, conscious or unconscious, behind the archive as an institution. This relates to the new historicist belief that objectivity is impossible, and that every culture is embedded with its own ways of thinking.[118] As Julie Bacon notes, while documentation may exist to provide an inventory of the archive, narrate its historical trajectory, and explain access policy, 'the entirety of the motives of the archive founder, and the archivist's hands thereafter, is no more fully known to them than any individual can see the entire shape of their imagination and agency.'[119] Foucault sees the archive as a set of discourses that has been considered true 'knowledge' in a certain period, implying a bias and process of selection that belies its apparent objectivity.[120] The archive becomes a centre of control from which some practices or types of knowledge are included and some are excluded, depending on current attitudes.[121] What he calls 'practices' which Thomas Flynn describes as 'the intelligible background for actions' – establishing norms and controls, and thus making a distinction between true and false discourse possible – become 'positivities': unexamined beliefs or enduring discourses that seem factual and not intentional.[122] As a result of this, the archive organises knowledge according to what was allowed to be deemed true.

---

[117] Gidley, p. 252.
[118] Gallagher and Greenblatt, pp. 5-7.
[119] Julie Bacon, 'Archive, Archive, Archive!', *Circa Art Magazine*, No. 117 (2007), 50-59 (p. 51).
[120] Thomas Flynn, 'Foucault's Mapping of History' in *The Cambridge Companion to Foucault*, ed. by Gary Gutting, 2nd edn (Cambridge: Cambridge University Press, 2005), pp. 29-48 (pp. 30-31). Cambridge Collections Online ebook.
[121] Ibid.
[122] Flynn, p. 31.

Taking the discipline of science as an example, the process of organising knowledge led to certain types of research being classed as one set or field – science – and others not to be.[123] The seemingly unrelated areas of clinical medicine and geology thus become linked, and would be categorised as science in an archive. From this we can see that not only is discourse unreliable in terms of objectivity, but that the apparent cohesion of fields and disciplines is not a natural thing. The archive is not an objectively gathered set of documents but part of a system of control.

An archive is never natural and always constructed: Peter Fritzsche views it as the production of a group of 'heirs' to memory and history; 'a group that knows itself by cultivating a particular historical trajectory.'[124] Francis X. Blouin mirrors these views, arguing that archives can implicitly reinforce political and cultural constructs through the presentation, selection and organisation of records.[125] Some records, being deemed more culturally valuable or important, may be highlighted in more detail or made easier to access through better organisation. For example, many hundreds of letters concerning the GPO Packet Service are filed in the National Archives under one archive number, given the title 'Letters from the Post Office', and a two-line description that gives little idea what the record really contains beyond the basic information: 'Admiralty, and Ministry of Defence, Navy Department: Correspondence and Papers. ORIGINAL SERIES (1st group): 1660-1839. POST OFFICE. Letters from the Post Office.'[126] However, the catalogue entry for a collection of papers relating to Second World War bomb damage, arguably a much more popular topic with the public, is accessed directly from a list of the archive's key sources, given the title 'Ministry of Home Security: Research and Experiments Department, Registered Papers' and accompanied by a seven line paragraph of descriptive text which details precisely what is included in the record.[127] It is difficult to mediate this particular problem, though making oneself

---

[123] Flynn, p. 32.
[124] Peter Fritzsche, 'The Archive', *History and Memory*, 17 (2005), 13-44 (p. 16).
[125] Francis X. Blouin, Jr., 'History and Memory: The Problem of the Archive', *PMLA*, 119 (2004), 296-298 (p. 298).
[126] 'ADM 1/4071', *National Archives*,
<http://discovery.nationalarchives.gov.uk/SearchUI/s/res?_q=ADM+1%2F4071&x=0&y=0> [accessed 9 October 2012].
[127] 'Series reference HO 192', *National Archives*,
<http://www.nationalarchives.gov.uk/catalogue/displaycataloguedetails.asp?CATLN=3&CATID=7747&SearchInit=4&SearchType=6&CATREF=HO+192> [accessed 9 October 2012].

aware of it and conducting a thorough search through material that may not be well signposted is one method of mitigating its effects. In this instance, when receiving a large box of historical records, the approach adopted has been to consult every one in the box in order to pursue a line of enquiry through to the end of what the archive can offer. Documents such as undelivered soldiers' letters or Packet Ship voyage paperwork, which in some instances comprises many hundreds of pieces and may not be considered historically important in a general sense, must be viewed in this way.

The sheer quantity of material available in archival research can also pose an issue. Sifting through the aforementioned hundreds of Packet Service letters can naturally lead to investigator bias as the material must somehow be consolidated, or the most useful items prioritised over others which seem less so. This highlights once again that archival research cannot and should not be considered objective. Just as the motives of the archivist or authors of documents cannot be always be discerned, the researcher themselves may be influenced by many factors that shape the resultant selection and interpretation of documents. This problem is difficult to mitigate, but can be made clear at the outset of this research: while based in fact and the material available for this period of history, the thesis should not be considered an objective history but a subjective account.

When working with primary sources, the potential subjectivity and bias inherent within the first-hand accounts of events themselves must also be borne in mind. One of the predominant problems associated with archival research and so-called 'objective' investigation and representation of findings, is that one can never be sure that the documents being studied are actually objective or accurate in themselves. In the sense that almost all documents studied in archives – or otherwise – are produced by someone, they are all vulnerable to bias and their subjectivity should be taken into account. In the case of some – for instance, the journals of Caroline Fox – editing has already taken place on multiple levels in the production of material. Fox herself interpreted events as they occurred in an unavoidably biased way, as all people must, and further revisited and edited the scene when writing out a journal entry. Her original diary was destroyed on her death, after carefully selected and edited sections were published for public consumption. While the journal remains an extremely valuable resource for the historian, it can never be a window onto events as they happened during Fox's lifetime, but rather a view onto portions of the life and opinions of Fox herself. These are, as Himani Bannerji argues, distanced from the present through time and space, and ultimately Fox's work is a 're-presentation' of events influenced by some sort of political bias.[128] In many ways, the acceptance of this lends a subjective and personal view that is worth analysing every bit as much as the event itself might have been. This thesis frequently concerns itself with issues of identity relating to empire, and for this the study of individuals is paramount and their subjectivity embraced. In this thesis, the potential bias of the Foxes in their journals will be explored as a topic in itself, potentially revealing new interpretations of events.

A port of the first consequence[129]

The primary aim of this thesis is therefore to draw together many elements of empire and society within Falmouth to consider the extent to which, as a whole, they demonstrate an interaction between the town and the British empire during the first half of the nineteenth century. Its four main topics of interest: the maritime in the Napoleonic Wars, mining, horticulture, and travel, will each be explored in one chapter. Though seemingly disparate topics at first glance, each of these themes is intrinsically bound up in Falmouth's role as a port, and each contributes in some way to illustrating how the dynamics of power that were held at the heart of empire affected, or were affected by, the town and its people.

The power of the British empire was forged to a great extent in the Napoleonic Wars, in which Britain emerged as the victor against France in 1815. From this great success, new colonies were formed and global influence spread. Chapter One, 'Sightings, smuggling and secrecy: maintaining communications during the Napoleonic Wars' will examine the role that Falmouth and its Packet Service played in this conflict. During the period from 1803-1815, the town's Packet ships regularly

---

[128] Himani Bannerji, 'Politics and the Writing of History' in *Nation, Empire, Colony: Historicizing Gender and Race*, ed. by Ruth Roach Pierson and Nupur Chaudhuri (Bloomington: Indiana University Press, 1998), pp. 287-302 (pp. 287-288).

[129] A guidebook of 1815 notes with regard to Falmouth that 'As a sea-port, it is of the first consequence in the county.' Thomas, *A Falmouth Guide*, p. 35.

travelled into hostile areas to deliver mail, and the service was resourcefully transformed from a simple postal system to a vehicle for intelligence. This chapter will explore the differences between tactical and strategic intelligence, highlighting the ways in which Falmouth contributed to both. On a tactical level, its ships were able to quickly report on the location and condition of British and enemy vessels, providing information useful in an immediate setting. The Packet Service also had a valuable role to play in the practice of strategic intelligence. It functioned as a part of the General Post Office's little-known 'Secret Office', intercepting mail for covert study. The Service also adopted its own counter-intelligence measures to protect government dispatches from falling into enemy hands. Considering strategy at home in addition to on the seas, this chapter will conclude with a discussion of maps produced during this period, which highlight the importance of Falmouth in warfare.

The second chapter, 'Science, technology and trade: exporting Cornwall to the empire', will move on to consider the topic of mining – for which Cornwall has long been famous – in the underexplored context of Falmouth. By charting the formation of the Royal Cornwall Polytechnic Society, a group dedicated to innovation in mining matters, it will discuss how knowledge produced in Cornwall was made valuable and exportable due to its geographic origins. This powerful, economically important knowledge, whether contained in technology and papers or within the body of the Cornish miner himself, afforded the British empire a means of entry into locations such as Latin America and South Australia. This chapter will draw upon the work of Daniel Headrick in *The Tentacles of Progress* to consider how the transfer of technology can relate to the spreading of power into new areas.[130] It will argue that by transferring people and technologies from the British mainland to new territories, the empire was able to establish sites of informal and formal empire, and to contain the power that knowledge created, rather than sharing or relinquishing it. Though this export would ultimately damage the Cornish economy by creating overseas competition, its legacy can still be observed today in communities of Cornish descendents around the globe.

---

[130] Daniel R. Headrick, *The Tentacles of Progress: Technology Transfer in the Age of Imperialism, 1850-1940* (New York: Oxford University Press, 1988)

Science in the noisy, industrial realm of mining and engineering will find its counterpart in the natural world of plants and horticulture. The wealth and power enjoyed by those involved in exporting Cornwall's mining industry was invested and displayed through importing exotic plants. Chapter three, 'The empire garden: plant hunting and hierarchies of power' studies how horticulture came to be a means for the creation and reinforcement of power hierarchies in Falmouth. Fragile and exotic products of the empire were imported through the port's maritime industries – such as the Packet Service and East India Company – and used to create grand subtropical gardens that marked their owners out as some of the richest and most powerful in the region. Utilising ideas in Victorian writer Thorstein Veblen's *The Theory of the Leisure Class*, published only fifty years after the period of discussion,[131] the chapter will consider the hierarchical aspects of plant hunting and horticulture, positing that groups such as the Royal Horticultural Society of Cornwall were formed to allow the wealthy to share and discuss specimens, and thus to demonstrate their own social rank. The poorer classes were encouraged to enter into this discursive space to a limited extent, but were denied the opportunity to possess or exhibit the valuable plants of empire. The power dynamics of plant owning will thus be explored in an attempt to demonstrate the effect of these colonial imports in creating a hierarchy based on access to empire, which was ultimately dependent on social power and wealth.

The power dynamics of empire also permeated everyday life and perception to the extent that they affected how the residents of Falmouth viewed themselves and others; as already touched upon. The fourth chapter, 'Bringing the empire home: identity and the Other', will focus on Falmouth as a contact zone for encounters between the British and the foreign. As a busy port with travel routes stretching across the world, Falmouth welcomed visitors of many nationalities. This chapter will argue that, whether consciously or unconsciously, these encounters between the peoples of home and abroad took place within a context of power and ideological representation. Through meetings in or from the town, residents such as the Fox family were able to situate the people they met within an existing colonial dialogue – albeit a negotiable one – in order to generate perceptions of their own identity and

---

[131] Thorstein Veblen, *The Theory of the Leisure Class* (London: Penguin Books, 1994)

define those that were other to it. Taking as its theoretical starting-point Catherine Hall's 2008 work 'Culture and Identity in Imperial Britain', in which she discusses the process of Othering in relation to British identity,[132] this chapter will progress to discussion of more specific races, or areas of identity, such as that of Indian visitors to Falmouth. These individual case studies will consider the work of other academics such as Edward Said,[133] Derek Bryce,[134] and Vincent Brown.[135] Analysis will take place using the first-hand accounts of individuals such as Barclay and Caroline Fox, and the Packet Service surgeon James Williamson. Through these sources, it will be made clear that a complex mixture of face to face encounters and existing stereotypes led the empire to profoundly impact on British identity.

This introduction, despite having only touched upon Falmouth's imperial connections, provides a strong indication of the busy and vibrant place it had become during the first half of the nineteenth century. One of the major contributors to the volume of traffic through the town was its Packet Service. Though founded in the late seventeenth century, it was during the Napoleonic Wars that this service expanded dramatically to connect the town, and Britain, with sites all over the world. During this conflict, the Packet ships of Falmouth braved dangerous conditions, often in enemy territory, to deliver mail and dispatches. More than this, however, they also became a vital part of the war in the sphere of intelligence.

---

[132] Catherine Hall, 'Culture and Identity in Imperial Britain' in *The British Empire: Themes and Perspectives*, ed. by Sarah Stockwell (Oxford: Blackwell Publishing, 2008), pp. 199-217.
[133] Edward Said, *Orientalism* (London: Penguin Books, 2003).
[134] Derek Bryce, 'The Absence of Ottoman, Islamic Europe in Edward W. Said's *Orientalism*', *Theory, Culture & Society*, 30 (2013), 99-121.
[135] Vincent Brown, *The Reaper's Garden: Death and Power in the World of Atlantic Slavery* (Cambridge, Massachusetts: Harvard University Press, 2008)

Chapter 1: Sightings and secrecy: maintaining communications during the Napoleonic Wars

> Falmouth's maritime success was based not on bales of wool loaded for export, nor on the products of the Cornish mines, nor sugar or tobacco or wine or slaves, nor on the presence of a naval fleet, but on an abstract commodity that would grow in importance over the coming centuries. Falmouth's trade was *information*.'[1]

Today, one of the legacies of Falmouth's Packet ships during the Napoleonic Wars lies in an image that depicts a captain and his crew in the thick of battle. The painting *Captain William Rogers Capturing the 'Jeune Richard', 1 October 1807*, by Samuel Drummond (Fig. 1) depicts Falmouth master Rogers[2] as an heroic figure, fighting off several French privateers. Surrounded by a light that seems to emanate from him, Rogers is unperturbed by the sword that is about to be brought down upon his head, or by the dead body his enemy stands on. The portrait represents the events of October 1807, when Rogers' Packet ship *Windsor Castle* was attacked by the *Jeune Richard* on a voyage to the West Indies.[3] Though, in Rogers' own words, 'every exertion was made to get away', the Packet could not escape and at noon, the privateer 'got within gunshot, hoisted French colours and began her fire'.[4] Their attacker was a far more powerful ship and had over three times as many crew. An attempt by the French to board the *Windsor Castle* was successfully resisted with pikes, before the Packet fired upon it with 'double grape, cannister, and one hundred musket balls' and Rogers and five crewmembers boarded the ship.[5] Not only did Rogers, only an acting commander, effectively prevent capture of the ship and seizure of his cargo, he and his twenty-seven compatriots managed also to take the *Jeune Richard* for the British and to kill or wound fifty-five of its crew.[6] Fifteen uninjured men aboard the *Windsor Castle* then secured the remaining thirty-eight on the privateer, putting each in irons.[7] On his return, Rogers became a hero, celebrated

---

[1] Marsden, p. 148.
[2] Who was contradictorily named as John Rogers, not William, in the GPO's version of events. London, National Archives, ADM 1/4073.
[3] London, National Archives, ADM 1/4073.
[4] W. Jago, 'The Heroes of the Old Falmouth Packet Service' in *Journal of the Royal Institution of Cornwall* (Truro: Lake and Lake, 1895), XIII, pp. 204-208 (p. 206).
[5] Jago, p. 207.
[6] London, National Archives, ADM 1/4073.
[7] Sabine Baring-Gould, *Cornish Characters and Strange Events* (London: John Lane, 1909), p. 624.

not only with a painting but with the thanks of the Postmaster-General, one hundred guineas, a share of the prize money, promotion to Captain, the freedom of the city of London, and an illuminated address and sword of honour.[8]

Fig. 1: Painting of William Rogers

Samuel Drummond, *Captain William Rogers Capturing the 'Jeune Richard'*, *1 October 1807*. National Maritime Museum, Greenwich, London, Greenwich Hospital Collection.

Drummond's portrait, painted in the wake of the battle, is indicative of the brief fame Rogers and his ship enjoyed. Its style places it firmly in the genre of eighteenth and early-nineteenth century history painting, which dramatically re-created important

---

[8] Jago, p. 207.

events and stories.⁹ Depictions often focused on highly significant characters, such as politicians, biblical or classical figures, and royalty, showing them within the setting of famous events.¹⁰ Rogers joined such illustrious company as Oliver Cromwell, Elizabeth I and Anne Boleyn, painted by David Wilkie Wynfield, and Alexander the Great, the Archangel Michael, and Admiral Lord Nelson, by Benjamin West. Drummond himself also painted the death of Nelson, in addition to more traditional portraits of high-ranking officials such as the Chief of the Bank of England and the Duke of Sussex.¹¹ The painting of Rogers points to the public appeal that the capture of the *Jeune Richard*, and the victory of the weaker party, held.

The defence and subsequent attack of 1 October 1807 was undoubtedly impressive, and from contemporary accounts Rogers emerges as a brave and capable commander. It is little wonder that he and the *Windsor Castle* have been preserved on canvas. Equally indubitable, however, is the fact that his actions made very little lasting difference to the outcome of the Napoleonic Wars. Though the French privateer was taken off the seas as an enemy, and the Packet crew protected their vessel and its cargo, the legacy of the fight was, in the context of the wider conflict, minimal. Drummond's painting, commissioned as a celebration of the Packet's triumph, is impressive but misleading. While Packet ships did engage with the enemy during the wars, this was not their primary contribution to British victory. Becoming embroiled in combat, though tempting due to the prize money ships could command, was a last resort when fleeing was no longer possible.¹² The reason for this was that for the duration of the wars, the Packet ships were charged with seeking out, conveying and protecting a highly valuable commodity that was not to be risked: information. Their involvement in the wars was generally less sensational than the occasional skirmish, but far more significant.

---

⁹ 'Tour: British and American History Paintings of the 1700s', *National Gallery of Art*
<https://www.nga.gov/collection/gallery/gg61/gg61-main1.html> [accessed 19 September 2014]
¹⁰ Ibid.
¹¹ 'Your Paintings', *BBC*
<http://www.bbc.co.uk/arts/yourpaintings/paintings/search/painted_by/samuel-drummond-10674> [accessed 19 September 2014]
¹² Mudd, p. 22.

The various types of information that travelled through Falmouth, from mail to scientific knowledge and discourses of identity, will underlie the main arguments of this thesis. It is, in effect, a work concerned with the transfer of information and the consequences this had on Britain and its people. This chapter will focus on intelligence; one type of information that was crucial to the interests of the British empire. As much as guns, cannon and men mounted on horseback, intelligence is a key, though relatively silent, component of warfare. Its gathering has been an integral part of military operations for hundreds of years.[13] This chapter will explore the many ways in which Falmouth, and most specifically its Packet Service, contributed to the intelligence practices in the Napoleonic Wars, from 1803-1815, and during the years following.

The effective use of information played an important part in Britain's success in the conflict. British victory, aided in the realm of intelligence by the Packet Service, had a direct influence on the expansion of its maritime empire and overseas colonies. By providing systems of intelligence for the military, Falmouth was therefore engaged with the expansionary interests of empire. Victory over Napoleon in 1815 led the French and Dutch to surrender many territories[14] and left Britain a predominant maritime and imperial power.[15] The wars led to the most extensive expansion of the British empire since the earlier creation of colonies in Ireland and America in the seventeenth century.[16] In 1792, the British empire contained twenty-six colonies, but by 1816 it contained forty-three.[17] Andrew Porter argues that the British empire consisted of three separate spheres: the early empire of white settlement, the empire in India, and the 'dependent empire', gained by conquest and wartime acquisition.[18] It was therefore the realm of the dependent empire that saw the greatest growth in 1815. It will be here shown that Falmouth's Packet ships, in their function as a

---

[13] John Murphy, 'Timeline of Intelligence' in *Encyclopedia of Intelligence and Counterintelligence*, ed. by Rodney P. Carlisle (New York: M.E. Sharpe, 2005), Credo Reference ebook.
[14] P. J. Marshall, 'Introduction', in *The Oxford History of the British Empire*, ed. by P. J. Marshall, 5 vols (Oxford: Oxford University Press, 1998), II, pp. 1-27 (p. 19).
[15] Michael Duffy, 'World-Wide War and British Expansion, 1793-1815' in *The Oxford History of the British Empire*, pp. 184-207 (p. 184).
[16] C.A. Bayly, *Empire and Information: intelligence gathering in India, 1780-1870* (Cambridge: Cambridge University Press, 1996), p. 100.
[17] Andrew Thompson, 'Empire and the British State' in *The British Empire*, ed. by Sarah Stockwell (Oxford: Blackwell Publishing, 2008), pp. 39-62 (p. 42).
[18] Andrew Porter, 'Introduction' in *The Oxford History of the British Empire*, ed. by Andrew Porter, 5 vols (Oxford: Oxford University Press, 1998), III, pp. 1-30 (p. 4).

vehicle for intelligence, contributed, in their own way, to the victory that inspired this growth.

The Packet Service, formed in 1688 or 1689,[19] was one of the town's primary industries.[20] Deriving its name from the French 'paquet', meaning package,[21] it transported state letters and dispatches, commercial mail, and even passengers, from Falmouth to ports around the world. Though other Packet stations existed, in Harwich, Dover, Great Yarmouth, Plymouth, Holyhead, and Milford Haven, Falmouth was the principal: in the early nineteenth century it received four times as many mail ships as any other location.[22] Originally, until the 1680s, Dover was the main English port through which letters passed for the continent: one route running from Dover to Ostend or Nieuport, and one from Dover to Calais.[23] Another service ran from Harwich to Hellevoetsluis. These routes were slow and unreliable, and when war broke out in 1689, the Falmouth station took over, with one route running to Spain.[24] In 1705, a service to the West Indies was introduced, and by 1764 more ships were employed to travel to America. By 1782, the Falmouth station had twenty two ships running.[25] Norway, in his history of the Packets, was scornful of the other British stations. He observed that during the Napoleonic Wars the Harwich Packets were useful only when Napoleon's 'hostile influence' spread into the Baltic and North Sea, that Holyhead 'confronted no dangers worth speaking of', Milford Packets 'offer[ed] very little detail worth speaking of' and 'the boats between Portpatrick and Donaghadee were still less interesting.'[26]

The Napoleonic Wars and the early years of the nineteenth century could certainly be hailed as the glory days of the Falmouth Packet Service. Periods of war had traditionally heralded a great increase in the number of routes, with many new sea links being made for the delivery of military mail or information. At the outbreak of

---

[19] Accounts differ, though the Falmouth Packet memorial, located on the Moor in Falmouth, states the date of formation as 1688.
[20] Norway, p. 5.
[21] Pawlyn, p. 8.
[22] Susan Gay, *Old Falmouth* (London: Headley Brothers, 1903), p. 140.
[23] Peter Fraser, *The Intelligence of the Secretaries of State and Their Monopoly of Licensed News, 1660-1688* (Cambridge: Cambridge University Press, 1956; repr. 2011), p. 61.
[24] Philbrick, 'Some Falmouth Packet Captains 1729-1832', p. 56.
[25] Dunstan, p. 69.
[26] Norway, p. 14.

the Seven Years' War in 1756, new sailings between Falmouth and both North America and the West Indies were established.[27] In 1806, after the British success at the Battle of Trafalgar, a new route into the Mediterranean was formed, followed by one to South America in 1808.[28] Overland extensions of the Packet Service mail delivery were also created. Once ships had carried the post into the Mediterranean, it was taken from Alexandria in Egypt, where British forces fought the French, overland to India and the East Indies, where further campaigns were carried out.[29] An edition of the *West Briton* newspaper from 4 September 1812 reported the re-establishment of a route to Corunna, 'so that we may expect increased facilities in the transmission of intelligence from the head-quarters of our army in Spain.'[30] During the Napoleonic Wars, the service was in such high demand that temporary ships had to be drafted in, with the total number growing to around forty.[31] Their destinations included Lisbon, San Sebastian, the West Indies, Gibraltar, Malta, Brazil, Surinam, Halifax and New York.[32] Passenger numbers also increased significantly during wartime, due to the lack of alternative means of transport. In 1774, 230 passengers travelled aboard the Packets, but by 1814 this number had risen to 1,864.[33]

The Service provided an invaluable means of communicating with colonies and forces engaged in the wars overseas. Government dispatches, containing important and potentially time-sensitive information, were delivered by the Packets. The office in Falmouth was charged with identifying dispatches in its sorting of the mail, and ensuring that they were sent on to the relevant departments in as little time as possible.[34] In addition to sending dispatches from overseas on to London, ships in Falmouth also carried dispatches from London overseas: these were taken to Cornwall by coach, where they could be loaded onto the Packets with the other mail. In 1811, the Packet agent at Falmouth wrote in a message to London: 'I wish that the coach [carrying dispatches] might be kept to good time, particularly on Friday, in

---

[27] Philbrick, 'Some Falmouth Packet Captains 1729-1832', p. 56.
[28] Ibid.
[29] Whetter, *The History of Falmouth*, p. 52.
[30] *Life in Cornwall in the Early Nineteenth Century*, p. 33.
[31] Pawlyn, p. 90.
[32] Norway, pp. 8-10.
[33] Pawlyn, p. 88.
[34] Howard Robinson, *Carrying British Mails Overseas* (London: George Allen & Unwin Ltd., 1964), p. 85.

order that I may continue to dispatch the Lisbon packets always on Friday.'[35] The importance of maintaining this link between the British government and countries and colonies overseas is illustrated by the increase in new sailing routes, which were created for the conveyance of dispatches. Rather than the Packet Service simply meeting the government's postal requirements in the course of its usual service, the function of the Packet Service was altered to fulfil the needs of a country at war. The delivery of dispatches was not an incidental task, but an integral one. Reynolds, the Packet agent at Lisbon, which sent and received mail to and from Britain via Falmouth, handled such a volume of army dispatches that he became known as the 'Army Postmaster'.[36] During the Napoleonic Wars, when fewer vessels were able to travel across Europe to Britain's empire, a clear line of communication was also important for those fighting away from home, who wished to keep in touch with loved-ones. The Packet ship, hoving into view, became a reminder of Britain and home to sailors, and many popular ballads of the time were inspired by letters sent to and from these sailors.[37]

Though these services were vital, Falmouth's Packet crews also took on additional duties more directly related to warfare. For it was during the Napoleonic Wars that the Packet ship changed from being a carrier of news and mail to a fully-fledged military vessel: a vehicle for intelligence. It is this role, and the remarkable activities of the Packet Service, that this chapter will explore in more detail.

The meanings and definitions of intelligence are manifold, and it may be useful to briefly clarify the interpretation put upon the word in this context. The practice of information gathering in a political or military context is known as intelligence, and the information itself can also be described as such. It can be a metaphysical commodity: a fact or piece of knowledge that is passed on by word of mouth, or it may be a physical piece of information, such as a note or an intercepted letter. In his *Encyclopaedia of Intelligence and Counterintelligence*, Rodney Carlisle defines it as 'all the information, both secret and open, that can be employed by a nation's

---

[35] Robinson, p. 89.
[36] Robinson, p. 91.
[37] *The People's Post: A Narrative History of the Post Office*, Episode 3, BBC Radio 4, 7 December 2011.

decision-makers to reduce the risks to national security.'[38] Those in receipt of intelligence are generally able to gain foreknowledge of any threats, both internal and external.[39] Human intelligence, often abbreviated to HUMINT, is information gathered by humans, such as the debriefing of emigrants, contact with foreign governments, or spying.[40]

In the late eighteenth century, as Britain's empire expanded, the quality of military and political knowledge was, as Bayly states, 'a critical determinant of success in conquest and profitable governance.'[41] The practices of intelligence and counterintelligence are ancient, with stories dating back as far as ancient Babylon and the Bible.[42] Through networks of spies, interception of mail, reconnaissance and code breaking, nations have developed the ability to keep watch on their friends and enemies at home and abroad. The multipolarity of the West at this time, and the complexity of international relations, meant that information of many types had a premium.[43] The delicate balance of power in the West could be assessed by examining such information.[44] This would have been the case to an even greater extent during periods of war. Many contemporary figures such as Napoleon Bonaparte and Arthur Wellesley, Duke of Wellington, saw great value in intelligence of many varieties and used it to their advantage. As this chapter will argue, intelligence gathered by the Packet Service could be highly useful.

Napoleon is today respected as one of the greatest facilitators of intelligence services of his age. In addition to championing technologies such as the optical telegraph, he

---

[38] Rodney Carlisle, 'Introduction' in *Encyclopaedia of Intelligence and Counterintelligence* (para. 2 of 13)
[39] Carlisle, (para. 2 of 13)
[40] Montgomery McFate Saponey, 'human intelligence' in *Encyclopaedia of Intelligence and Counterintelligence.*
[41] Bayly, p. 1.
[42] Carlisle, (para. 1 of 17). The history of intelligence is a lengthy one and cannot be elaborated upon in any great detail here. In the time of Emperor Augustus Caesar, who ruled from 27 BC to 14 AD, Rome had its own imperial intelligence service; a system that will be explored in more detail later. In August 1586, British intelligence in action was demonstrated by the arrest of Mary Queen of Scots, after a code used between the Queen and her alleged conspirators was deciphered by England's 'spymaster' Francis Walsingham. Carlisle provides a detailed timeline of events relating to intelligence, from which it becomes clear that the practice has long been an accepted and vital element of warfare.
[43] Jeremy Black, *The Power of Knowledge: How Information and Technology Made the Modern World* (London: Yale University Press, 2014), p.
[44] Black, *The Power of Knowledge*.

has become known for his 'mastery of deception' and fully appreciated the value of intelligence and counter-intelligence.[45] In campaigns he shrouded the movements of his Grand Army in mystery wherever possible, and devoted many resources to gathering knowledge of his enemies.[46] Napoleon was a master of what we now call strategic intelligence, which is much broader in scope and can encompass many nations and 'many possible theatres of operations'.[47] Its counterpart, tactical intelligence, instead focuses on one individual battle or situation.[48] Strategic intelligence, more long-term as opposed to the short-term nature of tactics, could include methods such as deception, counter-intelligence, smuggling and spying.[49] Napoleon's administration saw spies planted around Europe, the smuggling and translation of foreign newspapers, and the operation of a deciphering branch for handling coded messages.[50]

Though France's use of intelligence during the Napoleonic Wars is well documented, the British forces also made good use of similar techniques. During the early years of the Napoleonic Wars, the Duke of Wellington served as the British army's intelligence officer, with all information in the field being directed to him for consideration and analysis.[51] By the latter years of the war, however, Wellington appreciated the value of intelligence enough to create a department dedicated entirely to this practice.[52] In the maritime sphere, Lord Nelson also promoted its use. Maffeo, in his history of British intelligence during the Napoleonic Wars, describes him as 'a superb intelligence officer' who was constantly seeking out and analysing intelligence.[53] While British intelligence was gathered by and for the British military, it will be argued here that the Packet Service, which was not an official military organisation, nevertheless became an unofficial intelligence body. Strategic measures such as those adopted by Napoleon were also at work within Britain during the wars, with Falmouth's Packet Service at their heart.

---

[45] Victor M. Rosello, 'Clausewitz's Contempt for Intelligence', *Parameters*, (1991), 103-114 (p. 105).
[46] Rosello, p. 106.
[47] Maffeo, p. xx.
[48] Ibid.
[49] Manuel De Landa, *War in the Age of Intelligent Machines* (New York: Zone Books, 1991), pp. 182-183.
[50] De Landa, p. 183.
[51] Rosello, p. 108.
[52] Ibid.
[53] Maffeo, p. xvi.

The practice of intelligence gathering in the eighteenth and nineteenth centuries did have its detractors, however. The military theorist Carl von Clausewitz took a negative view, declaring that it was too 'unreliable and transient' to be trusted: '[m]any intelligence reports in war are contradictory; even more are false, and most are uncertain'.[54] In describing the circumstances in which it is problematic, Clausewitz locates his example in the thick of battle, 'with reports streaming in', and with a commander of troops being forced to decide whether contradictory reports should be believed.[55] Clausewitz primarily imagines intelligence being utilised at 'the scene of action', and as part of individual military operations and battles, when it is most difficult to assess due to fear and 'the pressures of the moment'.[56] In short, what Clausewitz describes under the blanket term of intelligence is land-based tactical intelligence only; tactical intelligence being defined by Steven Maffeo as 'military intelligence which is often gathered and produced in the field during actual hostilities.'[57] Tactical intelligence is only one type of knowledge. It does indeed have its weaknesses, but should not be used as a means of discussing or dismissing the concept altogether. Indeed, even the tactical intelligence that Clausewitz seems to malign could have real significance and value during the Napoleonic Wars.

Tactics: keeping watch

In addition to its obvious function as a carrier of the mail, at the beginning of the nineteenth century the Packet ship was also publicly known as a vehicle for intelligence.[58] While fighting in India from 1799-1804, the Duke of Wellington, aware of the benefits of insight, took over pre-existing intelligence systems and made them his own to form a local reconnaissance corps.[59] Similarly, during the wars the Admiralty mirrored his actions, utilising the existing Packet Service and its crews by charging them with observing and recording as much as possible while

---

[54] Carl von Clausewitz, *On War*, trans. by Michael Howard and Peter Paret (London: David Campbell Publishers Ltd., 1993), p. 136.
[55] Ibid.
[56] Clausewitz, p. 137.
[57] Steven E. Maffeo, *Most Secret and Confidential: Intelligence in the Age of Nelson* (London: Chatham Publishing, 2000), p. xx.
[58] *Life in Cornwall in the Early Nineteenth Century* (Truro: D. Bradford Barton Ltd., 1970), p. 33.
[59] John Keegan, *Intelligence in War: knowledge of the enemy from Napoleon to Al-Qaeda* (London: Hutchinson, 2003), p. 19.

travelling on their usual routes. By asking Packet crews to report back to it, the Admiralty moulded an existing service into a reconnaissance corps, separate from naval vessels already caught up in fighting battles. Admirals, as Keegan notes, did not take warmly to sending their battle-ready ships out on reconnaissance missions, preferring to keep them together in anticipation of action.[60] Individual units within a fleet were not necessarily powerful; it was a mass of ships that equated power, and individual, isolated vessels sent out on observation were much more vulnerable to defeat.[61] To counter this problem, the Admiralty used smaller, faster frigates for observation, though there were never enough of these and those that were with a fleet were given a multitude of tasks aside from reconnaissance.[62] The Packet ships, like these frigates, were also designed to be fast: in the 1790s their design was amended specifically so that they would be able to outstrip the enemy.[63] By utilising ships that had to sail regardless of the war, the Navy was able to increase its maritime presence and create a greater British power on the sea: the need for 'maritime strength' and 'a superior Force at Sea' having been identified by the Tories as primary sources of power for the nation back in the mid-eighteenth century.[64]

Packet ships, travelling regularly back and forth to Europe and beyond, were well positioned to report on the location and condition of the British and foreign vessels they encountered during their voyages. Each ship had a journal for the recording of details and observations, and were able to communicate with each other from a distance using flag signals, a practice that increased the amount of information they were able to record and report back.[65] During the period of the Napoleonic Wars, this information could be useful in charting enemy vessels and anticipating actions. The conflict, as Nigel West argues, was 'heavily dependent on accurate information

---

[60] Keegan, p. 31.
[61] Ibid.
[62] Keegan, pp. 31-32.
[63] M.E. Philbrick, 'The Post Office Packet Service from Falmouth' in *History around the Fal* (Exeter: Fal History Group/University of Exeter, 1980), pp. 1-26 (p. 6).
[64] Geoffrey Till, 'Introduction: British naval thinking: a contradiction in terms?' in *The Development of British Naval Thinking: Essays in Memory of Brian McLaren Ranfit*, ed. by Geoffrey Till (London: Routledge, 2006), pp. 1-18 (pp. 4-5).
[65] Robinson, p. 85.

about the seaworthiness of ships and conditions in blockaded ports.'[66] Good intelligence could often tip the balance in favour of one protagonist, as this was a war in which major sea battles were rare and those which occurred often depended on the element of surprise to give one force an upper hand.[67] When a Packet ship had completed its journey and returned to Falmouth, extracts of its journal were sent to the Postmaster General, and often also to the Admiralty, for their reference or action. If a particularly important event had occurred during the ship's voyage, a letter was often sent in addition to the journal extracts.[68]

This type of intelligence, dealing with short-term events and the things that ships have seen, is tactical. Michel De Certeau argues that tactics is movement located within the field of vision of the enemy, and carried out in the space controlled by him.[69] While strategy operates within a space of power, or the operator's own spatial "property", tactics 'must play with the terrain imposed on it'.[70] The Falmouth Packet ships didn't always operate within terrain that was under their control. The routes followed were often dangerous, and could frequently throw vessels into the paths of hostile forces. This much is clear from the frequency of attacks made upon Packet ships. Between 1793 and 1815, nineteen Falmouth Packets were captured by enemy vessels.[71] Between 1812 and 1815, over six hundred American privateers were commissioned, making American vessels, as well as French, a threat.[72] Shortly after the United States declared war on Britain in 1812, the Packet *Prince Adolphus* was captured by an American privateer during a journey from Martinique to Falmouth.[73] Few ships survived the Napoleonic Wars unscathed; many entered the safe haven of Falmouth 'battered, blackened and damaged, with hulls, spars and sails shattered, and with ensigns half-masted in honour of the dead.'[74] As already noted, it was under wartime conditions that many new Packet Service routes were introduced, meaning

---

[66] Nigel West, *Historical Dictionary of Naval Intelligence* (Plymouth: Scarecrow Press, 2010), p. xxvii.
[67] West, p. xxvii.
[68] For instance, London, National Archives, ADM 1/4073.
[69] Michel De Certeau, 'On the Oppositional Practices of Everyday Life', *Social Text*, 3 (1980), 3-43 (p. 6).
[70] Ibid.
[71] Malcolm Archibald, *Across the Pond: Chapters from the Atlantic*, (Caithness: Whittles Publishing, 2001), p. 118.
[72] Robinson, p. 100.
[73] Ibid.
[74] Mudd, p. 49.

that captains were forced to sail into strange and unfamiliar territory that could not yet be claimed as British.[75] Venturing so regularly into dangerous waters, the Packets were designed to make a fast getaway and were not equipped with the aim of fighting back unless absolutely necessary.[76] Commanders received a firm instruction to run on sight of an enemy vessel, and to fight only if they could no longer run.[77] In this, the knowledge pursued by the service conforms with Eva Horn's perception of intelligence: its task being, both metaphorically and physically, to 'penetrate into the forbidden and protected space, cross borders and investigate the enemy's territory.'[78] The spaces investigated are, by necessity, those that are traversed and reconnoitred,[79] and the Packet ship, as intelligence agent, was concerned with penetrating and investigating this space.

An advantage of Packet ships operating within a potentially hostile terrain, separate to that which they could control, was rather obvious: they were often given the opportunity to see and hear of things relating to the enemy. The following letter, written on 12 May 1801 by Captain Dorset Fellowes of the *Lady Hobart*, was addressed to Francis Freeling, Secretary of the General Post Office (GPO).

> I have the Honor to enclose you the presented paper, filled up with such Names of Ships as were spoken by us on our Passage out. I think it proper to inform you that the Semillante French Frigate of 36 Guns, is now shifting in Norfolk Harbour preparing for Sea, two of her Officers are at this time in New York. She is expected to be in readiness for Sea in a short time & it is reported here that HM Frigate the Boston is cruizing off that Port waiting her coming out.
> An American Ship arrived here yesterday from Canton, & has brought Intelligence that she fell in with the Centurion, Victorious, Brave & Sybelle in Malaua Roads on 16th Jan. last they informed him that they had raised the Siege of Batavia but of no other particulars.[80]

---

[75] Pawlyn, p. 34.
[76] Mudd, p. 22.
[77] Ibid.
[78] Eva Horn, 'Knowing the Enemy: The Epistemology of Secret Intelligence', trans. by Sara Ogger, *Grey Room*, 11 (2003), 58-85 (p. 73).
[79] Ibid.
[80] London, National Archives, ADM 1/4043

In this instance, Norfolk Harbour, being an American port, is an uncomfortably neutral terrain, receptive to the Packet ship as mail carrier but entrenched in the history of the recent American Revolutionary Wars, in which the French were allied with America and British colonists were ejected.[81] Intelligence such as this depended heavily upon what De Certeau calls 'occasions'.[82] Operations were very much 'blow by blow', and relied upon chance instead of planning. Ships happened to be in certain ports, or sailing off certain coastlines, and the Packets happened to see them there. When sailing their routes, they worked in a space without a powerful British base, which offered mobility and allowed for surprises. In order to take full advantage of this mobility, commanders had to be ready to 'utilize the gaps which the particular combination of circumstances open[ed].'[83] Opportunities for coming across intelligence of the enemy must be seized, and the 'temporal chance and luck' of tactics appreciated.[84] This example highlights the Navy's wise use of Packet commanders for reporting intelligence, epitomising what Geoffrey Till phrases 'the traditional British naval wariness' of excessive analysing and doctrine, preferring instinct based on experience.[85] In matters of tactics, where situations could change rapidly, it was this instinct that was useful.

Sending information about enemy ships back to the Admiralty was an essential element of warfare as, to some extent, it reduced the possibility of British ships being surprised by an enemy force. Reports of the weapons carried on board an enemy ship, and of the ship's condition, allowed British vessels to more accurately assess the danger it might pose. On 15 July 1805, a letter was sent to the Postmaster General and the Admiralty from Falmouth, detailing a possible threat that had been observed by a Packet ship:

> For the Information of My Lord the Post Master General and of the Admiralty, is this inclosed, to say that on 6th June, I left Ribadeui[86] – There lay in that Harbour a Ship, the Leola French Privateer under Spanish Colours, mounting twenty two Nine Pounders on the lower Deck, she having a flush upper one, and only six in the

---

[81] 'America's Story', *The Library of Congress* <http://www.americaslibrary.gov/jb/revolut/jb_revolut_francoam_1.html> [accessed 9 August 2012].
[82] De Certeau, p. 6.
[83] Ibid.
[84] De Certeau, pp. 6-7.
[85] Till, p. 9.
[86] Possibly Ribadeo in Galicia.

Forecastle and Quarter Deck. She carries her Guns very low & cannot use them in bad weather – She had then on Board 130 or 140 Men, means not to sail with lefs than 200 – her Complement to be 260, which she will never get there – the Crew and the most of the officers sleep on shore every Night – She may be easily put out – the Port a very weak one, on the West Side has 12 Guns in bad order, and the soldiers in shocking bad order also – not more than 40 or 50 altogether. On the East Side there is not a Thing to annoy – It is a nest for Privateering. They have Agents for 14 French. I gave this information to Mr Allen the British Consul at [indecipherable] – to Mr Warr at Oporto, and to Capt. Barry of HMS Ship Brilliant, which we spoke in Lat. 47.30 N and Longitude 09.50 W.[87]

It is clear from the level of detail included in this letter that the information is provided in order to grant British forces the upper hand in any future conflict. Due to the way that the weaknesses of the *Leola* are described, the sender John Mudge gives the British every opportunity to launch an attack. Ambush and the use of surprise have long been accepted as valuable forms of warfare,[88] but are practices dependent on good intelligence. Mudge supplies what Eva Horn describes as the 'positive raw data':[89] in this instance the enemy strength and weapons. This raw data, when combined with knowledge of the present political situation – that France and Britain are at war and actively fighting – would be transformed into a scenario where the pros and cons of attack could be debated.[90] Details of a ship could also be vital in planning defences against it, however. As Richard Harding argues, the results of an attack depended on whether the enemy were seamen in a merchant ship, landsmen in merchant or warships, militia, professional soldiers, and so on.[91] Britain's focus on planning defences was also longer-term and strategic, with its focus on this serving as a real advantage over enemy forces.[92]

Mudge's information could, in the future, have therefore had some strategic importance: the previous year, enemy ships were already being observed, detailed

---

[87] London, National Archives, ADM 1/4073
[88] Sun Tzu, *The Art of War*, trans. by Lionel Giles (El Paso: El Paso Norte Press, 2009), p. 3.
[89] Horn, p. 61.
[90] Ibid.
[91] Richard Harding, *Seapower and Naval Warfare 1650-1830* (London: UCL Press, 1999), p. 283.
[92] Harding, p. 283.

and categorised according to size for the Admiralty, for the purposes of defence.[93] Though the *Leola* was a privateer rather than an official naval vessel, this information may nevertheless have come in useful if an attempt was made to estimate accurately the French fighting force. Collecting information about the location of ships was also standard Navy practice. In 1805, Lord Nelson relayed information to the Admiralty about the location of French ships and the extent to which they were manned.[94]

The way in which Mudge's letter is written displays experience in intelligence on his part. Some of the information in the letter is based on observations made either from the water or from the land, such as the guns being low, but also implies a foreknowledge of ships used in warfare. Only a sailor experienced in fighting, or in tactical intelligence, would know a gun's weight from observing it, and know that guns being in a low position mean that they cannot be used in bad weather. The nautical experience of the ships' crews therefore makes them a good choice of intelligence agent. The letter also implies that the captain has actively sought out intelligence in other ways, perhaps by mingling with crew members on shore, or by speaking to local people. This is evident from the report that local people will be hard to recruit; either because the public attitude is not in favour of the French, or because there simply are not enough fit men in the locality. Knowledge that the ship means to sail with two hundred men suggests that the captain has either somehow infiltrated its crew, or obtained the information from a 'middle party' such as a local person in the port. As the ship does not have a full crew, and so does not yet intend to sail, an attacking force could feel confident that it might remain in the location described for some days more.[95] In this, it is possible to discern elements of spying or deception – commonly associated with strategic intelligence – being incorporated into the gathering of tactical intelligence. Clearly, the crew of the Packet ships were not just passive observers, but active intelligence seekers and potential spies: in fact, 'living agents' of HUMINT, who were able to infiltrate territory occupied by the

---

[93] Roger Morriss, *The Foundations of British Maritime Ascendancy: Resources, Logistics, and the State, 1755-1815* (Cambridge: Cambridge University Press, 2011), p. 44.
[94] Morriss, p. 51.
[95] Sadly, it has – to date – been impossible to trace whether the Admiralty acted upon this information.

enemy and to spy on them.[96] In a conflict dependent on manpower, with France drawing on the population of Europe, this represented what Christopher Hall terms 'the best possible use of [Britain's] human resources.'[97]

Wherever they went, Packet commanders observed proceedings and sought out the latest news, in order that they might relay it to those at home. This was done under orders; commanders were obliged to inform themselves of affairs in every country they visited, and if military or naval operations were being planned, to be able to provide a full account of the campaign.[98] On a ship's return to Falmouth, its journal and any other memoranda were sent immediately to London. The Packets became, as Arthur Norway would say in 1895, 'the regular vehicles of news'.[99] Because of the speed and regularity of the overseas postal service, their journals 'frequently contained news later and more authentic than any which had yet reached London', and so often contained the first indicator of an event.[100]

At this, the height of the Packet Service's functioning, arrivals in the port were frequent, each bringing personnel and passengers along with a varied cargo of personal luggage, mail, bullion and other freight.[101] The Falmouth agent for the Post Office carefully recorded every detail relating to each ship, including the money received for letters, both 'homewards' and 'outwards', the value of freight carried, 'the third to the office' (namely, the commission received by the Packet Service for its transport) and the numbers of any passengers travelling aboard.[102] Due to the increased need for weaponry aboard the ships, before departure the agent also oversaw the arming of the Packets, and their supplies of what are recorded as 'wartime stores', which included gunpowder and sheepskins.[103] In this way, all possible knowledge – economic, military, or otherwise – was diligently contained, with no information of any kind allowed to slip through the town unrecorded.

---

[96] Horn, p. 62.
[97] Christopher David Hall, *British Strategy in the Napoleonic War, 1803-15* (Manchester: Manchester University Press, 1992), p. 1.
[98] Norway, p. 6.
[99] Norway, p. 6.
[100] Norway, p. 37.
[101] London, British Postal Museum and Archive, POST 4/22.
[102] London, British Postal Museum and Archive, POST 4/21.
[103] Ibid.

While the Falmouth Packet agent and his clerks were kept busy recording the arrival, victualling and departure of the service's ships, other bodies were also active in the port, including the East India Company, which had an agent and stores in the town[104] and made payments to its Customs officials for goods landed there.[105] There was also a Naval Office in Falmouth, which formed an administrative and supply base for the Admiralty, from which wages were paid and ships' stores replenished.[106] Stationed there were a master-attendant, store-keeper and master shipwright, among others.[107] In 1813, Falmouth formed an important base for the re-supply of Wellington's army in Spain, with his Lordship requesting in dispatches that goods be kept there for specific army use only.[108] This constant activity would have created a space teeming with information gathered from across the seas; the most interesting sections of which were recorded in letters and sent on to the Admiralty. In February 1810, for instance, a letter was sent to inform the lords that the purser of the HMS *Arethusa* had 'this moment landed' with intelligence that the vessel had run ashore nearby.[109] During a time of war, this culture of both methodical and immediate reporting ran through the onshore activity of the maritime services as well as influencing them at sea.

On 20 January 1802, while Britain was at war with France, a letter was sent to Francis Freeling, secretary of the GPO, from a Packet ship in Lisbon, reporting the movements of two French craft.[110] The *Le Duquesne*, a seventy-four gun ship, and the *La Cornelia*, a forty gun ship, had been travelling from Brest to St Domingo with troops, when a gale had separated them from the rest of the French fleet off Cape Finisterre. Instead of continuing on their journey, they had instead put into Cadiz in Spain, a location at that time belonging to neither Britain nor France.[111] Though chance had played a large part in the acquisition of this intelligence, it could nevertheless be useful. Not only did it allow the Navy to keep an accurate record of

---

[104] London, British Library, IOR/L/AG/1/1/30/f.338(1).
[105] London, British Library, Add MS 38769.
[106] London, National Archives, ADM 42/645.
[107] George Alexander Cooke, *Topography of Great Britain: or, British Traveller's Directory: Cornwall* (London: Brimmer & Co., 1810), p. 87.
[108] *The Dispatches of Field Marshal the Duke of Wellington, during his various campaigns in India, Denmark, Portugal, Spain, the Low Countries, and France, from 1799 to 1818*, ed. by John Gurwood, 12 vols (London: John Murray, 1838), X, p. 518.
[109] London, National Archives, ADM 42/645.
[110] National Archives, ADM 1/4073
[111] Ibid.

enemy movements, it also informed them that two ships could potentially move or attack from a previously unexpected direction, or that the two ships could be attacked, as they were weaker for being separated from the fleet. In addition to this, the information could allow those charting the movement of the fleet to more precisely estimate its gun power: with two ships separated, the fleet was now one hundred and fourteen guns less powerful than it had previously been. This type of insight could be highly valuable to those within the conflict.

While tactical intelligence, as outlined here, is a useful commodity, it is also undoubtedly a problematic and precarious one. As already stated, Clausewitz highly distrusted its veracity,[112] and De Certeau critiqued it as 'an art of the weak', though he also recognised its value.[113] The predominant weakness of tactical intelligence is its time sensitivity. Operating in a 'blow by blow' fashion means that Packet ships reporting tactical information had to be aware of its short expiration date and act quickly to seize the opportunity provided by the moment. Timeliness is a key part of the second of five fundamental stages for useful intelligence, as outlined by Keegan: delivery.[114] After a Packet captain acquired intelligence, he reached the delivery phase of the process, which Keegan singles out as the most difficult of the five.[115] In delivery, the sender – being in this instance the ship or its captain – is under immense time pressure, as the longer the time gap between intelligence being acquired and passed on, the less value that intelligence has.[116] John Churchill, the first Duke of Marlborough and a soldier in the late seventeenth and early eighteenth centuries, thought highly of tactical intelligence, if received in good time, stating that '[n]o war can be conducted successfully without early and good intelligence.'[117]

De Certeau also highlights the timeliness of intelligence, arguing that the value of tactics depends upon 'the circumstances which a punctual intervention transforms into a favourable situation or conjecture'.[118] This is what Keegan calls 'real-time

---

[112] Clausewitz, p. 136.
[113] De Certeau, p. 6.
[114] Keegan, pp. 3-4. The five stages of intelligence he outlines are acquisition, delivery, acceptance, interpretation, and implementation.
[115] Ibid.
[116] Ibid.
[117] Keegan, p. 9.
[118] De Certeau, p. 7.

intelligence': '[w]ho knows what in sufficient time to make effective use of the news'.[119] Though Packet ships were comparably fast for their time, even naval intelligence of the Napoleonic era was constrained by distance, as greater distances naturally meant longer delivery times. One of the main advantages of using the Packet Service as a vehicle for intelligence was its size. The extensive network of Packet ship routes, with up to forty vessels at a time on journeys to and from outposts of the British empire, not only meant that the ships were fast and relatively reliable for communicating messages, but also meant that if one ship gained news while heading away from Britain, it could potentially pass this news on to the first Packet ship it encountered that was inbound. Much time could be saved in this way, as messages arrived sooner than they would have done if one vessel had to complete its outbound journey before returning with its news. Essentially, the ships formed an early communications web or network, able to pass information back and forth to ensure speed. Consequently, though tactical intelligence is problematic, there were instances in which information gathered by the Packets was received in time to make a difference to proceedings. In 1778, for instance, the *Grantham* packet ship saved British forces at Philadelphia from being attacked by the French fleet; providing warning of enemy movements in time for the British to withdraw to New York.[120]

These examples demonstrate that tactical intelligence was of high value to Britain, and could have been instrumental in securing the victory of 1815, which expanded its empire. By supplying timely information, the Packets could save ships from destruction, preserving the fighting force, and offer up intelligence useful in battle, defence or ambush.

Strategy: Deception, interception and the 'Secret Office'

While tactical intelligence could be useful, strategy was prized before and during the Napoleonic Wars as an alternative to dealing with purely time-sensitive information.[121] The term strategy as it used here, denoting strategic intelligence, refers to information of a more general nature, such as the capability of the enemy,

---

[119] Keegan, p. 20.
[120] Kenneth Ellis, *The Post Office in the Eighteenth Century: A Study in Administrative History* (London: Oxford University Press, 1969), p. 61.
[121] Keegan, p. 21.

the size of its lands, and the type of terrain it operates on. This could allow commanders to learn more about their opponents and, if necessary, supplement tactical intelligence with educated guesses about the action the enemy is most likely to take.[122] These guesses are what De Landa calls 'strategic estimates.'[123] N. A. M. Rodger argues, however, that the term strategy was not widely used at this time: in fact, that 'naval strategy' as a term was not used until the late nineteenth century.[124] Its use here is therefore retrospective; this section analysing practices that historians nowadays would view as strategic.

Strategy, knowing one's enemy or potential enemy, and having a system in place for the gathering of useful information about it, is useful in times of peace as well as times of war. This section will explore how the Falmouth Packet Service contributed to strategic intelligence gathering, both in the Napoleonic Wars and in peacetime. It played a part in both the accumulation of foreknowledge, and in deception; in one particular capacity merging the two in the acquisition of information through deception. In this instance, deception was used not to hide Britain's true intentions from the enemy, but to spy on foreign communications under the guise of providing a postal service.

Knowledge of the enemy's ability and intentions is thus often accompanied by another key facet of strategy: deception. De Landa states that the value of foreknowledge and deception lies in having 'the foreknowledge needed to make strategic estimates for a campaign, as well as the deceptive means to conceal from a potential enemy one's true dispositions and ultimate intentions.'[125] One of the most covert ways in which intelligence was gathered specifically by the GPO was through the founding of an office for the interception and inspection of foreign mail. This office was quite independent of that responsible for inspecting inland mail, and allowed for the detection of any potential threats to national security.

---

[122] Ibid.
[123] De Landa, p. 179.
[124] N.A.M. Rodger, 'The idea of naval strategy in Britain in the eighteenth and nineteenth centuries' in *The Development of British Naval Thinking: Essays in Memory of Brian McLaren Ranfit*, pp. 19-33 (p. 19).
[125] De Landa, p. 179.

On 18 May 1748, John David Barbutt, Secretary to the Post Office, was subject to an enquiry carried out by a secret committee in the House of Commons in relation to the sums of money paid to employees of a secret office for the inspection of foreign correspondence. An account of this enquiry gives some idea of the history and importance of this office, and its standing during the Napoleonic Wars.[126] The money allocated to pay the expenses of the secret department was awarded by warrant from the Crown, and the wages paid – listed in the account – were sums sufficiently generous to imply that the work of this office was both prized and carefully protected from the public gaze. Certainly until 1782, the running of the secret office was paid for by warrants signed by the king, with monies recorded as being for 'Our Secret Service'.[127] To offer some perspective on these payments, the average wage for a crewman on board a Packet ship in the first half of the eighteenth century was one shilling a day, or eighteen pounds and five shillings a year.[128]

> To the chief Decypherer, Mr. Willes, for himself and his son £1000. to the Second Decypherer Mr. Corbiens [?], £800. to the third Decypherer Mr. Lumps [?], £500. to the fourth Decypherer Mr. Zolman, £100. – to the Chief Clerk Mr. Le Favre, £650. to the four other Clerks, Messrs. Bode, Thouveis, Clark, Hemmitt; £300. each, - to the Comptroller of the Foreign Office, Mr. Day, £60. to the Door Keeper £40. or £50. but this examinant believes £50.[129]

During the enquiry, Barbutt revealed that to the best of his knowledge, payments of this kind had been made to workers employed in the secret office since the year 1718, though he felt that the date of the office's founding may have been far earlier: 'this Examinant cannot say as to the first establishment of this Office, having been but three years and a half himself in the Post Office; but he apprehends there was always an Office of this kind'.[130] Ellis dates the office to 1653, when it was managed by Isaac Dorislaus.[131] Secrecy seems to have been key in the running of this office, for obvious reasons. A department for the covert inspection of foreign mail could not draw attention to its practices without endangering its effectiveness by warning those

---

[126] London, National Archives, HD 3/17
[127] Ibid.
[128] Howard Robinson, *Carrying British Mails Overseas* (London: George Allen & Unwin Ltd., 1964), p. 46.
[129] National Archives, HD 3/17
[130] National Archives, HD 3/17
[131] Ellis, p. 65.

being investigated. If foreign governments suspected that their mail was being intercepted, they could choose to send it by messenger instead of using the GPO. Mail carried by messenger could not be as easily intercepted by the state, and this was therefore not a desirable outcome. Likewise, if there was no suspicion of mail being read in Britain, there was less need for foreign ciphers, which could take decipherers a great deal of time to crack, to be changed.[132] Even those employed within the GPO knew little or nothing about the secret office. Barbutt stated that he was 'a strainger to the business of the Office, having never been in it', and that while the Postmasters had a right to go into the office, its function was kept private and operated outside their remit, 'for they pretend to be independent, and to receive their instructions from the Secretaries of State, and carry their Intelligence to the Secretaries of State'.[133]

A memorandum on the subject of the office, written around 1844, asserts that its function was to detect treasonous correspondence. It was admitted that 'the Proprietors of a General System of Postal Communication' had identified a need for some control over the mail, in the interests of public welfare, and that the Secretary of State always had the power to intercept any correspondence that could be considered suspicious:

> They did not consider it to be the duty of Government to facilitate and protect the conveyance of Treason from one end of the country to the other; - nor, probably, do right-minded people of the present day think it is good for the State that the Postmaster General should propel the correspondence of wicked and designing men from Shetland to Scilly at the price of a Penny.[134]

It was the task of 'decypherers' and translators to read through correspondence selected for inspection and either decode or translate it into English, before sending the translation on to the Secretary of State. From around 1752-1799, it was the task of the Chief Clerk, in charge of the running of the secret office, to see all the letters passing through the Foreign Post Office and select 'all those which he considered it

---

[132] Ellis, p. 75.
[133] National Archives, HD 3/17
[134] National Archives, HD 3/17

his duty to examine.'[135] After 1799, this task fell to the Comptroller of the Foreign Letter Office. Until the inspection of the day's mail was complete, outbound post destined for overseas locations could not be dispatched for delivery. Letters could also be selected for inspection on the orders of the king, as demonstrated by a letter from Whitehall, dated 20 October 1755. A letter, addressed to Anthony Todd, the Chief Clerk of the secret office, and written by the Earl of Holdernesse, requested that certain letters be sent to him, by command of the king, stating: 'I am to desire, by His Maj:^{ty}. special command, that you would strictly examine the Flanders and French Mails of this night, and the subsequent ones, and to direct you to open and copy any letter you may find directed to Mr Barry, Capitaine au Regiment de Dillon à Dunherque'.[136]

Arrests were made in connection with intercepted mail, though very few records of this exist, making it difficult to illustrate the effectiveness of the GPO's secret office. Warrants could be issued demanding that certain foreign correspondence be sent to the secret office for inspection, but the details of these were rarely recorded and so cannot be linked to arrests or court proceedings. In her paper on postal censorship, Susan Whyman refers to a statement made in 1844 that between 1712 and 1798, 'it was not the practice to record such Warrants regularly in any official book'.[137] Warrants for intercepting mail for political reasons usually led to extracts of letters being copied, whereas mail detained on a criminal warrant usually involved detaining originals.[138] It can be surmised that criminal warrants were most commonly issued for mail sent within Britain, where senders could be prosecuted, whereas politically motivated interception could well include mail sent from overseas, in which situation prosecution was not possible and covert means were employed; essentially, spying. Warrants were addressed to the Postmaster General and were sometimes burned on arrival. In any case, very little records of them survive.[139] The interception of foreign mail certainly continued into the first half of the nineteenth century, as evidenced by the 1844 memorandum on the subject, which

---

[135] National Archives, HD 3/17
[136] National Archives, HD 3/17
[137] Susan E. Whyman, 'Postal Censorship in England 1635-1844' <http://web.princeton.edu/sites/.../censorship/postal_censorship_england.doc> [accessed 22 February 2012] (p. 14)
[138] Ellis, p. 63.
[139] Ellis, p. 63.

discusses the secret office as an active body, but no details of warrants can be found for this period. One very plausible reason for this could be that by 1844, knowledge of the office's activities had been brought to public attention, and was not a practice that found public favour. As Whyman argues, 'the myth of the heroic uncensored mail had come to an inglorious halt.'[140] The GPO sought to distance itself as much as possible from any perception that it was spying on Britons, commenting in an 1844 memorandum that:

> the Chief of the Secret Department does not desire (I may say, - never has desired,) to see any other letters but those <u>to and from the Foreign Ministers</u>. Inspection of Private Correspondence is altogether and entirely disclaimed, excepting in a very, very few cases, when the task has been imposed upon him by an Authority which he was bound to submit to.[141]

It can be reasonably supposed that details of the results of the secret office's findings are so scant because of the GPO's desire to portray interception of the mails, whether foreign or domestic, as a thing of the past. Almost certainly, the activities of the office increased during the period of the Napoleonic Wars, as seeking out potentially harmful foreign correspondence became of paramount importance. This conclusion is supported by observing the employment figures for the office from the mid-1770s, at the time of the American War of Independence, and 1815, when Britain's wars with France ended. Though the office had been established, according to the evidence of John Barbutt, for many years previous to 1718, from the early 1750s the number of people employed in its service steadily grew. In 1752, it had five employees, but by 1776, a year into war with America, there were 'ten persons doing duty in the Secret Office, besides three Decypherers, and two Translators'.[142] While most recorded information relating to the office frustratingly dates to the eighteenth century or 1840s, it is apparent that as tensions with France and the thirteen colonies of America, later the United States, grew, so too did the necessity for detecting anti-British exchanges. As the Napoleonic Wars dawned, the office had increased its staff: in 1799, there were eleven people employed.[143] In 1816, after the end of the

---

[140] Whyman, p. 14.
[141] National Archives, HD 3/17
[142] National Archives, HD 3/17
[143] Ibid.

Napoleonic Wars, the number was reduced to six, though between this time and the 1840s, the average in employ was nine or ten.[144]

Falmouth's Packet ships fit into this story as an important link in the information chain. Inbound letters arriving in Britain from overseas did so via the Packet Service. All mail from locations as widespread as New York, Quebec, Lisbon, Malta, Brazil and the Leeward Islands, came into the country through Falmouth. Packet commanders could be charged with seeking out certain correspondence, in order that it could be sent for inspection. As Howard Robinson notes, mail received at the Falmouth Packet station did not simply pass through it: anything arriving from overseas was carefully examined and sorted before it was allowed to progress to London.[145] In addition to seeking out smuggled letters and co-ordinating soldiers' mail, the Falmouth office was required to ensure that mail destined for the government, such as dispatches, was sent 'to the proper officials'.[146] This allowed those officials to read through the dispatches in order to spy on foreign affairs that may have relevance to them, and to detect any possible threats or weaknesses that might be strategically relevant.

Immediately after the Napoleonic Wars, a restructuring of the foreign postal system saw the establishment of government messengers as a means of delivering communications to chief cities in Europe. This meant that not all foreign mail passed through the GPO as it had once done. However, the memorandum of 1844 notes that 'the intercourse opened by Packet boats with the New States of South America and Mexico' afforded the office a greater length of time to examine the mail that did come through, which made up for a deficiency in man hours due to post-war staff cuts.[147] Thanks to the Packet ships, the secret office could continue its work with regard to some mail routes, and 'as long as letters for those countries were not received at the Post Office after 5. o'clock p.m. and not sent out till 8. – there was time afforded for doing a great deal'.[148] Speed was essential in dealing with intercepted mail, as any delay in delivery could lead to suspicions being raised.

---

[144] Ibid.
[145] Robinson, p. 85.
[146] Robinson, p. 85.
[147] National Archives, HD 3/17
[148] National Archives, HD 3/17

In the same way that strategic intelligence gathering was important to the British, counterespionage – 'denying the enemy access to sources of data'[149] – carried equal significance. The ships' cargo of mail, often including important government dispatches, was highly valuable in terms of the information it could contain, and Packet crew were charged with protecting it at all costs, in order that no sensitive information should fall into enemy hands. In a modern intelligence system consisting of spies, those who gain knowledge, and counterspies, those who protect it, as well as double spies, those who plant false information,[150] the Falmouth Packet ship would take the role of a counterspy.[151] Napoleon's main counterespionage strategy was the Continental Blockade, by which he sought to blockade trade and communications passing between Britain and the Continent.[152] With this blockade posing major difficulties for vessels travelling to the Continent, Packet ships were essential in maintaining communications between Britain and the armed forces.[153] Some routes, such as those to Gijon and San Sebastian, were run almost entirely for the delivery of dispatches, with very little domestic mail sent to these locations.[154] Naturally, delivering mail to military bases meant that Packets were put in close proximity to the danger posed by enemy forces, and could be targeted by Napoleon's forces in an attempt to stop communications.

The usual practice for delivering dispatches was to send the original document by one ship, and a copy of it by another.[155] This protected the information by ensuring that if the mail aboard one vessel was lost, the other might still be delivered. Protection of information not only involved transporting it safely to its destination, but also preventing it from being taken by the enemy, thus denying them the information. The portmanteau of mail was the last thing to board a Packet before its departure, and the first to leave the ship on its arrival at port.[156] It was thought to be far better that a mail bag be lost entirely, than that the enemy be given access to

---

[149] De Landa, p. 183.
[150] Ibid.
[151] Though as already noted, Packet crews could also be considered spies due to their gathering of information in ports.
[152] Ibid.
[153] Robinson, p. 89.
[154] Robinson, p. 91.
[155] Robinson, p. 89.
[156] Pawlyn, p. 85.

sensitive information, and so commanders were instructed to sink the mail if defeat was inevitable. During times of war the mail was kept on deck so that it might be quickly thrown overboard if the Packet seemed in danger of being overtaken by enemy troops.[157] Inside each mail bag were placed two GPO-issue lumps of pig-iron, which would ensure a faster sinking and prevent the bags floating on the surface of the water where they could be retrieved.[158] If another vessel had been sighted, the bags were suspended over the side of the Packet ship, so that the rope attaching them could be quickly cut if capture seemed inevitable.[159] Sinking the mails, or the possibility of it, is referred to in the records of many Packet vessels from this time, and prior to it. On 10 July 1801, the Packet *Penelope* sent a letter to the GPO informing the Postmaster General that it had been chased by a ship, which then tried to board her, and that as such the captain 'gave orders for the Mails to be thrown overboard'.[160] Similarly, in October 1810, the mail aboard the *Duke of Marlborough* was sunk not far from Pendennis Castle, when the ship was attacked by a French privateer.[161] The importance of denying enemy forces access to government dispatches need hardly be stressed. In a war of intelligence, protecting information could be every bit as important as gathering it: these measures served as a part of one whole.

This practice seems to have been standard not only for British vessels, but also for ships from Holland, which was essentially a satellite of France, with Napoleon Bonaparte's brother Louis ruling as king. On May 4 1811, the Packet *Townshend* succeeded in capturing the Dutch brig *Lucien Bonaparte*, which was carrying dispatches from Batavia to Bordeaux. In a letter sent to the Admiralty from Christopher Saverland, the Packet Service agent in Falmouth, it is noted that these dispatches 'were destroyed' before the ship was taken possession of by the *Townshend*.[162]

---

[157] Pawlyn, p. 85.
[158] Marsden, p. 148.
[159] Ibid.
[160] National Archives, ADM 1/4073.
[161] Marsden, p. 258.
[162] National Archives, ADM 1/4073.

Having explored how information at sea could be vital to Britain, attention must now be briefly paid to a final key element of strategic intelligence that instead took place on land.

Putting Falmouth on the map

In addition to the 'Secret Office' of the GPO, another predecessor to the modern-day intelligence and security services of MI5 and MI6 was the Depot of Military Knowledge. This department within the British War Office was formed during the Napoleonic Wars to gather information on the topography and resources of foreign countries, collecting maps and other related information that could lead to strategic estimates of a prospective enemy's actions.[163] Aside from the activities of this department, not all intelligence gathered during the wars provided information about an enemy. The practice could also extend to accumulating strategic intelligence about Britain, its resources and geography, in much the same way that general information about an enemy and its lands, practices and military potential was gathered. In 1813, the first Ordnance Survey map of Cornwall was produced as a direct consequence of its strategic importance during the Napoleonic Wars (see Fig. 2).[164] In comparison to previous maps of Cornwall, the 1813 production contained a great deal of coastal detail and information in addition to land detail.[165] The Burghley map of Falmouth Haven, produced around 1583, contains no information about the sea and is instead an artistic rendering of the land, with Pendennis Castle rising up out of the map as its clear focus, and the careful marking of field boundaries.[166] Similarly, another late seventeenth century map of Falmouth contains little coastal information but clearly shows field boundaries, each field or plot of land

---

[163] Michael Heffernan, 'Geography, Cartography and Military Intelligence: the Royal Geographical Society and the First World War', *Transactions of the Institute of British Geographers*, 21 (1996), 504-533 (p. 505).
[164] Simon Naylor, 'Geological Mapping and the Geographies of Proprietorship in Nineteenth-Century Cornwall' in *Geographies of Nineteenth-Century Science*, ed. by David N. Livingstone and Charles W. J. Withers (Chicago: University of Chicago Press, 2011), pp. 345-370 (p. 351).
[165] Truro, Cornwall Records Office, AD147/1
[166] 'Falmouth Haven', *British Library* <http://www.bl.uk/onlinegallery/onlineex/unvbrit/f/001roy000018d03u00016000.html> [accessed 8 July 2014]

being annotated with the name of its owner (see Fig. 3).[167] Earlier maps such as these tended to be produced in order to make clear the ownership of land.

Fig. 2: 1813 Ordnance Survey map

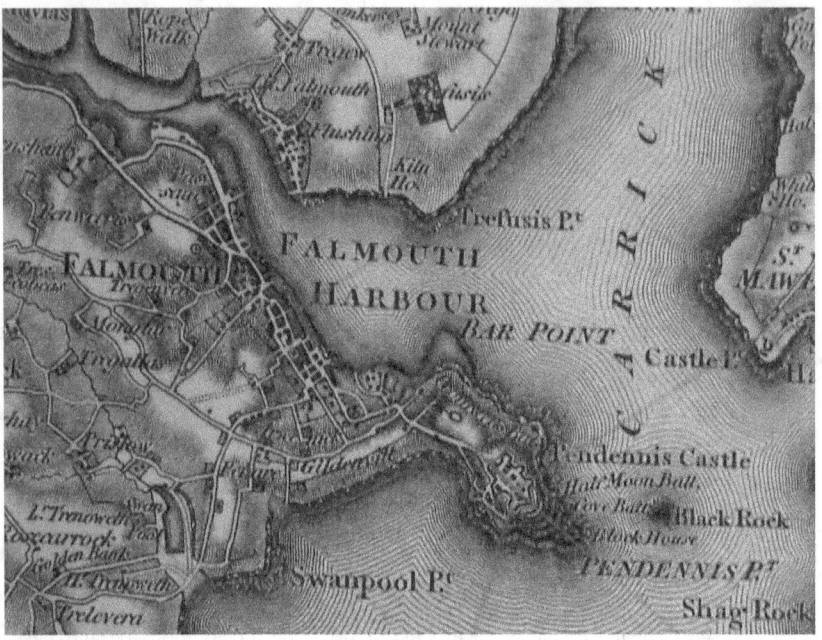

Detail from Ordnance Survey plans of 1813, showing Falmouth and surrounding areas. To the left of the Pendennis headland and between the words 'Falmouth' and 'Falmouth Harbour' lies the town of Falmouth, marked by roads and shaded areas of building. Truro, Cornwall Records Office, AD147/1.

---

[167] Truro, Cornwall Records Office, BRA1356/2

Fig. 3: Seventeenth century map of Falmouth

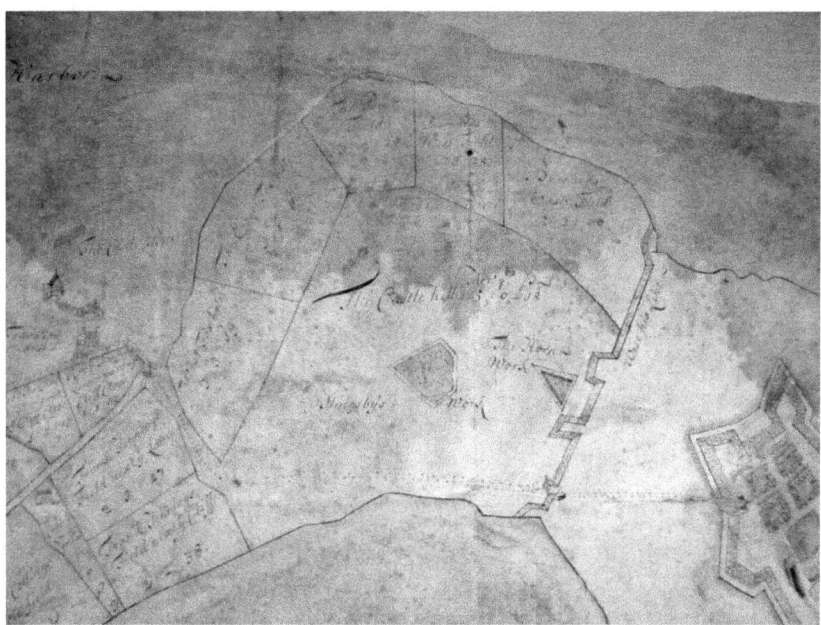

Detail from a late seventeenth century map of Falmouth, showing the demarcation of field boundaries between Pendennis Castle and Arwenack House. Truro, Cornwall Records Office, BRA/1356/2.

The Napoleonic Wars and the associated threat of invasion that came to pass in the late eighteenth and early nineteenth centuries created a necessity for detailed maps of the south of England for defence purposes.[168] Existing maps had so far been privately and locally produced, and showed only one county or area. As a result, they were not of a standard design and could not be fitted together to make one representative whole. In 1791 a large-scale project for mapping out the south began; a project that would take over twenty years to complete. In creating the maps, the director of the survey was instructed to deviate from the usual design of marking field boundaries, as this information was not useful for military purposes.[169] The 1813 Ordnance Survey map of Cornwall, showing Falmouth, is therefore remarkable

---

[168] James M. Garrett, *Wordsworth and the Writing of the Nation* (Aldershot: Ashgate Publishing, 2008), p. 79.
[169] Ibid.

for its difference to pre-existing maps of Cornwall. Instead of field boundaries, it displays detailed networks of roads, an accurate rendering of the coastline, and maritime information such as indicators of shallow water, buoys, and narrow inlets and coves.[170] The Ordnance was a military organisation, responsible for things such as artillery and fortifications.[171] In the late eighteenth century, early surveys had taken place in Scotland, to settle a dispute with France, and in Plymouth and the south-east, as militarily significant sites.[172] Likewise, during the Napoleonic Wars, the south-west of Britain was mapped to chart what Richard Oliver terms 'potentially helpful or obstructive ground'.[173] This Ordnance Survey was exclusively for military use: sale to the public was forbidden between 1811 and 1816.[174]

The production of these maps therefore contributed to strategic intelligence, generating foreknowledge of Britain that could help in the planning of defensive operations or campaigns, should an invasion come. It also reflected the importance of Falmouth and the maritime sphere to Britain's empire and the wars. The amount of topographical information contained within the Ordnance Survey meant that it would allow a greater accuracy in strategic estimates about the enemy's likely actions. This may include, for instance, knowledge of which areas of the coast were the most suitable for landing craft, which could be useful in making decisions about where defences should be placed. Having a visual guide to the road network of Falmouth would allow for easier planning for defensive action in the event of an invasion, as the movement of troops and goods along these roads could be designed in advance, and strategic estimates made as to the probable movement of enemy forces.

These maps therefore served a purpose: the intelligence they provided was skewed towards Britain's military interests. This is simply one example of a far more general bias in maps and surveys, which always serve a purpose of some kind. The first census of 1801, for instance, took place to track the population of Britain for the

---

[170] Truro, Cornwall Records Office, AD147/1.
[171] Richard Oliver, 'The Ordnance Survey in South-West England', in *Maps and History in South-West England*, ed. by Katherine Barker and Roger Kain (Exeter: University of Exeter Press, 1991), pp. 119-143 (p. 119).
[172] Oliver, p. 120.
[173] Ibid.
[174] Ibid.

purposes of war – estimating its fighting force – and tax, essentially gathering intelligence about people for military and economic benefit.[175] Maps are often representative of a 'reality' or fact that is shown only on the map itself, or that can be contested. Dennis Wood uses the example of land borders to make this point: often boundary markings appear only on a map, while on the actual land there is no indicator of moving from one place to another.[176] Property deeds mark out a certain area owned by an individual or individuals, serving their interests of ownership, but also determine the amount of tax due to the state, which translates into financial resources.

Overall, the various intelligence services described in this chapter, from straightforward observations to deceptive interception, contributed to the creation of Britain's maritime prestige. As already noted, success in the Napoleonic Wars led to the second great expansion of the British empire, and to the nation's dominance over the seas for many years following. Intelligence in its many forms was a critical part of military success, and also of peacetime power. Most of the practices here outlined, including the interception of mail and the completion of forms and sending of letters by Packet crews for the Admiralty, continued well beyond the victory of 1815 and were concerned with keeping a watchful eye on other European powers, such as Spain.[177] During the nineteenth century, Britain's maritime power, global presence and commercial network meant that it had the greatest opportunity to acquire information, and the greatest need of it.[178]

Mapping was one realm which continued to grow in importance, particularly for Cornwall, beyond 1815 and into the heyday of the British empire. Geological maps of the nineteenth century marked out the ownership of resources, such as minerals, and so were devoted to enclosing and owning a landscape, and keeping track of its economic potential.[179] As a location rich in minerals such as copper and tin, Cornwall had a great deal of potential wealth stored underground. An 1819 survey of the mining district of Camborne and Chacewater, printed in London, shows the

---

[175] Kathrin Levitan, *A Cultural History of the British Census: Envisioning the Multitude in the Nineteenth Century* (Basingstoke: Palgrave Macmillan, 2011), p. 49.
[176] Dennis Wood, *The Power of Maps* (New York: The Guilford Press, 1992), p. 8.
[177] For instance, London, National Archives, ADM 1/4074 and ADM 1/4075.
[178] Black, *The Power of Knowledge*.
[179] Naylor, pp. 345-346.

collective resources of the district, allowing for an estimate of its potential wealth and productivity, as well as the resources of individual mines.[180] This information would be valuable to the landowner for attracting potential shareholders, as the intimation of more ore would make a mine seem a more lucrative and secure investment. Maps in this instance therefore attracted wealth into the industry, and tracked its underground profit streams.

One of the primary functions that strategic intelligence through mapping served was thus to chart the military and economic potential of Cornwall, whether this was through marking out its safe waterways, or by determining the mineral ownership of individuals, groups, or the state. When it came to mineral resources, Cornwall had a great deal to offer the empire: metals originating from here could be used in the production of industrial machinery in colonised locations such as India.[181] As this chapter has demonstrated, Cornwall's skills, technology and resources were intrinsically also those of the empire, and it was through the harnessing of these that the region came to be part of a far wider global dialogue. While this is clearly true in the instance of intelligence, with Packet ships being used to help win Britain's fight for land, Falmouth's role as part of the empire continued well into peacetime with the glory and riches of its mining industry.

---

[180] Truro, Cornwall Records Office, CL/P/566
[181] 'Earth Treasures', *Cornish Mining World Heritage* <http://www.cornish-mining.org.uk/delving-deeper/earth-treasures> [accessed 14 May 2013]

Chapter 2: Science, technology and trade: exporting Cornwall to the empire

> At ½ past 8 one half of the beam was cast. It was a grand sight reminding one of Milton's 'burning Marl', whilst Richard Cloke's vociferations to his grimy Imps added not a little to the Infernal Character of the scene.[1]

The casting of a great new beam at Perran Foundry, witnessed by its manager Barclay Fox, was an event to draw crowds of spectators. On one occasion, Fox's sister Caroline, the author John Sterling, and Derwent Coleridge made the journey to Perran to view the wonder of creation.[2] What was essentially a scientific, industrial process came to be imbued with romance and glamour in the eyes of this audience, conjuring comparisons with Vulcan's forge and numerous classical works.[3] The whole population of Perran, drawn to the foundry, was said to be lit by the light of molten iron.[4] In Caroline's eyes, the foreman Richard Cloke was made beautiful in an 'agony of excitement'.[5] Sterling found Cloke a Celtic hero: an archetypal Cornishman.[6] To Coleridge, a casting represented the triumph of man in creating such machinery, and the amazing progress from ignorance to scientific ingenuity: 'all science begins in wonder and ends in wonder, but the first is the wonder of ignorance, the last that of adoration.'[7] The beam, a key part of the impressive Cornish beam engine, controlled the up and down motion of a steam-powered piston and could be spectacularly large. An engraving advertising beams, or 'bobs', to buy in a Perran Foundry catalogue circa 1870 depicts a man standing next to a beam that is in parts as tall as he is, and almost eight times as long.[8] The beam described here by Barclay, so large that the foundry was required to make it in halves, was destined for Tresavean Mine in Lanner, near the great copper-producing district of Camborne, Pool and Redruth. In the first half of the nineteenth century, output from the mine was high: by the date of its closure in 1858 it had become one of the largest copper

---

[1] Barclay Fox, p. 295.
[2] Caroline Fox, p. 60.
[3] Caroline Fox, p. 60.
[4] Ibid.
[5] Ibid.
[6] Ibid.
[7] Caroline Fox, p. 61.
[8] *Illustrated Catalogue of Pumping & Winding Engines* (London: Williams Perran Foundry Co., [1870(?)]; repr. Cambridge: Polyhedron Printers Ltd., 1976), p. 29.

producing mines in Cornwall.⁹ Sterling's adoration of Cloke as a Cornishman in this event is significant, for this was a uniquely Cornish endeavour and triumph. Mining was an industry in which the Cornish had become world famous and in which they could sail to glory.¹⁰

While the casting of a new beam at the foundry was a grand occasion, it was by no means a rare one. The Fox family had been on the site since the 1760s, unloading coal and timber imported from Britain and abroad at purpose-built quays to feed their smelting business.¹¹ Within two years of the family gaining a lease on wasteland in Perranarworthal, they had laid the foundations for what would become a key part of Britain's global mining industry in the nineteenth century.¹² For it was not just in the mines of Cornwall that the beam engines manufactured by Perran Foundry were to be found. As Cornish mining practices, and the men and equipment to accompany them, began to be exported around the world from the 1820s onwards, the foundry began to fulfil orders for clients based thousands of miles around the world. In 1847, Henry Ayers of the South Australian Mining Association wrote to its agent in Liverpool requesting that he procure:

> a second hand steam engine as used in the mines of Cornwall. It is to have a fifty inch cylinder with eight or nine feet stroke and seventy fathoms of pitwork complete, including ten inch plunger lift, matching pieces, seatings, buckets, windboxes, strapping plates, castings for balance bob, pulleys for shears, centres for capstan, lathe, and *two new boilers* which had better be shipped in parts and put together here¹³

As such an engine could not be found second hand, the work of manufacturing a new one fell to Perran Foundry. Presumably this order was fulfilled and sent out to the Burra Burra Mine, as the advertisements for engines and pumps in the Perran

---

⁹ Henry George Dines, *The Metalliferous Mining Region of South West England*, 2 vols (London: H.M. Stationery Office, 1956; repr. 1994), I, p. 366.
¹⁰ This alludes to a song sung by Cornish emigrants to Australia, referred to in Philip J. Payton, *The Cornish Miner in Australia: Cousin Jack Down Under* (Trewirgie: Dyllansow Truran, 1984), p. 21, which contains the lines: 'And to glory we will sail, We'll sail, And to glory we will sail.'
¹¹ 'Cornwall Industrial Settlements Initiative PERRANARWORTHAL (Truro Area)', *Cornwall County Council* <http://www.historic-cornwall.org.uk/cisi/perranarworthal/cisi_Perranarworthal_report.pdf> [accessed 7 February 2013] (p. 10)
¹² Ibid.
¹³ Philip Payton, *The Cornish Overseas: The epic story of the 'Great Migration'*, 2nd edn (Fowey: Cornwall Editions, 2005), p. 169.

Foundry catalogue of twenty years later boast of supplying the mine with '3 Engines and Pumps' of eighty inches and '1 Engine and Pump' of fifty inches.[14] From this small village location, which never employed a great number of men for its work, Perran Foundry became, as described by a 2005 heritage report, 'hugely important on the global stage'.[15]

As Britain made increasing links with the rest of the world in the form of colonial possessions, new opportunities arose for those investing in mining in Cornwall. The region not only supplied the empire with metals such as copper, but it also exported technology, men, and knowledge to extract its mineral wealth. This chapter will argue that Falmouth's role as a port and a trade centre was crucial to the formation of intellectual networks and the global export of Cornish mining. This in turn assisted in expanding Britain's formal and informal empires, and increasing its mineral wealth and potential for industrial growth, which was vital for the development of colonies such as India.

In this study of Falmouth's role in the creation and circulation of mining knowledge and technology, the facilitation of a global trade in science and minerals, and the formation of new territories within formal and informal empire, it will be occasionally necessary to consider the role that Cornwall as a whole, and the Cornish as a people, played. Falmouth, while the overall focus of this thesis, did not and could not exist in isolation from the rest of the region, and in the instance of Cornish mining in particular, was part of a wider narrative. Rather than considering only and narrowly the role that Falmouth played in the story of Cornish mining and empire, this chapter will instead show how the town acted as the catalyst for new power relationships between the British and other nations overseas. The power struggle between Britain and informal empire, and the transfer of Cornish mining knowledge on a global scale, would not have occurred as it did without Falmouth, and as such an examination of this is essential to an accurate exploration of its interaction with the British empire.

---

[14] *Illustrated Catalogue of Pumping & Winding Engines*, p. 5.
[15] 'Cornwall Industrial Settlements Initiative PERRANARWORTHAL (Truro Area)', p. 16.

The mining industry affected large areas of Cornwall, most notably but not exclusively those around Camborne, Redruth, Gwennap, and St Just. The role of Falmouth in the industry is rarely made clear; it does not appear in guides to the Cornish Mining World Heritage Site[16] and does not have a significant number of mines associated with it. It would appear, on consideration of the vast amount of literature concerning Cornish mining, that the town is not relevant in the story of this industry, and yet it was an integral location within it. This section will not seek to undermine the importance of mining areas such as those previously mentioned, but will take an alternative view of the connections between Cornish mining and the British empire, by considering the importance of maritime trade links and communications in the export of both raw materials and more complex 'packages' of men, machinery and knowledge. It will examine the extent to which Falmouth contributed to the industry of mining within the empire; and the affect that this involvement had on the town, Cornwall, and the empire itself.

As touched upon briefly in the previous chapter, mining was a sphere that held enormous economic power for Cornwall: the literal mapping of geological resources was testament to the wealth held beneath Cornish soil. This mapping, most likely initiated by the mapping of other valuable information such as road networks, which, as discussed, began in Falmouth, led to a more accurate understanding of Cornwall's resources. It was the task of men such as the Foxes to use this information to access the potential wealth and transform it into a valuable – and additionally, exportable – commodity. Although both geological mapping, and the literal, still-visible landscape of engine houses and abandoned mine shafts are proof that resources could be found all over the county, the process of exporting the results of mining – resources such as copper and technological innovations such as the beam engine – began in Falmouth.

From the eighteenth until the late nineteenth century, Cornwall was a leading region within Britain's industrial revolution. The mining industry here made fortunes for a new upper class of humble origins and adventurous spirit, so-called 'mineral lords' such as William Lemon, the Williams family, and the Foxes. Being rich in minerals,

---

[16] 'Areas, Places & Activities', *Cornish Mining World Heritage* <http://www.cornish-mining.org.uk/areas-places-activities> [accessed 15 May 2013]

Cornwall was a profitable area to mine and this industry was a welcome one, as the wealth and employment it generated slowly began to benefit the poverty-stricken and rapidly expanding Cornish working classes by the middle of the eighteenth century.[17] Originally, tin was the primary metal mined: a tin mining industry had been in existence in Cornwall since the Bronze Age. However, from the eighteenth century, the copper mining industry also began to gain prominence, and from around 1750 to 1850, copper was arguably the most important mineral in the region.[18] The mining of copper in great quantities was advantageous to the East India Company, which purchased two thirds of the total copper produced by Cornwall in 1789/90.[19] Around this time, the Company required large quantities of metal for the coppering of its ships' bottoms.[20] As colonial possessions such as India became increasingly industrialised, copper was also needed as a building material and for the manufacture of machine fittings.[21] The vast quantity that could be supplied by Cornwall also allowed the Company to retain its monopoly over 'sub-continental' markets in the early years of the nineteenth century.[22] Ultimately, by the 1840s, the mining landscape of Cornwall and West Devon was producing half of the world's copper.[23]

To begin to consider why Falmouth is so important in this context, we must first look to its physical geography and trade connections. Richard Drayton considers maritime networks as fundamental to the expansion and administration of the British empire, as trade could easily be conducted along the coast or at the mouths of rivers, while inland penetration was more difficult.[24] Due to this, he argues, global maritime networks had their foundations in what were naturally the easiest routes to take, 'where it was easiest to move fastest'.[25] Imperial trading routes were therefore based on the principles of speed and resistance. Those located within an easy route of

---

[17] Bernard Deacon, *Cornwall: A Concise History* (Cardiff: University of Wales Press, 2007), p. 104.
[18] 'Copper', *Geevor Tin Mine Museum* <http://www.geevor.com/index.php?object=138> [accessed 22 May 2013]
[19] H. V. Bowen, *The Business of Empire: The East India Company and Imperial Britain, 1756-1833* (Cambridge: Cambridge University Press, 2006), p. 266.
[20] Ibid.
[21] 'Earth Treasures', *Cornish Mining World Heritage* <http://www.cornish-mining.org.uk/delving-deeper/earth-treasures> [accessed 14 May 2013]
[22] George Unwin, *Observations upon the Export Trade of Tin and Copper to India* (Truro: T. Flindell, 1811), pp. 13-14.
[23] 'An Introduction to the Cornwall and West Devon Mining Landscape', *Cornish Mining World Heritage* <http://www.cornish-mining.org.uk/> [accessed 22 May 2013]
[24] Richard Drayton, 'Maritime Networks and the Making of Knowledge' in *Empire, the Sea and Global History*, ed. by David Cannadine (Basingstoke: Palgrave Macmillan, 2007), pp. 72-82 (p. 73).
[25] Drayton, 'Maritime Networks and the Making of Knowledge', p. 78.

travel were more connected to the empire and globalisation, both in terms of communications and in sympathy or loyalty. Those located within difficult, resistant routes could become regionalised, or 'marooned'. In this belief Drayton essentially agrees with Massey, whose theory of time-space compression allows for the existence of those who do not fit within the network of increasingly fast communications, and become isolated within the local as a result.[26] It is thus clear that within the British empire there were varying degrees of involvement: those located in a network of fast travel and communications had a greater experience of connectivity and involvement in empire than those located outside of it. In an age of sea travel, an age of the *maritime* empire, Falmouth's connection to the world was naturally and geographically superior to inland towns such as Camborne.

Falmouth also had natural advantages that rendered it a key location within a maritime network based on rapid travel, advantages that placed it far above other ports and harbours within Cornwall and Britain. In 1742, Daniel Defoe described it as, next to Milford Haven in Wales, 'the fairest and best road for shipping that is in the whole isle of Britain'.[27] The waterway leading into Falmouth is secure, wide, and calm for sailing ships entering it, making it an easy one to enter, with navigable creeks, and a safe harbour to be in if weather should worsen. It was originally chosen as a base for the Packet Service due to the fact that it has an exceptionally deep natural harbour, which also makes it ideal for mooring large vessels such as trading ships. On one day in December 1847, local businessman Alfred Fox observed in his journal that there were 190 vessels in the bay.[28] Its location in the extreme south west of Britain meant that it was the first suitable port reached by ships on return voyages from Europe and beyond. When Falmouth, or Smithwick as it was then, was being considered as a location for a new port around the year 1613, it was considered to have 'many advantages [...] in point of situation',[29] compared to nearby coastal towns such as Penryn.

---

[26] Massey, p. 148.
[27] Daniel Defoe, *A Tour Thro' The Whole Island of Great Britain*, 4 vols (London: J. Osborn, S. Birt, D. Browne, J. Hodges, A. Millar, J. Whiston, and J. Robinson, 1742), I, p. 345.
[28] *Jottings from Alfred Fox's Journal*, Truro, Cornwall Record Office, AD 854/72/1.
[29] R. Thomas, *History and Description of the Town and Harbour of Falmouth* (Falmouth: J. Trathan, 1827), pp. 55-56.

From these natural maritime routes based on ease of passage – speed and resistance – came trade links. As Drayton argues, human networks grow out of maritime geography.[30] In his *Magna Britannia*, published in 1814, Daniel Lysons comments that the extensive trade of Falmouth, exceeding at that time any other port in Cornwall, was due to 'its advantageous situation'.[31] While the Packet Service brought great prosperity to Falmouth, its rapid growth as a town was, argues Whetter, most directly a result of the trade carried on in the port.[32] From a hamlet consisting of Arwenack House and some fishermen's huts in the year 1600, Falmouth in 1664 had expanded to contain two hundred houses,[33] this growth attributable to the trade and supply function of the port. The ease with which ships could travel to Falmouth led to strong trade links with overseas countries as early as the end of the seventeenth century, and so in Falmouth geographic advantage resulted in linkage to a maritime trade network. The town became a major trading port and its business was increased by new connections made with foreign countries through the formation of the British empire. By 1814, the port took large deliveries of timber, hemp, wine, spirits, and sugar, and exported tin, copper, pilchards, woollen goods, and cotton, the latter being sent from Manchester to Falmouth to be exported to Malta, which had officially become a British colony in that year under the Treaty of Paris.[34] With colonial compression occurring in this way in Falmouth, the area became an increasingly important trading port, and large companies, agents and merchants from elsewhere in Britain established themselves in the town.

During the second half of the eighteenth and first half of the nineteenth century, the East India Company, representing imperial trade on a global scale, established agents in British communities that might be particularly useful to it.[35] Many of the locations chosen were ones that had been significant during wartime, and the introduction of an agent highlighted an area's growing strategic importance to war, the empire, and trade. Ports equipped for service during war could provide defences for ships and

---

[30] Drayton, 'Maritime Networks and the Making of Knowledge', p. 79.
[31] Lysons, p. 101.
[32] Whetter, *The History of Falmouth*, p. 28.
[33] *A Panorama of Falmouth* (Falmouth: Cornish Magazine Office, 1827), p. 15.
[34] Lysons, p. 101.
[35] James H. Thomas, 'East India Company Agency Work in the British Isles, 1700-1800' in *The Worlds of the East India Company*, ed. by H. V. Bowen and others (Woodbridge: The Boydell Press, 2004), pp. 33-48 (p. 33).

valuable cargoes and a safe haven for those in danger, in addition to supplies and repairs.[36] The wartime significance of Falmouth has already been discussed, and as a location important to both war and trade, initially influenced by its natural advantages, it retained an East India Company agent from 1765-1817.[37] Agencies worked in maritime communities as the eyes and ears of the Company, reporting any occurrences in the port that might affect its interests, collecting and distributing its mail, checking and managing provisions on ships, and liaising with Company employees on board. Duties undertaken by the agent at Falmouth in a year from August 1776 to 1777 included such things as care of ships in the form of repainting, and forwarding letters.[38] James Thomas, in his study of East India Company agents, describes the port as 'a 'natural' community for the Company' due to its physical features such as navigability, and the facilities it could offer ships.[39] The presence of the Company in the port reiterates its importance as a commercial location within the British empire. Thus far it has been demonstrated that, as Drayton argues, the initial stages in the formation of maritime networks linked to Falmouth are the physical maritime geography of shipping routes, upon which are built human trading routes.[40]

In the formation of a maritime network based on the fastest travel routes between Britain and overseas, and the subsequent establishment of trade routes and trading ports, we can begin to see the creation of time-space compression, a concept already mentioned briefly but now of particular relevance and warranting further investigation throughout this chapter. Time-space compression, the shrinking of time and space through the speeding up of movement and communications, is not necessarily a modern phenomenon, although it is especially relevant in today's world of instant global communications. Massey, writing in 1994, described her present as 'an era [...] when things are speeding up, and spreading out',[41] though this phrase could easily be applied to the period studied within this thesis. The ability to travel greater distances in less time than previously, as well as access to the products and

---

[36] J. H. Thomas, p. 35.
[37] J. H. Thomas, p. 35.
[38] J. H. Thomas, p. 46.
[39] J. H. Thomas, p. 37.
[40] As a point of interest, Milford Haven, mentioned earlier as another example of a harbour naturally suited to shipping, was also made an important port for the Navy, communications, and trade in the eighteenth century, with an East India Company agent, due to its physical geography.
[41] Massey, p. 146.

cultures of places geographically far away from home were experiences applicable to many within the British empire at this time. Equally, this experience was not universally shared, and many were not included among the areas of society blessed with the ability to travel or purchase exotic products from the empire.

From the seventeenth century onwards, with the introduction of mail routes from Falmouth to Europe, the port of Falmouth had the potential to become a key location within Britain for the experiencing of time-space compression. With the formation of the Packet Service, as discussed previously, communications became more efficient, faster, and international. As trade routes were formed for import and export, products such as tea and sugar came to be consumed in Falmouth, and consequently also around Cornwall, thousands of miles away from their natural environment. By the first half of the nineteenth century, greater numbers of mail and trade routes, extending further across the world to places such as the East and West Indies, led to the crossing of a far larger space from Britain. In discussing maritime trade connections, therefore, it becomes clear that one of the by-products of connecting Falmouth to the empire was the experience of time-space compression in and around the town. Having the facility within Falmouth to traverse greater distances than before and to communicate with geographically distant locations opened up the potential within Cornwall for scientific innovation and economic growth based on industry. Without the trade and communications links of Falmouth, Cornwall's gateway to the empire might not have been created, and its far-reaching reputation for mining skill and knowledge might not exist. It is to this notion, that Falmouth was an instrumental location in the expansion and exportation of Cornish mining knowledge and technology because of its maritime connections, that attention will now turn.

The formation of trade networks based on the fastest and easiest shipping routes is of paramount importance to the formation of intellectual networks. These networks can be viewed as the third tier of a structure in which natural routes form, followed by trade routes, which in turn support intellectual circuits.[42] Interactions between nations, or indeed simply between towns, are generally motivated by an initial desire

---

[42] Drayton, 'Maritime Networks and the Making of Knowledge', p. 79.

to trade, and it is for this reason that communications begin. The passage of men and mail from one country to another for the purpose of trade then leads to the passage of ideas, and of books or pamphlets. Knowledge is thus traded, or rather exchanged, while goods and money also change hands.

This is true in the case of the Dutch East India Company, as Siegfried Huigen notes. 'The commercial networks of the Dutch trading companies', he argues, 'provided an infrastructure which was accessible to people with a scholarly interest in the exotic world.'[43] Huigen takes as an example the Dutch trading post of Deshima, in the harbour of Nagasaki, from 1635-1853. At this point, Dutch East India Company employees could acquire information and knowledge relating to Japanese geography, science and culture, while the Japanese could use it 'as a window to Europe', after the country had been isolated from the rest of the world by the shoguns.[44] Here, the trading links made through the Company allowed knowledge to circulate and to be generated. To have knowledgeable men travelling along trading routes became a scientific ideal. In his 1772 preface to the Louis de Bougainville book *A Voyage Round the World*, Johann Reinhold Forster voiced a wish that 'our English East India Company, prompted by the noble zeal for the improvement of natural history [...] might send a set of men properly acquainted with mathematics, natural history, physic, and other branches of literature' to their colonial possessions in the Indies.[45] He also called for Company employees to purchase Hebrew, Persian and Brahmanic manuscripts, in order that the British should be able to learn more about foreign countries.[46] The sharing of knowledge through what were originally trade routes can be seen throughout history, reaching as far back as pre- Roman Empire. An ancient example lies in the method of winemaking in France around 500BC. Researchers have found that French wine making was actually of Etruscan – Italian – origin, and that the skill was passed from one civilisation to another as goods were shipped from Italy to France.[47]

---

[43] Siegfried Huigen, 'Introduction' in *The Dutch Trading Companies as Knowledge Networks*, ed. by Siegfried Huigen and others (Leiden: Koninklijke Brill, 2010), pp. 1-16 (p. 1)
[44] Huigen, p. 2.
[45] Johann Reinhold Forster, 'The Translator's Preface' in Lewis [sic] de Bougainville, *A Voyage Round the World*, trans. by Johann Reinhold Forster (London: J Nourse, 1772), pp. v-x (p. viii).
[46] Forster, pp. viii-ix.
[47] Jason Palmer, 'French wine 'has Italian origins'', BBC News (2013)
<http://www.bbc.co.uk/news/science-environment-22758119> [accessed 5 June 2013]

Trading routes could also lead to a stimulation of knowledge production, as a greater ability to share information, and to share technology that came out of it, created a greater demand. The expansion of Cornwall's mining industry, and the market for Cornish copper during the century leading to 1850, influenced by the British empire, resulted in a demand for greater knowledge relating to minerals and mining. In 1849, the British *Mining Almanack* called for an increase in scientific study relating to mining in order that the industry should become more economically rewarding.[48] Mining was viewed as an industry of great value to the nation, but with the potential to become even more profitable. 'Imperfect knowledge of the character of the natural material, and slight acquaintance with the appliances which have been made, lead too frequently to considerable expenditure of ingenuity, time, and money, upon an object which turns out to be useless', state the authors of the volume. 'Never was there a period when it became so imperative a necessity to enlist all the knowledge, scientific and practical, that we possess, in and of our mineral productions in all the operations of mining and metallurgy.'[49] A move towards contributing greater knowledge relating to mining had been made in Cornwall around sixteen years earlier. It should be noted, however, that the intellectual heart of the Cornish mining industry did not lie in the industrial heartlands of Camborne, Redruth or Gwennap, but in Falmouth.

In 1833, the Cornwall Polytechnic Society, later to become the Royal Cornwall Polytechnic Society (RCPS), was formed in Falmouth at the suggestion of Anna Maria Fox, 'who was anxious to encourage a number of clever workmen who were then employed by several members of her family'.[50] These workmen in need of encouragement were based at Perran Foundry. The 1834 manifesto of the society stated that the aim of its foundation was to 'encourage industry, and to elicit the ingenuity of a community distinguished for its mechanical skill'.[51] While the society also exhibited artistic work from its members, including women, the most active areas of research and display were in engineering and mining technology. In 1835,

---

[48] *The Mining Almanack for 1849*, ed. by Henry English (London: The Mining Journal Office, 1849), p. 89.
[49] Ibid.
[50] Wilson Lloyd Fox, *Historical Synopsis of the Royal Cornwall Polytechnic Society* (Falmouth: Lake & Co., Printers, 1882), p. 3
[51] Ibid.

the society's success in recruiting members and producing work of note was celebrated by *The Mechanics' Magazine*, which observed that:

> perhaps, looking at the intelligent and enterprising character of the population on whom it threw itself for support, and the intimate connexion of their prevailing pursuits with some of the grandest practical applications of science, there was really nothing surprising in the matter.[52]

Clearly, practical science relating to mining was to be encouraged in Cornwall, and its people were seen as being in a particularly advantageous position for generating mining knowledge.

Caroline Fox, sister to Anna Maria, is often credited with coining the name 'Polytechnic',[53] although the term was in existence as an adjective in France in 1795, being used in reference to the name *École Polytechnique*, meaning an educational institution dealing with several different technical subjects.[54] In his history of the society, Wilson Lloyd Fox claims that the RCPS was the forerunner to many other 'kindred institutions' which were formed around the same time.[55] Indeed, the use of the phrase Polytechnic Society as a noun is first credited to Caroline Fox in 1836 by the *Oxford English Dictionary*, although it is difficult to say for certain that it was the first ever society of this kind; it may simply be the first mentioned as such.[56] Laying aside this issue of provenance, the Cornwall Polytechnic Society was certainly among the first of these bodies to be formed in Britain, though not the only one. The society reflected a growing interest among the population in the sciences, and the accumulation of knowledge of many types.

---

[52] *The Mechanics' Magazine, Museum, Register, Journal, and Gazette, April 4 – September 25, 1835*, 13 vols (London: J. Cunningham, 1835), XXIII, p. 214.
[53] Wilson Lloyd Fox, p. 3.
[54] 'Polytechnic' in *Oxford English Dictionary* <http://www.oed.com.ezproxy.falmouth.ac.uk/view/Entry/147402?redirectedFrom=polytechnic#eid> [accessed 6 June 2013]
[55] Wilson Lloyd Fox, p. 3.
[56] Polytechnic' in *Oxford English Dictionary*

One motivation behind the pursuit of knowledge and its popularity was its link to piety and revelation: it was viewed as 'a moral ideal for the world'.[57] Ignorance was to be despised in a civilised Christian society such as Britain's. *The Polytechnic Journal* of 1840 bemoaned lack of education, fearing that 'ignorance is begetting crimes and disorders, and [...] the list of sufferers is not yet full.'[58] Originally, science was pursued by amateurs and volunteers, but was not officially sponsored by the state. Private societies and clubs were formed to allow gentlemen to share ideas, specimens, and overseas contacts.[59] Gradually, however, the usefulness of intellectual pursuits for state interests became apparent, as the so-called Scientific Revolution highlighted the scientific rationality that could be applied to governing.[60] Representatives of state began to collect information in earnest, mapping land and collecting data relating to natural resources and the population. From around the end of the eighteenth century, societies that had once been the sole concern of amateurs began to receive state patronage, and bodies such as the Admiralty began to work alongside scientists to drive forward discovery and invention.[61] The interest of the state in matters of science and knowledge can be seen in the rapid patronage granted to the Cornwall Polytechnic Society. The prefix 'Royal' was awarded in 1835, less than two years after its first exhibition, making it the Royal Cornwall Polytechnic Society: still a group of amateurs, but one with official backing.

The surge of interest in science led to a new era of lectures, publications, and, of course, scientific and polytechnic societies. The RCPS was not the only group in Cornwall to highlight research relating to mining. The Royal Institution of Cornwall (RIC), based in Truro and formed in 1818, sought to promote 'knowledge in natural history, ethnology and the fine and industrial arts, especially in relation to Cornwall'.[62] The RCPS and RIC were able to coexist in an often mutually informative fashion. Robert Were Fox, father to Anna-Maria, Caroline and Barclay, is listed among the RIC Vice-Presidents in 1847,[63] and publications by the RIC

---

[57] Richard Drayton, 'Knowledge and Empire' in *The Oxford History of the British Empire*, ed. by P. J. Marshall, 5 vols (Oxford: Oxford University Press, 1998), II, pp. 231-252 (p. 236).
[58] *The Polytechnic Journal* (London: Office of the Polytechnic Journal, 1840), p. 2
[59] Drayton, p. 239.
[60] Drayton, pp. 245-246.
[61] Drayton, p. 249.
[62] <http://www.royalcornwallmuseum.org.uk/> [accessed 20 June 2013]
[63] *Twenty-Ninth Annual Report of the Royal Institution of Cornwall* (Truro: J.R. Netherton, 1848), p. 12.

carried articles about research funded by the RCPS. One main difference between the societies lies in their scope: members of the RIC appear to have had broader interests, of which industrial arts was just one area. At the time of the formation of the RCPS, the RIC was essentially a society for the prosperous, excluding the working classes. Only in 1847 is there any mention of 'the less opulent classes', in a brief comment made that 'the fundamental design of this Institution may be advanced by opening our Museum and our meetings at a secondary rate of subscription', though this was recommended only on the proviso that 'the privileges of the proprietary and ordinary members' may be protected.[64] While the RIC provided a space for the privileged classes to discuss scientific ideas of varying content, the RCPS sought to explore more practical science, drawing on the working experience of actual labourers in the relevant fields. While Truro was a fashionable town for the upper classes, Falmouth was a hive of industry, hosting seamen, traders, and travellers of many classes and nationalities. Lower class men and women could, from the very first exhibition, submit their work to the RCPS. It is the emphasis on the practical application of science that marks the Polytechnic as separate from many other scientific societies, and it was the economic implications of science that enabled the RCPS to exist and thrive. Without Falmouth's links to trade and overseas markets, the purpose of the RCPS would have been negated.

Having a society that promoted and funded useful research was not an entirely new concept. The Royal Society, one of the earliest scientific societies, carried out practical scientific work after being founded in 1660. Members of the Lunar Society of Birmingham, formed around 1765, carried out practical experiments in fields such as geology, meteorology, and engineering.[65] It is arguably one of the earliest to embrace the science associated with the Industrial Revolution in Britain. While the Royal Society and Lunar Society are examples of early scientific groups, it wasn't until first half of the nineteenth century that their number began to increase significantly. The British Association for the Advancement of Science (BAAS), formed in 1831, aimed to promote discussion and connection between men of science, and became a forum for the discussion of major new ideas of economic, as

---

[64] *Twenty-Ninth Annual Report of the Royal Institution of Cornwall*, p. 14.
[65] 'The Lunar Society', *Library of Birmingham* <http://www.libraryofbirmingham.com/article/archivesofsohofigures/thelunarsociety> [accessed 7 July 2013]

well as scientific, benefit to the nation.[66] Within the BAAS, James Joule discussed his experiments on the mechanical equivalent of heat in 1847; a theory that would go on to have great significance for thermodynamics and consequently engineering and steam engines.[67] The RCPS fits into this story as one of the earliest provincial societies, being based in Cornwall and far from the busy cities more commonly associated with the Industrial Revolution: areas such as London, Manchester, Birmingham, and Swansea. This is in itself remarkable; that Cornwall should have such a dynamic society as early as 1833 is initially surprising, but becomes less so when it is remembered that Falmouth was a well-connected port and Cornwall an area that was significant for mining and its associated technologies.

After the formation of the RCPS came the Geological and Polytechnic Society of the West Riding of Yorkshire in 1837, founded to explore the geology of the local area but also, taking inspiration from its Cornish counterpart, to 'devote itself to the practical working and economy of coal-mines, their products, and ancillary industries'.[68] Much later, in 1865, the Worcester Polytechnic Institute was formed to 'create and convey the latest science and engineering knowledge in ways that are most beneficial to society.'[69] The notion of the Polytechnic Society was not confined to Britain. In Norway, the *Polyteknisk Forening* (Polytechnic Association) was created in 1852, with the aim of making the natural sciences applicable to society, encouraging cooperation between intellectuals and those working in industry.[70] Many other societies of this kind were also formed, but evident from these examples is the link between the pursuit of scientific knowledge and its practical application and potential benefit to society. In Yorkshire, coal mining was paramount as this could have the greatest economic impact on the local communities; in Norway, the

---

[66] 'Our History', *British Science Association* <http://www.britishscienceassociation.org/about-british-science-association/our-history> [accessed 6 June 2013]

[67] *Concise Encyclopedia of the History of Energy*, ed. by Cutler J. Cleveland (San Diego: Elsevier, 2009), p. 39.

[68] Jack Morrell, 'Economic and ornamental geology: the Geological and Polytechnic Society of the West Riding of Yorkshire, 1837-53' in *Metropolis and Province: Science in British Culture, 1780-1850*, ed. by Ian Inkster and Jack Morrell (London: Hutchinson & Co., 1983), pp. 231-256 (p. 236).

[69] 'About WPI', *Worcester Polytechnic Institute* <http://www.wpi.edu/about/index.html> [accessed 7 June 2013]

[70] Bjørn Pedersen, 'NORWAY: A Group of Chemists in the Polytechnic Society in Christiania. The Norweigan Chemical Society, 1893-1916', in *Creating Networks in Chemistry: the Foundation and Early History of Chemical Societies in Europe*, ed. by Anita Kildebaek Nielsen and Soňa Štrbáňová, (Cambridge: The Royal Society of Chemistry, 2008), pp. 223-235 (p. 228).

emphasis lay instead with chemistry. In Cornwall, as is now taken for granted, the economic potential of the region lay in mining and mineralogy.

Cornwall's role as one of the empire's foremost hard rock mining areas had made it a locus for invention, as problems in mining, or areas for improvement, were identified and solutions found. Here, as early as 1725, the Newcomen atmospheric engine was invented by Joseph Hornblower. This was one of the earliest machines to harness the power generated by steam, and was used in pumping water out of mines so that men could work deeper under the ground. A later improvement on Hornblower's engine, using significantly less fuel and so being far more economical, was pioneered in Cornwall by James Watt in 1769. Further improvements were made by Richard Trevithick, and in 1800 the first high-pressure steam engine was installed at Stray Park in Camborne. This invention increased the power of the engine, making it around ten times more powerful than the Watt engine.[71] While other locations within the region may have seemed a more natural home for a community of inventors and researchers, after the formation of the RCPS Falmouth became the intellectual base for the industry because of its place within the maritime network of the British empire. It was because of Falmouth and its fast connection to the rest of the world that the markets for Cornish copper could be accessed, in the form of export within, but also outside of, the East India Company.

The connection of Falmouth to intellectual networks informed by trade was important to the interests of the town, and to Cornwall as a whole. At this point in the 'Scientific Revolution',[72] it was not enough for a local society simply to produce an arbitrary collection of research, shared only between its members. In a national context, the *sharing* of knowledge was an ideal, shown in the formation of the Society for the Diffusion of Useful Knowledge in 1826, and in the great number of publications concerned with science and education that were created around this time. The British empire, in the minds of its proponents, was a scientific, civilised, thinking entity, and knowledge was produced to be shown and shared. Papers and

---

[71] The developments in steam technology made by those involved in the mining industry had a major impact on Britain and the world during the Industrial Revolution. Not only did steam power significantly speed up mining, and allow for deeper excavations, but it also laid the foundations for many innovations in travel, including steam ships, locomotives, and portable engines.
[72] Richard Holmes, *The Age of Wonder: How the Romantic Generation Discovered the Beauty and Terror of Science* (London: Harper*Press*, 2008), p. xvi.

annual reports were sent between different societies to become a part of their libraries. Often, extracts or full articles were re-printed in other societies' publications. This was not a practice confined to Britain: in 1842, a quarterly meeting of the American Philosophical Society noted the receipt of the *Ninth Annual Report of the Royal Cornwall Polytechnic Society* for its library.[73] In London in 1844, the Royal Society for the Encouragement of Arts, Manufactures and Commerce (RSA) acknowledged receipt of three items from the RCPS, including a report on a society-funded research project, a copy of its annual report, and an appendix to its Transactions.[74] Science had become a discipline concerned not only with knowledge and research, but also with networking and correspondence: sharing information that might be useful around Britain and the world. The reports sent to the RSA meeting, and the aforementioned interest in the 'Polytechnic', show that the practical application of science for economic interests (as seen in the name of the RSA) was important, and that a culture of sharing useful information was at the heart of science during this time.

The reading and reviewing of research was integral to its authentication: not everything, as David Livingstone notes, will be considered as valid scientific knowledge.[75] Research must be approved by the relevant scientific public to secure the status of 'true' knowledge. Livingstone points to the 'showing' of knowledge in display or demonstration as part of its process of verification,[76] and indeed this is true for practical experiments carried out by the RCPS. As a second layer, upon this localised display of an experiment, however, can be added a textual 'showing' for those not located in Cornwall, or even in Britain. The reports of public experiments, such as the trial of an engine at Tresavean Mine, as well as other reports of meetings, were thus created and shared in order that a wider scientific community might peruse the experiment and be part of the process of its verification. For the effective communication of knowledge, a location that was well connected to the rest of Britain, and the rest of the world, was vital. Falmouth's fast communications and

---

[73] *Proceedings of the American Philosophical Society*, 2 vols (n.p. n.d., 1842), II, p. 209.
[74] 'PRESENTS RECEIVED BY THE SOCIETY FOR THE YEAR ENDING JUNE 12, 1844. WITH THE NAMES OF THE DONORS', *Transactions of the Society, Instituted at London, for the Encouragement of Arts, Manufactures, and Commerce* , 55, (1843-1844), 204-212 (p. 206).
[75] David N. Livingstone, *Putting Science in its Place: Geographies of Scientific Knowledge* (Chicago: The University of Chicago Press, 2003), pp. 18-19.
[76] Livingstone, p. 24.

travel links were therefore important in promoting the research of the RCPS, and so the intellectual networks that had been built upon trade routes assisted in disseminating and authenticating this research. Such networks were crucial for creating a credibility and value that could be attached to knowledge, a concept that will become one of the main ideas in the remainder of this chapter.

While intellectual networks were, to some extent, dependent on correspondence and effective communications, face to face interaction and scientific discussion was also common. The town of Falmouth, a hotspot for trade and travel, played host to many important people from the worlds of science and business. While its trade links stimulated the production and sharing of knowledge, the networking opportunities that it offered also played a part in making it an intellectual base. The journal of Barclay Fox offers an interesting insight into the people his family and the RCPS met due to Falmouth's functioning as a port and their own mining connections. On 21 July 1838, the Foxes dined with a Colombian mines commissioner named Dagenhert, whom Barclay describes as 'a man of much science & general information'.[77] The group discussed the design of engines for raising and lowering men in the mines, which was a project very much at the heart of the Society's research interests and one that will be revisited in more detail later in this chapter. On 18 August 1840, Count Von Beust, the Director General of Mines in Prussia called at the Fox office in Falmouth 'to ask for introductions to the Mines'.[78] Being based in Falmouth, the Society was able to attract noteworthy people, who might be passing through the town and waiting for a ship, to visit its lectures and exhibitions. In April 1842, two captains and two officers, about to embark on a 'voyage of survey and scientific discovery', attended a lecture given by Barclay's uncle George Croker (often abbreviated to GC) Fox.[79]

The intellectual networks of which Falmouth was a part were important in disseminating research, verifying it, and giving it an exportable quality. These networks could tell the world that Cornish miners were able to work more efficiently than men elsewhere, and that Cornish mines were safer to work in because of their

---

[77] Barclay Fox, p. 132.
[78] Barclay Fox, p. 206.
[79] Barclay Fox, p. 265.

new equipment. If this information could be distributed, so too could the knowledge and technology associated with it; though perhaps at a price. The RCPS could identify an intellectual or technological deficit in the mining industry and communicate its success in fulfilling this need, thus creating a demand for the resultant product. Of course, this economic angle to science could only be successful if the research carried out by society members was of real use. The Cornish mining industry, and the demand for Cornish minerals for the empire, therefore had a strong influence on the RCPS's research interests.

Falmouth being an important port, a second research area was shipping, and improvements to vessels or travel. In 1834, for instance, Robert Were Fox received a medal in the annual society exhibition for his invention of a method for copper sheathing boats.[80] This invention had particular relevance for both the Cornish mining industry, as metals produced from its minerals would be used in the practice, and in Falmouth's overseas trading interests, as companies such as the East India Company purchased large amounts of copper in order to sheath their ships. Members could pursue their own lines of scientific enquiry such as this, but particular areas of study were also promoted heavily by the awarding of financial prizes for improvements in certain fields. The decisions made regarding which areas of research were to be given a monetary value are in need of investigation for the ways in which they relate to the needs of Cornwall and the wider British empire.

Creating the legend of Cornish mining

Here, I have touched on the concept of certain types of science having a locality, or indeed, localities relating to a certain branch of science. The idea of science being intrinsically linked to its locations of production and consumption is one that has been explored by writers such as Livingstone and Simon Naylor,[81] although prior to studies such as Livingtone's the discipline was often, as he himself acknowledges, seen as 'an enterprise untouched by local conditions [...] a universal undertaking,

---

[80] 'Cornwall Polytechnic Society', *Royal Cornwall Gazette, Falmouth Packet & Plymouth Journal*, 1 November 1834.
[81] Livingstone, and Simon Naylor, 'The Field, the Museum and the Lecture Hall: The Spaces of Natural History in Victorian Cornwall', *Transactions of the Institute of British Geographers*, 27 (2002), 494-513.

not a provincial practice.'[82] Contrary to being placeless, scientific knowledge in its many different forms is shaped by the setting in which it is produced. Livingstone argues that if that knowledge did not in some way resonate with its setting, it would not be allowed to reach the stage by which it is expressed, verified or supported.[83] The actual process by which research or hypothesis becomes knowledge is very much dependent on the site of its production and discussion, be this a society meeting hall, a field excursion, or a laboratory. The latter is carefully designed to be as placeless as possible, but as a consequence has an implied code of practice and system for verification that shapes the work being carried out from its formative stages. Scientific discourse is thus enabled and constrained within certain spaces. The knowledge associated with mining that was produced within Cornwall is therefore reflective of its location. It had both a local and global application and relevance, as this section will explain. It was indeed shaped by the space in which it was produced, but also transferable to other locations with similar mining conditions around the world. The dual local and global quality of technology and knowledge related to mining is typified by the Cornish Mining World Heritage Site strapline: 'Our mining culture shaped your world'.[84] Here, the local character of knowledge is clear, but equally clear is its global significance.

It is my argument that it is only by acknowledging and investigating the influence of the local on branches of science and technology such as mining, which went on to be of global significance for the British empire, that we can understand how that empire functioned. It is all too easy to view the empire as a homogenous whole, with scientific knowledge as an objective ideal, when it was clearly constituted by a number of separate localities – rural as well as metropolitan – all with their own role to play in its operation, spread, and influence. In this section, I will argue that the Cornish mining industry, with an intellectual heart in the Royal Cornwall Polytechnic Society, came to be globally significant during the British empire, and that the knowledge produced and carefully contained by it was vital in the empire's economic quest to exploit the resources of lands overseas. Far from consisting of objective, placeless truths, the knowledge and technological insight relating to hard

---

[82] Livingstone, p. 1.
[83] Livingstone, p. 7.
[84] <http://www.cornish-mining.org.uk>

rock mining was, for a time, so intrinsically located in Cornwall and with the Cornish that its provenance gave it a global value and prestige. The forthcoming section of this chapter will examine several points. The first is how research carried out in Cornwall was shaped and influenced to serve the region's needs, as well as those of the empire, in the context of productivity and economics. The second area of interest will be a concern with value: how value came to be attached to knowledge specifically produced in Cornwall – how it became exportable – and how this knowledge contributed to British colonial and economic interests overseas. Finally, it will examine the effect of exporting knowledge on the empire and the people of Cornwall.

The research interests of members and associates of the RCPS were shaped to suit a certain agenda relating to trade and empire. The motives of the society, in the context of its research, warrant examination. What did the society want to achieve by promoting certain types of knowledge and invention? An initial answer to this lies in the society's own account of itself, and its aim to:

> impart to the Society a more important character; by pointing out the most desirable field for research; by calling the attention of the public to the greatest desiderata in art and science, especially as connected with the permanent interests of the county.[85]

The reference to the interests of the county alludes to the furthering of Cornwall's economic strength; science that might promote the industries which maintained so many Cornish households. Chief among these industries was, of course, mining. Rather than allowing members to pursue any line of enquiry, the society has acknowledged its own wish to increase its importance and credibility by channelling research towards certain subjects beneficial to Cornwall. In this, we can begin to see the formation of a Cornish identity based around mining expertise. This identity would go on to be a source of pride and encouragement to the Cornish, but also to add value to the region's knowledge, skill and equipment in the context of export.

Further evidence of potential underlying motives in the society's research can be seen in the structure of the society itself. The 1838 annual report of the RCPS lists

---

[85] Wilson Lloyd Fox, pp. 3-4.

the various committees that constitute it, which are defined by district.[86] Eleven committees based on place are included. The largest, unsurprisingly given the society's location, is that of Falmouth and Penryn, with thirty members. Other large committees are those of Penzance and Marazion, St Austell and Fowey, St Day and Chacewater, Redruth, and Truro. Smaller committees existed for Camborne, Helston, Hayle, Liskeard and Bodmin. These locations, spanning almost the whole of Cornwall, are all areas with links to mining.[87] As such, the committees of the RCPS mirror the most significant mining areas within Cornwall, excluding only St Just and the Tamar Valley in the extreme southwest and north of Cornwall respectively. It would be natural that the interests of these members, representing their localities, would be in some way geared towards mining and the economic health of Cornwall.[88] With such a strong mining presence in the very makeup of the society, we can begin to see a potential direction in its activities. This becomes yet clearer if the society's activities are considered. Each year, the RCPS held an exhibition of work by its members and any non-members paying a fee to exhibit. The categories by which contributors' work were sorted would in themselves have directed endeavour towards certain fields. Some were artistic, appealing to women as well as men, and to the arts as well as science,[89] but the main scientific categories were 'Inventions and Workmanship', 'Models of known Machines', 'Naval Architecture', and 'Charts and Maps'.[90] In the first annual exhibition, entries for the invention and models categories were decidedly in the field of mining and engineering, with

---

[86] *The Sixth Annual Report of the Royal Cornwall Polytechnic Society* (Falmouth: Jane Trathan, 1838), pp. 2-3.
[87] Redruth, Camborne, St Day, Chacewater, Bodmin, Liskeard, Helston, Marazion, and St Austell were all mined areas. Hayle's link to the industry was in its port and foundry, and Fowey and its surrounding areas were similarly linked through their function as a port, and to a lesser extent as a mining district. Truro was another port, and also a stannary town and administrative centre for the industry: a location where metals were brought to be tested, stamped and taxed. Penzance had a large tin smelting works at Chyandour, and a second nearby at Stable Hobba in Newlyn.
[88] Indeed, if the members themselves are considered, their interests become yet more obvious. Many had mining interests of some kind, such as the Foxes of Falmouth, Samuel Moyle of Truro, Edward William Wynne Pendarves of Camborne, the Williams family of St Day and Chacewater, James Plomer of Helston, and Thomas Teague of Redruth. In each large committee, and several of the smaller ones, there sat at least one, and in some cases many more than one, man with mining interests.
[89] In the first annual exhibition, artistic categories for entrants included water colours, pencil and ink, oil paintings, and fancy work. Both prizes for oil paintings were awarded to men, but all other artistic prizes were won by women.
[90] Wilson Lloyd Fox, p. 40.

exhibits including a water gauge for steam boilers, a locomotive steam engine, and a model of a mine.[91]

Direction was also given more specifically through the creation of prizes in certain areas. The first prize was offered by Charles Fox[92] in 1834, and relates to mining. Three rewards were offered, one of ten guineas, one of five guineas, and one of three guineas, for 'the best improvement in the method of ascending and descending Mines'.[93] It is useful to analyse in detail the motivations behind this funded research, as a means of showing how the society's activities were shaped by its relationship to empire and trade networks. Previous to this invention, miners were asked to ascend and descend mines using ladders. Due to the invention of steam technology for the pumping out of water from mines, works could descend to several hundred fathoms,[94] meaning that miners must exert a considerable amount of energy, and use a great deal of time, to reach lower levels before starting work. The Cornish system of tribute and tutwork meant that miners bid against each other to secure a mining job, for which they were paid a percentage of the value of the ore that they raised. They were, therefore, only paid for their time below ground and for the ore they obtained, not for any time spent getting to the ore. If a man could only work for a set amount of time, any time wasted in getting to his pitch on the lode would cost him money. The haste and exhaustion induced by climbing so many ladders led to many accidents, and local newspapers carried frequent reports of men having died by falling.[95]

The public impetus and justification for creating a man engine was therefore that the health of miners would be greatly improved by it. Whether the intentions of the RCPS were truly philanthropic or simply geared towards raising public opinion is impossible to determine absolutely, but the motivation to appear humanitarian is clear in literature that was produced about the engine. An account of Captain

---

[91] 'Cornwall Polytechnic Society', *Royal Cornwall Gazette, Falmouth Packet & Plymouth Journal*, 28 December 1833.
[92] A brother to Robert Were Fox, Alfred Fox (mentioned in a later chapter) and George Croker Fox.
[93] Wilson Lloyd Fox, p. 43.
[94] A fathom being equal to six feet, or 1.83 metres.
[95] See, for instance, 'Coroner's Inquests', *Royal Cornwall Gazette, Falmouth Packet & Plymouth Journal*, 7 July 1832, and 'Fatal Accident', *Royal Cornwall Gazette, Falmouth Packet & Plymouth Journal*, 20 July 1833.

Nicholas Vivian's testing of the engine repeatedly uses the word 'barbarous' in reference to the ladders in mines.[96] The employment of science and technological advances for the improvement of working conditions fits with the British desire at this time to be perceived as civilised. Indeed, the word 'barbarous', with its implications of immorality and wickedness calls to mind the antonyms of civilisation, culture, and humanity. The self-perception of Britain as a civilised nation was integral to its imperial mission: Britain carried the moral superiority and enlightened civilised ideas that justified its taming of supposedly savage and barbarous peoples. Here, the motives of the society clearly support the imperial national identity. The man engine therefore gains a moral value that informs the perception of British industry as progressive and supports the ideals of the empire. In showing concern for Cornwall's miners, the RCPS also sought to win favour with this large body of working class men that had been known to riot.[97] Here, science was thus also employed in an attempt to cater to the volatile masses, defuse civic unrest and dampen agitation: subduing the barbarous at home.

However, this gain to the miners was not inducement enough to mine owners. Despite the man engine being first introduced to the society in 1833, when it won its inventor Michael Loam the prize money, it was not until 1842 that a mine could be found to trial it (see Fig. 4).

---

[96] *The Mechanics' Magazine, Museum, Register, Journal, and Gazette*, ed. by J.C. Robertson (London: James Bounsall, 1844), p. 362.
[97] Miners' riots were commonplace in Cornwall, and occurred most notably in poor areas where conditions were harsh and food scarce.

Fig. 4: Drawing of man engine at Tresavean Mine

Drawing of the man engine at Tresavean Mine by William Henry Tregoning, created in 1842, the year that the engine was installed. Truro, Cornwall Records Office, TG/11/1.

The trial, at Tresavean Mine in Lanner, took place on 29 October, 1842, and was attended by '100 real miners & about ½ a dozen dilettante[98] ones'.[99] The man engine carried workers up and down the mine shafts using two rods, each with several platforms built into them, which allowed men to step back and forth from one rod to another to progress up or down. While this was promoted as a far healthier alternative to ladders, mine owners and captains had been reluctant to try the engine as they perceived little benefit to themselves, and little reward for the expense of installing an engine. If their miners were paid only for what they achieved while they were already in the mine, it made no difference to the investors if they had to take longer to get there. It was only when it was made plain that the mine owners would

---

[98] Interested amateur.
[99] Barclay Fox, p. 293.

themselves see an economic return from the innovation that the technology became accepted. In fact, the health benefit to miners was not as considerable as had been suggested in the formative stages of the research. Around five years after the introduction of a man engine to Tresavean Mine, a letter was written by William Francis[100] in which the author reports, with embarrassment, that 'I cannot show the effect of the machinery so clearly as I could desire.'[101] Though this and consequent letters contained many claims about health improvements, and blamed the unchanged 'sick fund' figures on lasting results of ladder usage, nevertheless it was not the spectacular result that must have been hoped for.

While the benefit to miners had been promoted, it was the mine owners that stood to gain a great deal from the machinery, a fact that cannot have escaped the astute minds of the RCPS committee. One of the primary benefits is described by Captain Joseph Jennings of Tresavean Mine in a letter dated 1 November 1847: 'the men can do full a third part more work for the money'.[102] In this letter Jennings also observes that men who are older or suffering from health problems can continue to work in the deeper levels of the mine due to the engine, where before they may have been prevented from doing so by the fitness required to climb the ladders. In essence, the man engine allowed the men to descend and ascend in less time and using less energy, so that they were able, firstly, to spend longer working to extract ore, secondly to extract more ore in a set time period, and thirdly to work longer in terms of years. The technology of the man engine, promoted and funded[103] by RCPS members, was therefore a form of time compression that could be used in the mining industry: the potential output of Britain in terms of raw materials could be increased. To further increase the economic benefit of the engine to the mine owners, those in charge reduced the tut and tribute rates that miners received to keep their earnings close to their previous levels; while the men were able to mine more ore in a set

---

[100] Whose identity and connection to the man engine project cannot yet be clarified.
[101] *Twenty-Ninth Annual Report of the Royal Institution of Cornwall*, p. 72.
[102] *Twenty-Ninth Annual Report of the Royal Institution of Cornwall*, p. 71.
[103] Several premiums were actually offered relating to the man engine: the initial premium outlined, and at least five others offered subsequently for improvements to the design by Michael Loam, and for reports on it. Yet more cash bonuses were offered by various members of the Fox family. In 1838, Charles Fox, George Croker Fox and Robert Were Fox collectively offered an additional £250 to the existing premium for that year of £30 10s.

time, they received less for it and so the mine owners gained considerably by paying the same wages while receiving more ore.[104]

The engine's value to Cornwall and the empire therefore lay primarily in the increase in productivity of the mines, and to a lesser extent in the marketing of British industry as sophisticated and progressive. Robert Were Fox himself, in proposing the research at a society meeting in 1838, did so 'on the score both of humanity & economy.'[105] The desire for Cornwall, and thus Britain, to be at the forefront of scientific research relating to mining was also highlighted by Fox at this meeting, as he drew the crowd's attention to the fact that Germany already used man engines in mining, 'call[ing] on his fellow countrymen not to let themselves be outstripped by foreigners.'[106] Here, the British wish to appear civilised, and the Cornish – and therefore British – ambition to be world experts in mining technology become a matter of regional and national pride. The prestige that would come to be associated with knowledge produced by the Cornish made British mining technology a desirable commodity for export.

Of great importance to the research produced within Cornwall, and particularly by the RCPS, was the idea of value. Cornwall was gradually gathering a reputation for mining expertise that looked set to place it firmly on the map in terms of industrial importance. As the previous example has illustrated, research projects promoted by the society were chosen to fulfil certain aims, often to increase productivity or to appear humanitarian, and to make Cornwall *the* place for mining knowledge and technology. Technology originating from Cornwall was proudly labelled as such to give it prestige. Philip Payton, discussing mining in South Australia, observes that there 'the term "Cornish" itself was used in innumerable situations – for instance, Cornish engines, Cornish captains, Cornish boilers, and Cornish stamps.'[107] In an 1839 statement about the improvements made in steam technology, Thomas and Joel Lean observed that the steam engine had been brought 'to the state of great perfection' in Cornwall, due to its 'deepest, most extensive, and most productive

---

[104] R Burt, 'The Man Engine', *Geevor Tin Mine Museum* <http://www.geevor.com/media/Man%20Engine%20R_Burt%20extract.pdf> [accessed 20 June 2013]
[105] Barclay Fox, p. 134.
[106] Ibid.
[107] Payton, *The Cornish Miner in Australia*, p. 32.

mines'.[108] Though this publication was written in Cornwall by men living and working within the mining community, and so could be considered very much biased in its favour, it nevertheless shows the extent to which the region promoted itself as being the home of mining technology. This would go on to have great implications for the export of mining packages overseas.

From Cornwall to Latin America: informal empire

The creation of value and sense of sophistication connected with Cornish mining skill, knowledge and technology led to the generation of a highly exportable commodity. During the nineteenth century, the Cornish were able to export complete 'packages' of mining expertise, including the miners themselves, mine captains, mineralogists, and engineers, along with engines and associated mechanical workings, techniques for mining, and designs for engine houses. By doing so, the British were able to exploit resources in areas rich in minerals, such as Latin America, as well as at home in Cornwall and west Devon. Ultimately, the export of miners and mining techniques led to the extensive mining of places such as South Australia, California and South Africa, where enterprising young men went in search of their fortune in the form of silver, gold, and diamonds. As the supply of ore from Cornish mines began to dwindle around the 1850s, due, in part, to the intensive workings they had been subjected to and to greater overseas competition, new sites were already established far away from the mining areas of West Cornwall.

The export of mining technology overseas was deeply problematic for those involved in the Cornish mining industry. Demand for engines to be sent to places such as Mexico and Brazil obviously created a profitable new market for companies such as Perran Foundry, and many Cornish businessmen invested in overseas mining companies as a speculative way of making money.[109] The ability to export to places such as this was a product of time-space compression. As shipping became faster and navigation improved, vessels sailing from Falmouth were able to cover greater

---

[108] Thomas Lean and Joel Lean, *Historical Statement of the Improvements Made in the Duty Performed by the Steam Engines in Cornwall, from the Commencement of the Publication of the Monthly Reports* (London: Simpkin, Marshall and Co., 1839), p. 1
[109] Lists of company directors are available in Henry English, *A General Guide to the Companies Formed For Working Foreign Mines* (London: Boosey & Sons, 1825)

distances than previously, and new connections were made with overseas ports such as Rio de Janeiro. Naturally, this compression allowed the British to trade with new markets and to gain trading power by broadening their potential customer field. The power granted or diminished by time-space compression, however, ultimately worked against the Cornish as the ability to trade on a global scale led to far greater competition, and the ultimate demise of the Cornish mining industry. If greater quantities of copper could extracted from metalliferously richer countries such as Chile, it made economic sense for British capital to be invested there instead of in Cornwall. One way for the Cornish to mitigate this problem was to embrace new mining areas overseas, as much as possible. Miners emigrated abroad to employ their skills for the British investors, and the branded beam engines of Perran Foundry and Harvey's of Hayle appeared in altogether more exotic landscapes.[110] By controlling, to some extent, the mining taking place overseas, the Cornish were able to grasp hold of the power created by time-space compression rather than losing it entirely.

The importance of Cornwall to mining on a global scale is something that is now widely appreciated, particularly since the granting of World Heritage Site status to the Cornwall and West Devon mining landscape. This status acknowledges not only the importance of the industry to Cornwall's heritage, but its worldwide significance. The WHS literature makes plain the 'truly global heritage' of Cornish mining, which from around 1700 to 1914 played a major role in 'changing the world forever through the mass movement of people and goods.'[111] This much is known; but where does Falmouth fit into this narrative? This chapter has already discussed Falmouth and the RCPS's role in creating the trade and intellectual networks fundamental to the communication and export of new mining knowledge, technologies, and people. This section will now consider in more detail how Falmouth became a key location in the actual export of these commodities to Latin America, and how the establishment of Cornish mining techniques overseas led to an improvement in products that would ultimately make the British more successful when establishing new colonies based around mining in locations such as South Australia.

---

[110] A beam from an 1836 Perran Foundry engine can still be seen on a beach in Virgin Gorda, in the Caribbean. <http://archiver.rootsweb.ancestry.com/th/read/CORNISH/2012-05/1336253317> [accessed 2 July 2013]
[111] 'About Us', *Cornish Mining World Heritage* <http://www.cornish-mining.org.uk/about-us-0#Why is CM a WHS?> [accessed 2 July 2013]

The investment of British capital in Latin America has already been the subject of histories by Sharron Schwartz and Philip Payton,[112] and it is to these texts that one may choose to turn for a highly detailed account of this. Latin America was one of the first locations for the investment of British money and expertise outside of the formal British empire, and from around 1812, gaining momentum into the 1820s, British companies bought land in countries such as Chile, Peru and Brazil and mined it using British technology and skill. An 1825 guide to the companies formed to work foreign mines contains details of twenty-nine such companies, with a combined share value of £25,540,000, excluding one company with French associates whose shares amounted to six million francs.[113] Falmouth's role in the export of ideas, goods and people lay, unsurprisingly, in its function as a port. The first forays into new mining zones were made from Falmouth: as Schwartz notes, '[a]lthough some men and machinery were dispatched from Swansea, Portsmouth, Plymouth and Liverpool, by far the most was exported through the port of Falmouth.'[114] A *West Briton* newspaper dated 18 February 1825, observed that 'The streets of Falmouth are at this time quite thronged, in addition to the usual bustle of packet passengers and other strangers, there is an influx of the agents and others engaged for the different mining speculations abroad, and who are about to sail for their various destinations.'[115] An edition dated 22 July 1825 noted the departure of the *Auriga*, a London ship, from Falmouth to Valparaiso in Chile, carrying on board mining materials and equipment, chief engineers, and a party of Cornish and Welsh miners.[116] Reports of men and goods sailing from Falmouth were common: the guide to foreign mining companies refers several times to the passage of miners, engineers, mineralogists, and tools, stores, and large items of machinery. It records sailings to the Mariquita Mines in Columbia of 'a large party, consisting of Miners, Mechanics, Engineers, and Mine Agents', followed later in the same month by 'an adequate

---

[112] Such as Sharron Schwartz, 'Creating the Cult of "Cousin Jack": Cornish Miners in Latin America 1812-1848 and the Development of an International Mining Labour Market', *The Cornish in Latin America*
<https://projects.exeter.ac.uk/cornishlatin/Creating%20the%20Cult%20of%20Cousin%20Jack.pdf> [accessed 2 July 2013] and Payton, *The Cornish Overseas: The epic story of the 'Great Migration'*.
[113] English.
[114] Schwartz, 'Creating the Cult of "Cousin Jack"' (p. 15)
[115] *Life in Cornwall in the Early Nineteenth Century*, p. 144.
[116] *Life in Cornwall in the Early Nineteenth Century*, p. 146.

supply of Tools, Mine Materials, and Machinery' from Falmouth.[117] From the town also sailed 'a party of between 40 and 50 individuals, comprising Miners, Assayers, Smelters, &c., with Mining Tools, Stores, and every necessary for the carrying into operation the intentions of the Company.'[118]

The networks and routes needed to travel and transport to Latin America from Falmouth had already been established by the Packet Service. In *The Tentacles of Progress*, Headrick argues that when a technology is being transferred from one place to another, it is often through transportation technologies that a first contact is made.[119] After transport links have been made between two locations, it is easier to introduce other technologies. In this instance, Packet routes often preceded export routes: a Packet Service connected Falmouth with Brazil in 1805,[120] prior to the formation of mining companies such as the Imperial Brazilian Mining Association, around 1824, and the Castello and Espirito Santo Brazil Mining Association in March 1825. Colombia became a Packet Service destination in 1823, becoming part of the route from Falmouth to Barbados, Jamaica and the Bahamas. This preceded the granting of a lease to the Bolivar Mining Company in October 1824, and the first meeting of Directors of the Colombian Mining Association in November 1824.[121]

Establishing mining locations in Latin America allowed the British empire to extend its trade in terms of the amount of ore it could access and the amount of land, worldwide, that it had interests in. However, the countries that Britain gained access to through mining were not formal British colonies, but instead belong to the group of nations and areas that has become known as Britain's 'informal empire'. Matthew Brown, in his work on the British-Latin American informal empire, sees 'commerce and capital' as providing the framework for this,[122] mirroring Schwartz's view that it is 'imperialism through trade'.[123] Informal empire is undoubtedly a term open to

---

[117] English, p. 80.
[118] English, p. 85.
[119] Daniel R. Headrick, *The Tentacles of Progress: Technology Transfer in the Age of Imperialism, 1850-1940* (New York: Oxford University Press, 1988), p. 12.
[120] *Falmouth Packet Archives 1688-1850*
<http://www.falmouth.packet.archives.dial.pipex.com/id47.htm> [accessed 2 July 2013]
[121] English, p. 14 and p. 80.
[122] Matthew Brown, 'Introduction' in Informal Empire in *Latin America: Culture, Commerce, and Capital*, ed. by Matthew Brown (Oxford: Blackwell Publishing, 2008), pp. 1-22 (p. 1).
[123] Schwartz, pp. 8-9.

interpretation and differing definitions. Some, Brown argues, view it as a less-threatening euphemism for imperialism, but essentially imperialism nevertheless.[124] His own definition, or 'broadly recognised meaning', is the one that will be accepted for the purpose of this section, and is one that Brown feels encourages interdisciplinary and cultural study. Thus, here we view the concept of informal empire as 'a powerful nation managing to control a territory over which it does not exercise sovereignty.'[125] It is perhaps limiting to consider informal empire purely as exploitative or as mutually advantageous. This section will instead look closely at the power relations formed between the British and certain Latin American regions, to consider how informal empire can be seen as taking place, and how this potentially uneasy relationship affected the British 'colonisers'. The primary location that will be considered, for the purpose of offering a case study approach rather than attempting an overview of all central and Southern America, will be Chile, though useful comparisons can be drawn with Cornish miners working in Mexico and Brazil. Ultimately, the power exercised was a negotiated version of the British ideal, in which the working practices of the settlers were reluctantly influenced by the native population. This compromise between absolute dominance and submission would, however, go on to be of benefit to the Cornish in broadening the worldwide applicability of their skills. It will be demonstrated that by the mid-nineteenth century Britain was well-positioned to expand trade influence into all corners of the globe, including its new colonies in South Australia. This was due to the trade links between Falmouth and the rest of the world, the reputation established for the Cornish as the 'hard rock miner par excellence',[126] and the ability to travel to, and set up industrial works in new overseas territories of informal empire: territories that would become the proving ground for different types of hard rock mining.

Brown's concept of informal empire depends upon a framework of commerce, capital and culture that is important to this chapter: he argues that for informal empire to exist in a location, there must be evidence of commerce and the investment of capital which shapes political and diplomatic relationships, and that there must be 'a demonstrable role for culture either in supporting those relationships [...] or as an

---

[124] Brown, p. 2.
[125] Brown, p. 3.
[126] Schwartz, p. 1.

independent variable (as in local consciousness of asymmetrical power relations).'[127] In some areas, the attempted exercise of power was relatively overt: under the guise of forming a mining company, the United Pacific Association took control of 'cultivated and well-peopled lands'[128] for the purpose of exploiting all resources and trade potential that stemmed from them. The area in question was the Sandwich Islands,[129] which at the time were not a formal colony, despite the British apparently being granted rights to take over all trade and produce there, and employ its people in their pursuits. The islands would go on to be a part of the empire, becoming officially British in 1908 and grouped with other territories as part of the Falkland Island Dependencies.[130] In other areas, such as Chile, power relations were more complex and subtle.

Working within Brown's framework, Chile from the 1820s onwards can be considered a territory within Britain's informal empire due to mining exports from Falmouth. By 1825, there were four British mining companies in Chile: the Anglo-Chilian [sic] Mining Association, the Chilian Mining Association, Chilian and Peruvian Mining Association, and the United Chilian Association.[131] Mining activities and the capital and commerce associated with them did affect political and diplomatic relationships. Consuls and company representatives were able to gain power and influence locally, with emigrants such as John James Barnard, the first secretary of a British traders' association, being consulted by the Chilean government on commercial matters.[132] The introduction of consuls to Latin American countries was in itself a political move made on a trade basis. Due to British involvement in Chilean trade, most notably the mining industry, the British had, by 1825, established consuls in Santiago and Valparaiso, respectively the country's capital city and a chief port, 'to protect British interests'.[133] These consuls predated British recognition of Chilean independence, however, and signify increased involvement by the British in Chilean affairs. Essentially, the consuls were

---

[127] Brown, p. 21.
[128] English, p. 70.
[129] Now known as the South Sandwich Islands.
[130] It is debatable how much influence the United Pacific Association had in this ultimate colonisation, as the project failed to receive investment and folded in 1825.
[131] English.
[132] Simon Collier and William F. Sater, *A History of Chile, 1808-1994* (Cambridge: Cambridge University Press, 1996), p. 44.
[133] English, p. 2.

put in place for trade purposes but did not accompany British recognition of Chile as an independent nation because it was viewed as having too unstable a government with too great an amount of unrest in the country. Without British recognition, Chile was viewed 'merely as a Province' and so no commercial treaties could be signed.[134]

In the view of Theodore E. Nichols, in a thorough 1948 history of British political involvement in Chile, British recognition was valuable to Latin American countries for two primary reasons: the economic benefits of British trade, and the protective potential of the Navy for newly-independent countries.[135] The need for protection was certainly valid: John Miers, in his 1826 account of travelling through Chile and La Plata, wrote of the panic in Valparaiso on hearing that a fleet of Spanish ships were in the Pacific.[136] In order for Britain to recognise Chile, it was required to conform to certain standards, such as abolition of the slave trade and continued independence from Spain.[137] Factors such as continued commercial interaction with Britain worked in its favour: English, writing in 1825, observed that because of the 'value of its commercial intercourse with Great Britain, there is every probability of its independence being shortly recognized'.[138] From this it is plain that trade with Chile, with copper at its heart, had serious political and diplomatic implications: the country was required to conform to British expectations to keep its commercial ties strong. It was encouraged to keep up a strong trade with Britain in order to gain the recognition that might provide the vulnerable new state with British naval protection and even stronger trade. Here, the mining industry granted Britain informal empire.

The second of Brown's criteria, the cultural role played by Britain in maintaining influence and unequal power relations in Chile, is easy to discern from accounts of the mining industry there. The sudden arrival of Europeans and their mining methods, which differed greatly from the methods previously employed, caused conflict and dissatisfaction between the two groups as the Cornish way was forced

---

[134] Theodore E. Nichols, 'The Establishment of Political Relations Between Chile and Great Britain', *The Hispanic American Historical Review*, 28 (1948), 137-143 (p. 138).
[135] Ibid.
[136] John Miers, *Travels in Chile and La Plata: including accounts respecting the geography, geology, statistics, government, finances, agriculture, manners and customs, and the mining operations in Chile*, 2 vols (London: Baldwick, Cradock, and Joy, 1826), II, p. 119.
[137] Nichols, p. 139.
[138] English, p. 2.

upon the native miners.[139] Though the Cornish and Chilean methods ultimately informed each other, as will become clear, the culture associated with Cornish mining was superimposed onto the Latin American landscape. This was enforced by the fact that it was often Cornish, or at least British, men who were placed in positions of power within the mines while the natives were sometimes referred to as only cheap labour.[140] A more thorough account of the fraught power relations that existed between Chilean and British workers will be offered shortly, but having established that the republic of Chile can be considered a part of informal empire according to Brown's criteria, it is now useful to widen the analysis of power to consider the relations between the two countries with regard to the import/export of technology and the exploitation of natural resources.

The benefits to Britain of mining Chilean resources are obvious: the land was rich with minerals that they believed could be extracted cheaply,[141] and mining overseas in addition to at home greatly increased the amount of metals it had access to for its Industrial Revolution. The benefits to Chile require more explanation. Why would a country with known resources, striving to create a better economy, allow the British empire to take away its source of wealth, along with the majority of the profits? Why import British technology rather than doing it for themselves? The answer lies in the amount of British capital that was available for investment, and in the supposed expertise of the Cornish in mining. It was felt that Chile was lacking in capital and willing investors for its mines, as well as in the technology and skill needed to mine them: in his guide for potential investors, English noted that the injection of 'British capital, skill, and machinery' would assist their success.[142] The mines in Chile were viewed as technologically poor, whereas the British, through the Cornish, had made a strong reputation for designing and manufacturing mining technologies. The Cornish miners themselves were viewed as superior and valued for their sophistication in drilling and working deep underground. This was the case in Colombia also, where the mine manager for the Colombian Mining Association stated that native labourers were 'but inferior miners, being but little accustomed to

---

[139] Schwartz, p. 22.
[140] English, p. 19.
[141] English, pp. 20-21.
[142] English, p. 19.

blast and break the ground'.[143] Britain therefore had things that the Chilean government both wanted and needed: capital, willing investors, and mining skill and technology. The technological gap between the importers, Chile, and the exporters, Britain, allowed Britain to gain the upper hand in the resultant power play. It is for this reason that the export of technology was conducted as what Headrick terms 'relocation', rather than 'diffusion'.[144]

Relocation of a technology involves the transfer from one location to another of the equipment and methods associated with the technology, in addition to the experts that know how to operate it. This allows the exporter to maintain, to a certain degree, control over the knowledge associated with it: no other person, namely the importer, needs to understand how the technology works if a representative of the exporter is on hand to operate it. Diffusion instead involves the transfer of the technology, along with the transfer of the associated knowledge and skills, to enable the importer to control it independently.[145] Naturally, the importer generally favours diffusion, while the exporter gains the most from relocation. Because the government of Chile needed and wanted the mining technology offered by the British, the exporters in this particular case were able to control the transfer of technology, and so chose to relocate rather than diffuse. As a consequence, the aforementioned 'packages' of machinery, mine captains, miners, engineers, mineralogists, and so on, were exported to Chile from the 1820s onwards. In March 1825, the general manager of the Chilian Mining Association, Charles Lambert, sailed from Falmouth in the Packet ship *Eclipse* accompanied by Cornish miners for the new mines, and a variety of mining equipment.[146] George Croker Fox and Alfred Fox were directors of the Chilian Mining Association,[147] and the Fox family consequently organised the emigration of Cornish miners from Falmouth.[148] The relocation of a mining package allowed the valuable knowledge that had been circulated and promoted from places like Falmouth to remain in the possession of the British and for them to maintain a sense of power and authority in their new outposts.

---

[143] Schwartz, p. 27.
[144] Headrick, p. 9.
[145] Ibid.
[146] Schwartz, p. 15.
[147] English, p. 19.
[148] Payton, *The Cornish Overseas*, p. 142.

The early days of export to Latin America were not entirely straightforward. The wholesale relocation of mining knowledge was perhaps initially too uncompromising and not diffusive enough to be entirely successful, as technologies and methods that had been perfected in Cornwall did not necessarily transfer exactly to a different climate and geography. One main problem, despite the speeding up of travel from Britain to Latin America, remained the distance between the two locations. Transporting masses of heavy machinery such a long way took a lot of time, and could be expensive. Time was also a factor in the ordering of replacement parts or amendments for machines. Because the manufacture still took place in Cornwall, if additional parts were ordered for an engine, for instance, many months could pass between a company such as Perran Foundry receiving this order and the mine receiving the product.[149] Steam technology was not always necessary, even if it had been shipped so many miles. In Chile, there was less water and copper was mined on a shallower level than in Cornwall, meaning that the water pumping engines were often superfluous.[150] Charles Darwin, when he visited Chile in 1834, commented that the mine workings were quiet compared to those in England: 'here no smoke, furnaces, or great steam-engines, disturb the solitude of the surrounding mountains.'[151] Clearly, British invention made little impact in this sphere. Steam technology did have more relevance elsewhere, however: Mexico had deep mines that flooded, making it prime territory for the engines.[152]

Another possibly unforeseen complication lay with the expertise of the miners themselves. Having been promoted as the ultimate in labour by societies such as the RCPS, the Cornish did not always live up to expectations. Hard rock mining in a country such as Chile was not the same as hard rock mining in Cornwall, and though the Cornish miner was rich in experience and intuition, this was not always enough to make a completely successful transition. Coming from a society in which, despite the best efforts of the RCPS, science remained the realm of the middle and upper classes, he was not gifted with the actual theoretical knowledge in the spheres of

---

[149] Schwartz, p. 23.
[150] Schwartz, p. 24.
[151] Charles Darwin, *Narrative of the Surveying Voyages of His Majesty's Ships Adventure and Beagle, Between the Years 1826 and 1836, Describing Their Examination of the Southern Shores of South America, and the Beagle's Circumnavigation of the Globe*, 3 vols (London: Henry Colburn, 1839), III, p. 316.
[152] Schwartz, p. 22.

mineralogy and geology that might have made his skills more broadly applicable. Arriving from Falmouth, with the backing of Robert Were Fox, did not make the average miner an expert. If the Cornish miner was to become the true global mining expert, he would need experience of working in different climates, and of mining for gold and silver as well as copper. This weakness in Cornish mining practices, imposed upon the Chilean workers who felt that they knew their own terrain better, made for an uncomfortable and volatile working environment.

Within the context of informal empire, one way to consider the intricate and complex power relationship between Britain and Chile is to examine the way that the working people, as well as administrators or government representatives, interacted with each other and supported or challenged certain power hierarchies. Brown draws attention to a need to look at the relationships between colonised and colonisers 'to understand the real nature of imperialism.'[153] He also highlights the cultural aspects of informal empire as being worthy of study:[154] in this setting, the way that the cultures of Cornish mining and Latin American mining were thrown together and informed each other.

Darwin, in his account of the Chilean mines, relates one story that highlights the bemused contempt held between the emigrant and native miners: 'The Chilian [sic] miners were so convinced that copper pyrites contained not a particle of copper, that they laughed at the Englishmen for their ignorance, who laughed in turn, and bought their richest veins for a few dollars.'[155] Indeed, the copper pyrites did contain copper and the Cornish miners with the benefit of their experience at home were able to extract this and so show their superiority in this instance. Clashes over mining practice were not uncommon: Chilean workers, unhappy at having their methods superseded by Cornish ones took action against them. Cornish kibbles for raising ore out of mines were dismantled by the natives, who preferred their own method of hiring men, known as 'apires', with bags on their backs.[156] Any assumption of authority and leadership, in a traditional colonial style, proved unpopular. In 1827, Royal Navy Lieutenant Grosvenor Bunster visited Chile's mines in the footsteps of a

---

[153] Brown, p. 6.
[154] Brown, p. 4.
[155] Darwin, p. 317.
[156] Schwartz, p. 26.

previous visitor, Captain Head, and found that his predecessor had been greatly disliked by the Chileans: 'I could not get a civil answer, nor the least attention, so displeased had they been at his military commanding behaviour.'[157] When assured of Bunster's own diplomacy and distaste for Captain Head, however, the local people lavished 'every attention and accommodation' upon the traveller. Clearly, the wholesale enforcement of European, or specifically Cornish, mining practices and colonial attitudes could not succeed in a territory of informal empire. Problems such as these were not confined to Chile: strikes among the native workforce broke out in Mexico in the 1820s around attempts to replace the Mexican "partido"[158] labour system with the Cornish tribute system.[159]

One of the main issues with the relocation of the mining skills, practices and technology pioneered in Cornwall appears to have been that there was not a great enough attempt to 'de-localise' it or amend attitudes for their new surroundings. Livingstone argues that the location of science's consumption is as important as the location of its creation: ideas must 'resonate' with their original environment, but they must also be able to migrate and undergo translation, not just to be replicated.[160] Essentially, the attempt to replicate science in Latin America created problems, as seen in the irrelevance of steam technology in Chile. The routes and intellectual networks created between Falmouth and Latin America, through which knowledge could be transferred, orchestrated a culture clash between the two regions as attitudes and mining cultures failed to keep pace, to successfully migrate, with the ships they travelled in. The Cornish, once in Latin America, were content to behave as if they remained in Cornwall, and the Latin American subjects now working for them resented the rapid intrusion of foreigners into their culture. While in some instances, such as the conveyance of parts for machinery, the time-space compression that occurred between Britain and the new Latin American informal empire did not

---

[157] Grosvenor Bunster, *Observations on Captain F.B. Head's "Reports Relative to the Failure of the Rio de Plata Mining Association"; with Additional Remarks and an Appendix of Original Documents*, 2nd edn (London: E. Wilson, 1827), p. 18.
[158] The Mexican mining system was complex and entrenched in tradition. Men called "buscones" mined the ore, and "tenateros" were hired to carry it to the surface, instead of using buckets or bags that could be raised. Mexican miners received half the ore obtained in this way, which was called the "partido". The Cornish tribute system also saw men receiving a percentage of the value of ore raised, but was seen as safer.
[159] Schwartz, p. 25.
[160] Livingstone, p. 11.

provide a fast enough link, in other ways time and space were compressed far too quickly. The transfer of British people, ideas, and culture into places like Chile occurred, it seemed, too dramatically, and both incomers and existing civilians found the change difficult. An 1826 letter written from Valparaiso complained 'This country is overrun with miners'.[161] The British came under fire for acting too quickly, sending men out to work in mines that had not yet been purchased. The *Western Luminary*, in 1826, printed a comment from Valparaiso that shows the scorn felt at this intrusion: 'They seem to think our mountains are made of gold and silver, and that they can carry them away at pleasure'.[162] Falmouth, in its function as a port at the centre of the British formal and informal empire, contributed to this maelstrom as its facilitator, the portal through which hundreds of unprepared Cornishmen were plunged, suddenly, into the literal and figurative heat of South America.

Clearly, the location of science's consumption had a great affect on the reception it received. Ideas that had been tried, tested, and approved in Cornwall, in places such as the RCPS with its own set of hierarchies and scientific and technological ideals, were viewed very differently in Chile. This example supports Livingstone's assertion that science can be affected by the cultural politics of imperialism.[163] Though he seems to be largely referring to the science produced in colonies by the colonisers, which was undoubtedly influenced by imperial ideals, the idea rings true in the consumption of science in the colonies (though informal) by the colonised. Railing against British intrusion, Chilean workers, as already demonstrated, were hostile to working practices and theories different to their own.

The problem was either consciously or unconsciously resolved by a process of compromise between the two parties. While some miners returned home, those that stayed began to listen to their Chilean co-workers, rather than simply trying to rule them.[164] Working alongside the Chileans, Cornish miners were able to learn about hard rock mining elsewhere than Cornwall. As already stated, they were strong in experience and intuition, and these qualities made them good miners. What they needed, and what they managed to accomplish, was greater experience of working in

---

[161] Payton, *The Cornish Overseas*, p. 120.
[162] Schwartz, p. 19.
[163] Livingstone, pp. 12-13.
[164] Schwartz, p. 28.

foreign climes. In some ways falsely promoted as perfection at the start of British ventures in Latin America, by the middle of the nineteenth century, the Cornish miner was beginning to fulfil the hype perpetuated by Cornish businesses and those trading in shares. Emigration to places such as Chile, Mexico and Brazil taught the Cornish miner additional skills that would stand him in good stead as he moved to new colonies in South Australia. In her history of the Cornish miner in Latin America, Schwartz concludes that 'without the migration of British capital, Cornish miners would not have been afforded the opportunity to acquire the essential skills in mining and dressing gold and silver [...] and acquire the reputation of being the best hard rock miners in the world.'[165] Though many of the early British mining companies in Latin America failed due to a variety of outside factors, including a stock market crash and civil unrest in the countries,[166] valuable lessons had been learned and, most importantly, Britain had a foothold in Latin America. Other mining companies would come to have success there, and British interests expanded with investment in, and control of, the Chilean railways.[167] Having been exported once, and thus improved, British mining knowledge became yet more exportable. Latin America marked the beginning of the global migration of Cornish knowledge and technology; all, arguably, sparked by the superior geographic and trading position of the small Cornish port of Falmouth.

Cornish mining on the global stage

> Come on, my brethren, let us sing,
> > Unto that city bright,
> There need not one be left behind,
> > For Christ does all invite,
> And to glory we will sail,
> > We'll sail,
> And to glory we will sail.[168]

---

[165] Schwartz, p. 30.
[166] Such as the Chilean Civil War of 1829-30.
[167] Salvatore Bizzaro, *Historical Dictionary of Chile*, 3rd edn (Lanham: Scarecrow Press, 2005), p. 634.
[168] Payton, *The Cornish Miner in Australia*, p. 21.

In the 1860s, after twelve years of working to extract Chilean copper, a Cornish miner by the name of Henry Crougey moved, via California, to South Australia, where many other Cornishmen emigrated to make a new life based on their skills and improved experience.[169] In 1834, South Australia was officially made a British province by an act of imperial parliament. The motivations behind the formation of a colony here were that it should be a free land (that is, not comprised of transported convicts as was the case elsewhere in Australia) and self-supporting.[170] For this, the colony would need to generate its own trade and a strong economy, and one of the main sources of income from the mid-1840s was mining. In 1843, rich mineral deposits were discovered, sparking a mass interest in mining in the province, and ultimately dramatically increasing land prices.[171] Francis Dutton, whose description of the South Australian mines was published in 1846, observed that even at this early stage in the industry the mines had 'a respectable and important footing in the English market.'[172] The emigration of Henry Crougey was not unusual: the riches to be found in South Australia tempted many men from countries of Latin America, which were seen to be far less profitable for miners and investors.[173] Perhaps part of the allure, besides the rich lodes reported in places such as Kapunda and Burra, lay in the fact that the colony in South Australia was technically British, and as such there was no native government demanding payment of a duty on ore as there had been in Latin America. There was also a sense of pride in the colony being British, 'with mines worked by Cornish hands', as reported in the *South Australian Gazette and Colonial Register* in 1845.[174] Cornish miners were tempted to emigrate by high wages: in the Burra Burra mine men could earn the same in a week as they would in a month in Cornwall.[175] As a result, the migration of men to South Australia has become known as 'the Great Migration'.[176] As with Latin America, men migrated from Falmouth to South Australia, though Falmouth was by no means the only port

---

[169] Payton, *The Cornish Overseas*, p. 22.
[170] Francis Dutton, *South Australia and its Mines, with an Historical Sketch of the Colony, Under its Several Administrations, to the Period of Captain Grey's Departure* (London: T. and W. Boone, 1846), p. 6.
[171] Dutton, p. 272.
[172] Dutton, p. 257.
[173] Dutton, p. 258.
[174] Payton, *The Cornish Miner in Australia*, p. 16.
[175] Ibid.
[176] Payton, *The Cornish Miner in Australia*, p. 12 and *The Australian People: An Encyclopedia of the Nation, Its People, and Their Origins*, ed. by James Jupp (Cambridge: Cambridge University Press, 2001), p. 227 are just two examples of this.

used. On 5 October 1846, the *Kingston* took sixty-six passengers from Falmouth, almost all of them bound for the Burra Burra mine.[177] It was the injection of Cornish labour, knowledge and technology that helped to ensure the survival of the colony, which had been suffering from major financial difficulties prior to the discovery of its mineral wealth. Payton argues that Cornish mining was 'crucial' to its well-being.[178]

Indeed, even today it is easy to see the evidence of Cornish mining and the transfer of mining knowledge in South Australia. The landscape, though different to that of Cornwall, is populated with Cornish-design engine houses, the architecture obviously imported from Britain along with the machinery that ran within them. The captains and supervisors employed in the mines were almost always Cornish, the labour and pay arrangements mirrored those used in Cornwall, and the language of the mines, using terms such as 'bal' and 'wheal',[179] was Cornish.[180] A Perran Foundry catalogue dating from the 1870s, when the company was owned by the Williams family, demonstrates through illustrations populated with palm trees and figures in sun-shading hats (see Fig. 5) that mining technology had spread all over the world. Thanks, in part, to the efforts of people like the Foxes, the prestige of Cornish mining had become a secure thing.

---

[177] Payton, *The Cornish Miner in Australia*, p. 17.
[178] Payton, *The Cornish Miner in Australia*, p. 32.
[179] Bal meaning 'a digging', thus a mine, and Wheal, also meaning a mine, being a prefix for many mine names, such as Wheal Prosper and Wheal Friendship in South Australia.
[180] Payton, *The Cornish Miner in Australia*, p. 32.

Fig. 5: Perran Foundry catalogue illustration

Illustration from a c.1870 Perran Foundry catalogue (p. 24) showing mining technology in an exotic landscape.

The influence of Falmouth on mining in South Australia is perhaps more distantly removed, though certainly traceable, than its influence on mining in Cornwall and Latin America. By the 1850s, Cornish mining knowledge and technology had spread and migrated away from places such as Falmouth and institutions or companies like the RCPS and East India Company. The foundations for a global mining market had been laid in Falmouth, and by the time of the Great Migration and the success of mining ventures in South Australia, the industry had evolved away from the town, and its importance had become less obvious. It is for this reason that this chapter does not focus on Australian investments and colonies in great detail: while Falmouth did undoubtedly influence this export of men and knowledge, its involvement was at the beginning of what had, by this time, become a structure of many levels. Without the foundations and earliest of these levels, however, those that came later would have had nothing to build upon. Falmouth can thus be seen as the springboard from which a global British mining industry, with interests in informal and formal empire, began.

The effect that migration had on the Cornish people themselves, and their sense of identity, lives on to this day in communities of Cornish ancestry in locations such as Mexico and South Australia. Livingstone, discussing regional identity as it relates to regional science, notes that constituents of identity include 'channels of intellectual exchange, linguistic heritage, educational customs, codes of cultural communication, forms of religious belief, and numerous other constituents of human consciousness'.[181] During the period of this study, the Cornish were viewed as distinct because of their mining skill – mining knowledge became a key part of the Cornish identity, and was heavily promoted as a local research interest by the RCPS, as we have already discussed – but when exporting labour in the form of people it was impossible to extricate intellectual exchange from the rest of the regional identity of Cornwall, meaning that all aspects travelled together. By making migrant populations in new mining sites primarily Cornish, the British empire also exported Cornish beliefs and customs that came to dominate their new homes in a lasting way. Because of the Cornish, for instance, Methodism spread to South Australia, reflecting a predominant religion amongst the working classes of Cornwall at the time of emigration.[182] In a perfect example of time-space compression, there are now people in Mexico eating Cornish pasties, known as pastes, almost two hundred years after the first waves of migration. Games such as rugby and football were first introduced to Latin America and South Africa by miners.[183] In ways such as this, the men and women who moved so far away sought to address the sense of dislocation they must have felt, while in the process creating what could almost be viewed as a Cornish colony within a colony. The reality of Cornish communities overseas is evident in the number of Cornish societies in existence worldwide: groups such as the Cornish Society of New South Wales, Victoria Cornish Association, Cuba Cornish Association, and the Cornish Mexican Cultural Society. Their members

---

[181] Livingstone, pp. 87-88.
[182] 'Religion', *Cornish Mining World Heritage* <http://www.cornish-mining.org.uk/delving-deeper/religion> [accessed 24 September 2014].
[183] 'Cornish Mining in South Africa', *Cornish Mining World Heritage* <http://www.cornish-mining.org.uk/delving-deeper/cornish-mining-south-africa> [accessed 5 September 2014] and 'Cornish Mining in Mexico', *Cornish Mining World Heritage* <http://www.cornish-mining.org.uk/delving-deeper/cornish-mining-mexico> [accessed 5 September 2014].

celebrate traditional Cornish anniversaries and festivals such as St Piran's Day, despite being located so far from their ancestral homeland. These communities illustrate, in a very tangible way, the blurring of the line between local and global that occurred as a result of mining.

One of the conditions of World Heritage Site status, awarded to the Cornwall and West Devon mining landscape in July 2006, is that the location must 'exhibit an important interchange of human values, over a span of time or within a cultural area of the world, on developments in architecture or technology [...]'.[184] The lasting importance of Cornwall's mining industry and the knowledge generated within the region thus lies within its transfer and the connections made between Cornwall and the rest of the world, notably the formal and informal British empire, through locations such as Falmouth, which was one of the first and most important ports through which exportation occurred. In an age where the compression of time and space was vitally important to industry, with a desire to extract as much as possible in as little time as possible, for the least cost, Cornish mining techniques and technology came to be a major asset to the British empire. While the present day focus of Cornish mining heritage continues to be located in places such as Camborne and Redruth, correctly recognised as important, Falmouth and the role that it played in this has become overlooked. Not of obvious mining relevance today, the town and port nevertheless represents the processes through which Cornish mining passed to become an exportable commodity that would revolutionise industry in many ways: not just in mining, but in other technological areas such as transport. Discernible in Falmouth's history are the funding and promotion of research fitting the economic prospects of Cornwall, the trade links vital for the movement of raw materials needed for the empire's Industrial Revolution at home and in places such as India, and finally the transfer through established sea routes of a 'package' of mining that allowed the empire to access the mineral wealth of other nations, establish a financial foothold and influence in places such as Latin America, and ultimately create new and lucrative colonies based on trade.

---

[184] 'The Criteria for Selection', *UNESCO* <http://whc.unesco.org/en/criteria/> [accessed 11 July 2013].

Within the complex and ever-changing interplay of power relations created by time-space compression and trade with both formal and 'informal' colonies, men such as the Foxes were able to harness the power and wealth generated by mining and empire for their own personal gain. Overseas business links made through Falmouth allowed them to take full advantage of their gateway to the empire and its plunderable natural bounty. Having explored in this chapter how power and wealth were generated through science and technology, I will now move on to consider how a hierarchically privileged position was displayed at home, also through science. This science, however, was of a different nature to mining and engineering, involving the import, naturalisation and hybridisation of exotic plant species. From the noise and steam of mining came the peace and beauty of the imperial domestic: the empire garden.

Chapter 3: The empire garden: plant hunting and hierarchies of power

> The woods rising on the opposite side of the stream belong to *Carclew*, the seat of Sir Charles Lemon, Bart., M. P. for W. Cornwall, the liberal and distinguished patron of science [...] [The botanist] will be delighted with the gardens, so richly are they stored with curious plants. For many years Sir Charles Lemon has cultivated a collection of trees and shrubs, and as the climate is peculiar, the result of his experiments on exotic trees is most interesting.[1]

Carclew today is undoubtedly a shadow of its former self. Where a sweeping drive or long avenue of trees once guided visitors to their destination, now the wanderer stumbles across what they are looking for. A path is followed, trees passed, and suddenly it is there. The briefest of glimpses might give the impression of a manor house among the trees and overgrowth, but prolonged observation reveals missing walls, fallen window frames, an empty façade (see Figs. 6 and 7). The house and its surrounding land are impressive, even majestic, but the ordered botany spoken of to travellers in 1851 (Fig. 8) is absent. Its appeal lies in the wild allure of ruins rather than the taming of nature and the display of curious exotics. However, traces of these exotics, which once made Carclew great, can still be found jostling side by side with ivy and sycamores as they both seek to colonise the remains. In the first half of the nineteenth century, the garden served as a visual symbol of the wealth and connections of its owner, Sir Charles Lemon. Wealthy through mining and overseas trade, Lemon pursued his interest in botany and mobilised his contacts to create an estate through which one could travel the world: plants plucked from the landscapes of South America, Asia and Australia grew together as a marker of their owner's prosperity and access to foreign lands. Whether intentionally or not, in creating a horticultural paradise Lemon made clear his position of power. That power has now long dwindled away, his fine house destroyed in a fire and his gardens left either to overgrowth, simplification, or redesign. The modern-day visitor to Carclew might find themselves in the position of Percy Shelley's traveller from an antique land,

---

[1] T C Paris, *A Hand-Book for Travellers in Devon and Cornwall* (London: John Murray, 1851), p. 203.

gazing on a representation of power that long ago ceased to be.[2] Yet much like Ozymandias' trunkless legs of stone, the creations of Lemon linger as a testament to what once occurred here.

Fig. 6: Carclew House in 1841

Print of a calotype of Carclew taken in 1841 by HF Talbot. Truro, Cornwall Records Office, X546/1c.

---

[2] Percy Bysshe Shelley, 'Ozymandias' in *Ode to the West Wind and Other Poems* (New York: Dover Publications, 1993), p. 5.

Fig. 7: Carclew House in 2013

The ruins of Carclew House in 2013.

Fig. 8: Sketch of Carclew gardens

This 1845 pencil sketch of the formal gardens at Carclew is sadly not detailed enough to indicate individual plant species but gives an impression of the carefully designed and managed beauty of the site. Visible to the right of the beds is a hothouse or greenhouse, which may have been used for growing exotic species. Truro, Cornwall Records Office, X546/3.

Sir Charles Lemon inherited Carclew, just five miles from the centre of Falmouth, in 1824, and during his ownership became known both locally and nationally for his interest and expertise in botany. Lemon was involved in the business of Falmouth through trading connections, friendship with the Fox family, and his official and unofficial roles as an MP for Cornwall and a local landowner.[3] His fortune was made through mining: his great-grandfather William Lemon began his working life as a miner but rapidly rose to riches through investment in the industry and died in 1760 worth £300,000, making him the equivalent of a multi-millionaire today.[4] William

---

[3] He is regularly mentioned in the journal of Barclay Fox, was President of the RCPS and part of the group responsible for establishing it, and in 1836 led a party from Falmouth petitioning against the removal of the Packet Service from the town.
[4] Joan Rea, 'The Great Mr Lemon at Home at Princes House, Truro and Carclew, Mylor, 1740-1760', in *History around the Fal: Part Five* (Exeter: Fal Local History Group/University of Exeter, 1990), pp. 29-54 (p. 44).

Lemon's wealth and privileged position in society allowed his descendent Sir Charles to take full advantage of the overseas links offered by the nearby port of Falmouth, as he had the economic power to travel or purchase rare and expensive imports. The same is true for the Fox family. Men such as George Croker Fox and Robert Were Fox technically belonged to the merchant class, being in Marxist terms 'bourgeois capitalists'.[5] They were much closer to trade and the making of their money than Lemon, who was a landowner and had inherited the majority of his fortune. Nevertheless, in a changing world of rising industrialism they were wealthy and had the business connections to purchase or commission imports. Wealth was an important condition for access to the world's products: as noted in the previous chapter, those who were powerless in society were largely excluded from time-space compression, and this certainly included the working classes, who were generally not wealthy enough to travel by Packet ship. Those who did, such as the Packet crew or the few emigrating miners, were not in control of their passage in the same way as wealthy travellers. As Massey observes, 'it is time, space and money which make the world go around, and us go around (or not) the world.'[6] If the capital and trade of men like the Foxes contributed to the formation of time-space compression between places such as Falmouth and South America, it was only natural that these things would determine who could benefit from this compression. Men and women without capital were thus excluded.

This notion of wealth, power and rank in society will be key to this chapter and the history of horticulture as it relates to Falmouth. The town created and led a regional group of plant enthusiasts interacting with the empire, and became recognised for its gardens at this time. Without the overseas maritime connections based on empire and trade, men such as Sir Charles Lemon and George Croker Fox would not have had the easy access to empire that they enjoyed, and consequently would not have been able to obtain plant specimens as they did. In this sense, the town was crucial to the horticultural knowledge that circulated within and around it. As Naylor argues, a 'localist approach' to writing historical geographies of science is highly important,[7] and as such this chapter will chart how the plant hunting and import of certain

---

[5] David Cannadine, *Class in Britain* (London: Penguin Books, 2000), p. 3.
[6] Massey, p. 147.
[7] Naylor, 'The Field, the Museum and the Lecture Hall: The Spaces of Natural History in Victorian Cornwall', p. 495.

exotics in the first half of the nineteenth century was intrinsically linked to Falmouth as a location. Naylor's own work focuses on the Penzance Natural History and Antiquarian Society, which prized indigenous flora and fauna and therefore provides a clear link between space and scientific knowledge. However, despite the fact that the studies of RHSC members were not dedicated to local plants, but rather to those that were imported, it can be argued that Falmouth was nevertheless a crucial component of the creation of knowledge due to its facilitation of import and thriving local society of horticulturalists. The mild climate around the town also created a specific set of sub-tropical conditions in which exotic plant life could thrive: creating an open-air growing space that might not have been possible elsewhere. In 1836, the *Gardener's Magazine* noted that 'the number of tender plants that are now growing remarkably well in the open borders at Mr. Fox's, Grove Hill, is surprising.'[8] This peculiarity of connectivity and climate rendered Falmouth, much like Naylor's late nineteenth century West Cornwall, 'a site of singular scientific importance.'[9]

This chapter will demonstrate that the local interest in horticulture in Falmouth led to the formation of hierarchical power relations within the town, which reflect a predominant ideology of the state and empire of the time: that of ruler and ruled. It can be divided into two main sections: the first will discuss the context of horticulture in the first half of the nineteenth century and explore how Falmouth facilitated an interest in this field, allowing for the procurement of exotic plant species from around the world. The second will examine the effect of empire gardens on the inhabitants of the town, considering how a visual display of power and wealth helped to define the roles of ruler and ruled within local society, leading to an attempt to 'civilise' the white working classes in much the same way that natives of colonies would be civilised. Ultimately, through examining the creation of sub-tropical gardens in and around Falmouth, and the effect that these had on the local population, we can discern a high level of interaction with the products and ideals of the British empire, even – to some extent – among the working classes who did not have the wealth to travel or to purchase products for themselves. Those who were

---

[8] John Claudius Loudon, *The Gardener's Magazine and Register of Rural and Domestic Improvement* London: Longman, Brown, Green and Longmans, 1836), p. 370.
[9] Naylor, 'The Field, the Museum and the Lecture Hall: The Spaces of Natural History in Victorian Cornwall', p. 508.

poor felt the consequences of horticulture as it affected their standing in society and the way that they were perceived. Far from being an objective or purely aesthetic science, ornamental horticulture had real consequences for the British subjects of the empire and played a key part in reinforcing important power structures and the way that the residents of Falmouth and surrounding areas thought of themselves and others.

Horticulture as it relates to the British empire is the focus of existing studies by writers such as Richard Drayton, Lucile H. Brockway and Max Bourke.[10] In the context of empire, however, the focus of studies often lies within the realm of economic botany, defined by G. E. Wickens as contributory to Man's survival on earth in terms of providing food, fodder or fuel, though other needs fulfilled by plants may also include medicines, chemical products, and fibres.[11] Men such as Joseph Banks, working at Kew, imported plant species from overseas and re-exported them to British colonies to be naturalised and grown for these purposes.[12] The usefulness of plants for the empire's economy was of primary concern in the field of botany from the eighteenth century: in a May 1880 speech given at the Colonial Institute, W. T. Thiselton Dyer, Assistant Director of the Royal Botanic Gardens, Kew, observed that plants could be seen as 'the botanical resources of the Empire', with colonies 'aiding the mother country in everything that is useful in the vegetable kingdom.'[13] The choice of Banks as central character is a familiar one, and a significant number of histories or analyses of plant hunting during the time of empire focus on Banks or his acquaintances William and Joseph Dalton Hooker.[14] These men were all connected to the gardens at Kew,[15] and indeed, histories of horticulture in nineteenth century Britain often have Kew as their geographic and

---

[10] Richard Drayton, *Nature's Government: Science, Imperial Britain, and the 'Improvement' of the World* (New Haven and London: Yale University Press, 2000), Lucile H. Brockway, *Science and Colonial Expansion: The Role of the British Royal Botanic Gardens* (New Haven: Yale University Press, 2002), and Max Bourke, 'Trees on Trial: Economic Arboreta in Australia', *Garden History*, 35 (2007), 217-226.
[11] G. E. Wickens, 'What is Economic Botany?', *Economic Botany*, 44 (1990), 12-28 (p. 12).
[12] Fulford, Lee and Kitson, p. 34.
[13] W. T. Thiselton Dyer, *The Botanical Enterprise of the Empire* (London: George E. Eyre and William Spottiswoode, 1880)
[14] Banks, Hooker and Hooker are the central characters in Drayton, *Nature's Government* and Banks features in Fulford, Lee and Kitson's discussion of plant hunting.
[15] Banks supervised the collection of specimens for Kew, William Hooker held the position of first official Director of the Royal Gardens from 1841, and Joseph Hooker succeeded his father William as Director in 1865.

institutional centre.[16] In addition to Kew's plant hunting 'celebrities', however, there was also a culture of the 'gentlemanly amateur': men with wealth and therefore leisure time, whose desire to collect and display fitted well with the new opportunities for exploration opened up by an expanding British empire. While Kew was certainly a highly influential leader in the field, far away from the metropolitan centre of London were other, smaller locations such as Falmouth which were similarly affected by Britain's expanding horizons. Today, Cornwall boasts a large number of sub-tropical gardens that were shaped by plant hunting expeditions during the nineteenth and early twentieth century. Despite this remarkable aspect to the Cornish landscape, the history of these Cornish gardens has not been the subject of vast academic study.[17] Sue Shepard's *Seeds of Fortune*, charting the history of the Veitch plant nurseries in Exeter from 1768, comes geographically close, though a discussion of Falmouth and Cornish gardens is nevertheless outside the book's remit.[18] While exotic gardens are now dispersed across the majority of the region,[19] some of the first were found in Falmouth[20] and its surrounding areas and the port's connection to the wider world was of vital importance.

Ornamental horticulture, as opposed to economic botany, is a term coined here to refer to the acquisition of plants that have an aesthetic value, rather than a primarily economic one. The term 'horticulture' is used instead of botany, as many people acquired plants from plant hunters without necessarily having a botanical interest in them, though in some cases this was also true. Ornamental plants are defined here as those which are not cultivated *primarily* as food, fodder or fuel. They may contribute to the economy, however, though they are not chiefly utilitarian. In addition to a literal value – typified by the lucrative craze for Dutch bulbs in the seventeenth century – ornamentals had a cultural value as part of the 'aestheticization of

---

[16] See for instance Livingstone, p. 55 and Drayton, *Nature's Government*.
[17] Popular guides to Cornish gardens include the website *The Great Gardens of Cornwall*, <http://www.greatgardensofcornwall.co.uk/> [accessed 12 September 2013], and Timothy Mowl, *Historic Gardens of Cornwall* (Stroud: Tempus, 2005).
[18] Sue Shepard, *Seeds of Fortune: A Gardening Dynasty* (London: Bloomsbury Publishing, 2003)
[19] Cornwall boasts sub-tropical gardens from Trengwainton and Trewidden in Penzance, in the extreme south-west, to Menabilly in the east and Pencarrow in the north of the county.
[20] Though there were also exotic gardens at Scorrier House, in Redruth, This was owned by the Williams family, who made their wealth in the mining industry and had at one time employed the future plant hunter William Lobb.

power'.[21] Prior to an eighteenth century focus on utility and economy, the value of ornamental plants was appreciated by those who saw the potential within them for displays of power and prestige. In *Nature's Government*, Drayton explores the symbolic value of exotic plants between the Tudor age and the eighteenth century, when ornamentals were used to create impressive gardens for royalty that projected the glory and might of a monarch and their reign.[22] Although Drayton's work falls in line with many existing studies in the way that it focuses on the utility and economic value of plants, takes Kew as a main setting, and chooses as protagonists the now-familiar figures of Joseph Banks, William Hooker and Joseph Hooker,[23] his discussion of ornamental plants and power is more unusual and interesting and will be continued in some way into the nineteenth century through the work in this chapter. The distinction between economic botany and ornamental horticulture will be maintained throughout this work for ease of definition, though the concepts are not considered to be entirely rigid and there should be no inference drawn that ornamental plants were or are without value, or that all enthusiasts of ornamental plants were not botanists.

The collection, cultivation and cataloguing of ornamental plants from around the world typifies a broader desire in the eighteenth and nineteenth centuries to 'collect' and study the exotic. From within the natural world, enthusiasts collected plants, insects, animals, shells and minerals, among other things.[24] As botany and horticulture became more broadly popular, horticultural societies were set up across Britain, along with various publications targeted at those with an interest in the subject. The Royal Horticultural Society of Cornwall (hereafter RHSC) had its first meeting in June 1832, and drew together plant enthusiasts, boasting that its rapid foundation was due to 'the support of the most influential men in the County.'[25] The wealthier classes were often the primary funders and proponents of botanical research and its accompanying expeditions and dissemination, as they sought to demonstrate their wealth and leisure time as part of a show of what Thorstein Veblen called 'conspicuous leisure', in which distancing themselves from work marks out

---

[21] Drayton, *Nature's Government*, p. 45.
[22] Drayton, *Nature's Government*, p. 43.
[23] Drayton, *Nature's Government*, p. xvi.
[24] Drayton, 'Knowledge and Empire', pp. 238-243.
[25] 'The Royal Horticultural Society of Cornwall', *Royal Cornwall Gazette, Falmouth Packet & Plymouth Journal*, 7 July 1832.

the superior pecuniary classes as honourable and decent.[26] This is a concept that will be explored in far greater detail within this chapter, as I argue that the activities of men such as Sir Charles Lemon, enabled through the overseas connections afforded by Falmouth, led to the reinforcement of social ideals that can be best understood by utilising Veblen's theories.

Though this chapter will focus primarily on Sir Charles Lemon, his garden at Carclew was just one of many in the Falmouth area that made an imperial display of exotic plants. Lemon has been chosen because his fondness for these plants appears to have been the greatest – he appears most of all in horticultural magazines[27] – but others, particularly the extensive Fox family, held impressive collections. For this was a passion unique to Falmouth, rather than Carclew: Alfred Fox's garden at Glendurgan features plants such as *Camellia Reticulata* 'Captain Rawes', named after the East India Company captain that transported it back from China in 1820.[28] With regard to ornamental plants, a strong parallel can be drawn between Carclew and Grove Hill, home to George Croker Fox. Situated within Falmouth and a short walk from the harbour, Grove Hill is a large property and was built for Fox in 1789.[29] The garden is mentioned frequently in relation to prizes awarded by the Royal Horticultural Society of Cornwall.[30] In a guide to Cornwall from 1851, the gardens around Falmouth are noted for their unusual plants, with Grove Hill mentioned in connection with 'upwards of 200 foreign plants'.[31] Those of other large estates elsewhere in Cornwall – with the exception of those owned by the Williams family, who were involved in mining and so had access to inbound ships – are not described as exotic. The gardens of Gyllyndune in Falmouth, which was owned by the rector Reverend Coope, contained many exotic plants. When the house and

---

[26] Thorstein Veblen, *The Theory of the Leisure Class* (London: Penguin Books, 1994), p. 35.
[27] As will later be described, in an edition of *The Gardener's Magazine* from 1840, Carclew is mentioned in fifteen out of thirty entries in a section relating to Australian plants, and the gardens of George Croker Fox in nine.
[28] William Beattie Booth, *Illustrations and descriptions of the plants which compose the natural order Camelliae* (London: John and Arthur Arch, 1831), plate 4.
[29] 'Grovehill House, Falmouth', *British Listed Buildings* <http://www.britishlistedbuildings.co.uk/en-460144-grovehill-house-falmouth-#.VVh8jPlViko> [accessed 17 May 2015]
[30] For instance, in 'Royal Horticultural Society of Cornwall', *The Royal Cornwall Gazette, Falmouth Packet and Plymouth Journal*, 24 July 1840 and 'Cornwall Horticultural Society', *Royal Cornwall Gazette, Falmouth Packet and Plymouth Journal*, 14 July 1843.
[31] Paris, p. 222.

grounds were auctioned in 1863, the public listings included '1,500 green and hot house plants'; among them camellias, fuchsias and cacti.[32]

The gardens of upper classes such as Lemon were for private or, as will become clear, semi-private consumption, and so were not of obvious economic benefit to the empire. Being almost entirely ornamental, the plants gathered and cultivated in grand gardens around Falmouth did not provide a benefit to mankind in terms of food, fodder or fuel, and because of this the motivations behind this ornamental horticulture are in many ways different to those of places such as Kew, which sought to further economic botany. This chapter will thus vary from much existing research in that it will seek to examine ornamental plants and their impact in small domestic settings within Britain, rather than studying economics and trade. While the latter topic is clearly relevant to the history of horticulture, this work will not seek to repeat studies already carried out, recognising instead that the effect on the British of importing and naturalising exotic plants is an under-researched area for investigation that is particularly interesting in the setting of Falmouth from 1800-1850. It will consider how conspicuous leisure and consumption are dependent on visual demonstrations of wealth, often achieved through extensive leisure time or great expenditure,[33] and how this need was fulfilled by the importation and display of exotic plants, which were only attainable by the upper classes.

Falmouth's function as a port opened many doors, both in trade and leisure, for men such as the Foxes and Sir Charles Lemon. In the case of the Foxes, their fortune was made because of the port's maritime connections: their business interests lay in shipping, mining, and consulships to foreign nations. As noted, Lemon's fortune was already made, but through Falmouth he gained positions of power and influence, and made networking connections with men such as the Foxes and important travellers to the port. The town's relationship to time-space compression has already been introduced and need not be elaborated upon in too much detail here: because of the long-distance travel afforded by the town due to its regular Packet Service and its accommodation of large passenger and trading ships, those with money were able to

---

[32] 'Sales by Auction', *The Royal Cornwall Gazette, Falmouth Packet and General Advertiser*, 3 April 1863.
[33] Andrew B. Trigg, 'Veblen, Bourdieu, and Conspicuous Consumption', *Journal of Economic Issues*, 35 (2001), 99-115 (pp. 100-101).

access countries overseas, whether this was simply to travel, or to trade with them in some way. Wealth granted its possessor the power to travel, but equally, travel provided the means to increase one's own wealth and power, as evidenced by the overseas mining trade carried out by the Fox family. This ability to travel, and to trade overseas, was vital for the acquisition of plant species. The importance of time-space compression in the context of horticulture cannot be understated. While many explorers gathered and transported seeds, which could be dried and preserved, many also chose to send living plant specimens, which could not survive especially long journeys on a ship. The fast maritime connections offered by Falmouth made it a port ideally suited to receiving such specimens. The RHSC, from its foundation, showed an interest in exotic plants that could not be matched by the other groups in existence, such as those from Bedfordshire, Cambridgeshire and Essex, which tended to focus on indigenous plants or those that were long-established in Britain.[34] The Devon and Exeter Botanical and Horticultural Society, which could draw upon the resources of the exotic Veitch Nurseries, was one other society to boast a range of rare plants at its exhibitions, due to this plant-hunting contact.[35] The RHSC is therefore significant as one of the first early groups dedicated to exotics, due to the proximity of its members to Falmouth.

Captains working for the Packet Service in Falmouth, were valuable contacts for those interested in horticulture. They appear to have undertaken work additional to their postal duties, also exploring the places they visited in search of new plant varieties. One specimen of Gesneria, *Gesneria Suttoni*, was even named after its discoverer, Captain Sutton. An 1834 report by the RHSC noted that:

> We owe the establishment of this fine plant to Captain SUTTON, of His Majesty's Packet Establishment, at Falmouth, who informs us that he found it growing in a wood, on a sloping hill, near the Bay of Bomviago, Rio de Janeiro, at an elevation of between 30 and 40 feet above the level of the sea, and not exceeding 40 yards from the water. Its beautiful flowers attracted his attention, and induced him to dig up the plant and bring it home. On his arrival in England, in March, 1833, he presented the choice collection of Orchideous, and other interesting plants he had found, to Sir

---

[34] *The Gardener's Magazine, and Register of Rural & Domestic Improvement*, ed. by John Claudius Loudon (London: Longman, Brown, Green, and Longmans, 1832), VIII, p. 746-751.
[35] Ibid.

Charles Lemon, Bart. M.P., and George Croker Fox Esq. Grove Hill, Falmouth, in whose garden the present plant flowered.[36]

This example makes it clear that captains in the employ of the Packet Service, being so frequently called upon to travel to and from exotic locations within a short time frame – the mail being naturally delivered in a timely fashion – were ideally suited to plant hunting and could be called upon by those with power and influence, such as George Croker Fox and Charles Lemon, to procure items for them. Many ships' crews did the same: Andrew Sinclair, co-founder of a museum in Auckland, was able to supplement its collections due to his former career as a naval surgeon, during which he collected botanical specimens from the Mediterranean, Africa and New Zealand.[37]

The Packet ships themselves were also useful to a plant-hunter, as carriers of packages and people. In 1840, William Lobb, who became a notable employee of the Veitch Nurseries in Exeter, began his career with the company by travelling from Falmouth to Rio de Janeiro on the Packet *Seagull*.[38] Plants gathered overseas by Lobb were sometimes sent back to Britain by Packet: in 1843, he sent specimens from Panama to Exeter via Falmouth.[39] Sir Charles Lemon had many links to the Veitch Nurseries, having employed and trained William Lobb and his plant-hunter brother Thomas in the stove-house at Carclew.[40] The Lobbs' father worked on the estate as a gamekeeper. The brothers, despite working for Veitch in Exeter and travelling abroad for long periods of time, always visited their family after returning from a voyage.[41] They would almost certainly have seen Sir Charles, such an avid collector and former acquaintance; though this is, of course, conjecture. Though the nursery forbade its collectors from sending specimens to any other source, Sue

---

[36] *The Floricultural Cabinet, and Florist's Magazine* (London: Whittaker & Co., 1834), II, p. 18.
[37] John MacKenzie, *Museums and Empire* (Manchester: Manchester University Press, 2009), p. 193.
[38] S. Heriz-Smith, 'The Veitch Nurseries of Killerton and Exeter c. 1780-1863: Part I', *Garden History*, 16 (1988), 41-57 (p. 49).
[39] S. Heriz-Smith, 'The Veitch Nurseries of Killerton and Exeter c. 1780-1863: Part II', *Garden History*, 16 (1988), 174-188 (p. 175).
[40] Matthew Biggs, 'Lobb's Cottage', *Cornwall Gardens Trust* <http://www.cornwallgardenstrust.org.uk/journal/2011-2/lobb%E2%80%99s-cottage/> [accessed 14 November 2013]
[41] Heriz-Smith, 'The Veitch Nurseries of Killerton and Exeter c. 1780-1863: Part II', p. 177.

Shephard, a biographer of the Veitch family, believes that William Lobb may well have covertly sent plants and seeds to his former employer.[42]

Travellers known to the men through their business or leisure interests could also be relied upon to share specimens if journeying through the port. One unique natural specimen still found at Penjerrick, home to Robert Were Fox, to this day is a brain coral, which can have a lifespan of several hundreds of years. This creature – not a plant at all, in fact, but nevertheless introduced to Fox's garden – was given to him by Captain FitzRoy of Charles Darwin's expedition ship HMS *Beagle*, when the ship and its crew landed in Falmouth in 1836. Captain FitzRoy visited the Foxes for tea on October 3, as recorded in the diary of Robert Were Fox's daughter, Caroline. The link between the men on this occasion appears to be Fox's interest in navigation and magnetism. Being a man of science, interested in much more besides horticulture, Fox had invented a 'dipping needle deflector' for navigation at sea, and FitzRoy was, according to Caroline, 'highly delighted' with it.[43] The captain also spent time sharing with the family some of the details of his voyage, and the discoveries that Darwin had made.

Being situated within a global trading network, Falmouth attracted a great number of ships en-route to exotic lands where plant specimens could be located. East India Company vessels regularly passed through Falmouth, and their captains became acquainted with Falmouth residents that had an interest in plants. During a meeting of the local RHSC in July 1835, George Croker Fox was congratulated on his acquisition of 'some choice exotics' sent to him by Captain Jenkins of the East India Company.[44] In May 1841, a further reference is made to Captain Jenkins supplying the society with seeds; in this instance Camellia sinensis, tea plants, from Assam.[45] The exchange of plants with the Company was a reciprocal one: in a meeting of May 1839, it was observed that Captain Jenkins had sent Sir Charles Lemon some live specimens from India with the request that the society return the favour by sending

---

[42] Sue Shepard, *Seeds of Fortune: A Gardening Dynasty* (London: Bloomsbury Publishing, 2003), p. 94.
[43] Caroline Fox, p. 9.
[44] *The Gardener's Magazine, and Register of Rural & Domestic Improvement*, ed. by John Claudius Loudon (London: Longman, Orme, Brown, Green, and Longmans, 1835), XI, p. 694.
[45] 'Royal Horticultural Society of Cornwall', *The Royal Cornwall Gazette, Falmouth Packet and Plymouth Journal*, 21 May 1841.

him plants from either South America or the West Indies.[46] This system of exchange was not unique: in museums and gardens around the world, natural treasures such as plants, fossils, and even human remains, were traded between societies.[47] In the 1850s, the Albany Museum in South Africa exchanged botanical specimens with Briton Peter McOwan, who sent plants from the Lake District and Scotland.[48] There was, as Naylor, argues, a sense of obligation for societies or interested parties to share information and specimens.[49] In the meeting of May 1839, the RHSC asked its members to consider sending samples of their own to one Dr Wallich, in return for his 'valuable contributions' to their collection.[50]

Clearly, within Falmouth, networking was an important part of acquisition. The Fox family had shipping interests themselves through G. C. Fox & Sons, their ship agents firm, and were part of the social life of the port through their roles as consuls.[51] Because of this, men such as George Croker Fox were well-positioned socially to commission captains – whether their own, those of the Packet Service, or those of other shipping companies – to share specimens with them, or obtain them on their behalf. It is possible that Sir Charles Lemon was introduced to these men through Fox, though he may also have met them through his own involvement in the social life of Falmouth.

Overseas contacts made through mining also proved valuable for procuring exotic plants. In March and April 1838, Lemon took delivery of plant specimens and a 'large collection of curious seeds' from John Rule, the superintendant of the Real del Monte mines in Mexico.[52] In this instance the value of informal empire to spheres other than the industrial becomes apparent. Because of incursions into Mexico made through the mining industry, the British were able to access other natural resources and export them back to Britain for collecting, cataloguing and naturalising. As John

---

[46] 'Cornwall Horticultural Society', *The Royal Cornwall Gazette, Falmouth Packet and Plymouth Journal*, 31 May 1839.
[47] MacKenzie, *Museums and Empire*, p. 108.
[48] Ibid.
[49] Naylor, 'The Field, the Museum and the Lecture Hall: The Spaces of Natural History in Victorian Cornwall', p. 497.
[50] 'Cornwall Horticultural Society', *The Royal Cornwall Gazette, Falmouth Packet and Plymouth Journal*, 31 May 1839.
[51] Dunstan, p. 48
[52] John Lindley, *Edwards's Botanical Register* (London: James Ridgway and Sons, 1838), XXIV, p. 53.

MacKenzie states in *Museums and Empire*, locations within the British empire that were already being exploited for natural resources – those connected by rail, road, telegraph and, I would argue, through necessity ship – inevitably saw travellers 'sucked into the fascinations' of sciences such as palaeontology, archaeology and, in this case, botany.[53] Improved communications of this kind frequently caused the overseas environment to 'bleed out its hitherto hidden treasures'.[54] Some specimens arriving due to the Falmouth/Mexico connection, such as the one received by Lemon in March 1838 – later named Commelina orchioides *Booth in litt.* – had not previously been discovered by the British. The entry for this particular species in *Edwards's Botanical Register* for 1838 contains a detailed description and a note from Lemon himself: 'I do not find any described species with which the plant can be identified.'[55] Falmouth's importance to ornamental horticulture during this time here begins to become apparent: due to the trade connections made from the port and the fast communications facilitated by it, in addition to the wealth and influence enjoyed by men such as G. C. Fox and Sir Charles Lemon, Britain was able to acquire entirely new plant specimens for its plant registers and exotic gardens. This is not the only example of a plant coming into Britain for the first time through Falmouth. In 1840, a new species of plant was named *Lemonia* in the *Botanical Register* in recognition of the number of new plants added to Britain's inventory through Sir Charles.[56] The entry reads: 'This very distinct and beautiful genus is named as a slight acknowledgement of the great benefits conferred, not merely upon science in general, but upon Botany in particular, by the large and well directed liberality of Sir Charles Lemon'.[57] Though this credit does not explain in detail precisely how Sir Charles has assisted the cause of botany, it seems likely that his 'liberality' lay in funding for expeditions and botanical work; yet another display of the finances at his disposal.[58] In this instance, his interest in plants, both personal and financial, is perceived to have had great benefits for the nation, and field, as a whole.

---

[53] MacKenzie, *Museums and Empire*, p. 3.
[54] Ibid.
[55] Lindley, p. 54.
[56] John Lindley, *Edwards' Botanical Register* (London: James Ridgway, 1840), XXVI, [no page number].
[57] Ibid.
[58] In this I do not mean to imply that Lemon did so only to display his wealth. He appears to have been a passionate horticulturalist and likely funded expeditions due to a desire to be at the forefront of acquisition.

Indeed, while Lemon had an interest in working with plants himself, as a wealthy man he was able to fund the work of others and so be involved, at a distance, in the plant gathering process. If useful networking contacts were made through work and industry, Lemon had equally valuable ones through his standing as a wealthy gentleman of leisure. His passion for exotic plants led him to become a correspondent of William and Joseph Dalton Hooker, and he was one of the sponsors of the latter's Himalayan expedition of 1847-1851. In return for his funding, he was one of the first to receive rare rhododendron specimens discovered by Hooker, though Robert Were Fox is also said to have received rhododendrons from this expedition, perhaps due to his friendship with Lemon.[59] These specimens were not simply to stock nurseries or meet demand: many were being introduced to Britain for the first time.[60] The fact that one of the specimens at Carclew was later named Rhododendron 'Sir Charles Lemon' is a testament to the fact that the plants grown in Falmouth as a consequence of this social connection and funding were unique and thus of great importance. Falmouth was not simply performing on a local stage, but a national one. In this sense, its gardens function as a variant form of museum: by MacKenzie's definition, reflecting 'the power, the technology, [...] the social relations [...] of a modern global system.'[61]

Living symbols of power

Clearly, wealth and social connections, to greater or lesser extents, were important for obtaining exotic plants from around the world. These plants, once obtained, served as either intentional or unintentional visual symbols of the power enjoyed by their possessors. It is not suggested that men such as Lemon procured plants entirely as markers of power. Lemon and the Foxes had personal motivations for pursuing this form of leisure over others, whether this was a genuine passion for plants, or religious or moral reasons.[62] What, then, were the consequences of owning and acquiring exotic plants? It has already been explained that acquisition of species is intrinsically and unavoidably tied into wealth and social power – the ability to travel

---

[59] Fox, *Glendurgan*, p. 63.
[60] 'Sir Joseph Dalton Hooker (1817-1911)', <http://www.kew.org/heritage/people/hooker_j.html> [accessed 18 November 2013]
[61] MacKenzie, *Museums and Empire*, p. 4.
[62] The Fox family were notable Quakers and, to some extent, shunned ostentatious displays of wealth, implying that there may have been other motivations for their interests in horticulture.

or to connect socially with those who do – and that Falmouth was often the location through which individuals were able to generate this wealth or social power. During the nineteenth century, there were several ways in which the moneyed were able to demonstrate their affluence to others. Veblen, writing in 1899, argues that since the very beginnings of a society in which people were able to own things and industry became settled, the dominant incentive was, and remains, 'the invidious distinction attaching to wealth', and the social ranking achieved through wealth and property.[63] Essentially, prosperity became 'intrinsically honourable.'[64] Though Veblen's comments on society and power were written after the time period studied here, they are nevertheless highly applicable in this instance; particularly because Veblen charted society through the ages, rather than confining observation purely to his own experience.

Integral to social position are labour and leisure. Freed from the necessity of working and the debasement that accompanies labour, the group within society that Veblen terms 'the superior pecuniary class', must 'put in evidence' their wealth and position by conspicuously proving that they do not work.[65] This show of distance from labour is what Veblen calls 'conspicuous leisure': a show of time that is spent non-productively. As no person's time can be spent always within the gaze of the public, the gentleman of leisure (Veblen refers to the gentle*man* in this instance) must somehow be able to show evidence that he abstains from productive labour when away from others. Often this can be seen in non-tangible results, such as quasi-scholarly or artistic knowledge in fields that are not directly useful to society, such as dead languages, art, dress or sports. Though botany had obvious scientific benefits, an interest in the science of ornamental plants can be considered largely as a conspicuous leisure activity, enjoyed by wealthy men such as Lemon. Having inherited his wealth, Lemon would have been socially very high-ranking, as inheritance was superior to wealth made directly through industry because of the increased distance the individual was able to claim from the labour that produced it.[66] The acquisition of exotic plants therefore conferred honour and social status on many levels: individuals must be wealthy and well-connected in order to obtain them

---

[63] Veblen, p. 26.
[64] Veblen, p. 29.
[65] Veblen, pp. 36-37.
[66] Trigg, p. 100.

in the first instance, but they also served as a means of demonstrating leisure time spent in a non-productive way as men like Lemon used species to pursue the science of botany.[67]

In discussing class and hierarchy within society an important note must be made regarding the contemporary view of these things. Class as most people see it today, consisting of upper, middle and lower, is generally accepted to be a product of the Industrial Revolution and changing social scene of the period 1780-1840.[68] Though the term 'class' had been used prior to this, it was only at this time that classes became self-aware.[69] The traditional, hierarchical view of society, in which everyone had a rank, began during this period to be slowly replaced by the three-class model.[70] An alternative view was that of two classes, the lower class and a mixed higher class consisting of the bourgeoisie and the original upper classes.[71] David Cannadine, in a discussion of class, states that all three possibilities were considered during this time of change.[72] References to the upper classes and lower classes in this chapter are therefore made for ease of definition, not to imply that either the three-class or two-class models were the only ones in contemporary use. It is certainly noteworthy, however, that the RHSC was formed during a time of such intense class struggle and social change, when the boundaries of class and the identity of its members were being defined and tried.

The way that plants were gathered and displayed in the contexts of conspicuous leisure and conspicuous consumption – the display of wealth through the consumption of goods[73] – has a historical precedent in the hierarchical courts of Europe. In early modern times, gardens symbolised the wealth and cultivation of their owners within the court, and were a space for vegetables, fruit, drugs and

---

[67] The cultivation and naturalisation of exotic plants is seen as non-productive here as the display of ornamental species was almost exclusively aesthetic and not useful to society in terms of providing food, fuel or fibre. Any useful scientific information gathered from the study of ornamentals was a by-product, rather than a prime motivation. Despite this, the work did, of course, have a value; particularly what could be termed an artistic value.
[68] Cannadine, *Class in Britain*, p. 57.
[69] Cannadine, *Class in Britain*, p. 3.
[70] Cannadine, *Class in Britain*, p. 3.
[71] Cannadine, *Class in Britain*, p. 58.
[72] Ibid.
[73] Trigg, p. 101.

perfumes.[74] The gardens of the rich and powerful came to represent their status as rulers, and botanical knowledge was seen as kingly: those who could command nature were made for wise government.[75] Horticulture received royal patronage and came to acquire an intellectual prestige.[76] Drayton notes that from the Tudor period onwards, gardens were closely associated with royal and aristocratic power.[77] Chandra Mukerji, in a discussion of early modern French court gardens, observes that gardens legitimised social status and inscribed affluence and power, being 'used to buttress the social claims of their owners and designers.'[78] Mukerji refers to gardens as sites for 'conspicuous collection': as trading horizons expanded, the wealthy collected exotic objects, including plants, as 'emblems of an impressive global reach.'[79] In this instance, the gardens of French courtiers attested to the glory of France, in addition to their owners' personal power.

The novelty and beauty of exotic plants remained, in eighteenth century Britain, an 'aestheticization of power' for monarchs such as King George III: a mask 'behind which arbitrary power could hide.'[80] However, Drayton argues that by the end of the eighteenth century, beauty and exoticism alone were not enough to reinforce the monarchy's divine origin and right to rule; their horticulture also had to be useful.[81] Gradually, the focus came to shift, as already described, from the ornamental to the economic. Another possible reason for this change is that by the beginning of the nineteenth century, exotic plants were starting to become more available to wealthy people outside of the royal court and aristocracy. In essence, what Veblen terms the 'trickle-down effect' was more possible. This refers to the emulation of conspicuous consumption by lower classes: each level of society seeks to emulate that above itself, attempting to live up to this ideal.[82] As global trade increased and plants came to be available to more people, it was possible for rich men such as George Croker Fox – from a family of merchants – to emulate the conspicuous consumption, or

---

[74] Drayton, *Nature's Government*, p. 26.
[75] Drayton, *Nature's Government*, pp. 26-27.
[76] Drayton, *Nature's Government*, p. 26.
[77] Drayton, *Nature's Government*, p. 26.
[78] Chandra Mukerji, 'Reading and Writing with Nature: Social Claims and the French Formal Garden', *Theory and Society*, 19 (1990), 651-679 (p. 653).
[79] Mukerji, p. 654.
[80] Drayton, *Nature's Government*, p. 45.
[81] Drayton, *Nature's Government*, p. 49.
[82] Trigg, p. 101.

conspicuous collection, of plants previously confined to the royal court. The consequence of this is that the status symbol loses some of its value. It no longer signifies only kingly power, and so is replaced by something new. From this is becomes clear that the pursuit and display of aesthetically pleasing and exotic plants did not cease entirely with the British empire's focus on economic horticulture; rather it moved down a level. Ornamental horticulture continued to have major implications for the reinforcement and creation of hierarchies of power, but the site for this power play had spread from an exclusive royal setting to include the gardens of the wealthy upper classes. Just as the gardens of the European courts symbolised the glory and global reach of the countries themselves, the gardens of Falmouth glorified Cornwall and Britain in their turn.

It should be noted that within Falmouth productive gardens could in some instances be considered exotic; much like the early court gardens in which productive but non-essential plants were grown. Although Glendurgan, like Carclew, housed rare ornamentals, its gardens also nurtured exotic fruit and vegetables. On her tour of the area in 1846, Queen Victoria was there presented with a grapefruit as a gift.[83] Similarly, Robert Were Fox's Rosehill accommodated over 300 species of lemon.[84] Clearly, these are 'productive' plants as opposed to ornamentals, but they would nevertheless have served as status symbols when compared with vegetable gardens of the poorer inhabitants of Falmouth. Their limited necessity when compared with practical, filling foods that might have been grown by others arguably renders them luxuries in the context of the nineteenth century.

From the public, visible courts of Europe, conspicuous consumption and leisure associated with plants thus trickled down to the private gardens of nineteenth century Britain. Yet the gardens, if conspicuous, could not be entirely private. While Lemon and the Foxes carried out much of their work with plants in the confines of their own properties, if we continue to gaze through the lens of Veblen's theory of conspicuous leisure their activities must have been publicly displayed in some way; and this is indeed the case. Though some traces of display have undoubtedly been lost to time,

---

[83] Charles Fox, *Glendurgan: A Personal Memoir of a Garden in Cornwall* (Penzance: Alison Hodge, 2004), p. 22.
[84] Fox, *Glendurgan*, p. 13.

even today, almost two centuries after they created their gardens, many examples of their contemporary public profile can still be found. With the formation of several publications on the topic of horticulture in the first half of the nineteenth century – magazines and journals such as *The Gardener's Magazine, and Register of Rural & Domestic Improvement*, *The Floricultural Cabinet and Florist's Magazine* and *The Gardener's Chronicle* – there were created many channels through which the gardens and plants belonging to British subjects could be described. In these publications, there can be found repeated references to George Croker Fox and Sir Charles Lemon in particular. An edition of *The Gardener's Magazine* dating to 1837 notes simply that under the direction of one Mr Beattie Booth, a new kitchen garden, flower gardens and shrubberies are being created for Sir Charles Lemon at Carclew.[85] Here, the useful production that is implied by the formation of a kitchen garden is kept away from Lemon by the clear mention of his employee undertaking the work, while the flower garden and shrubbery are probably of more interest to the landowner himself. This example does not highlight the conspicuous leisure time of Lemon, but is interesting because it shows that he, and Carclew, are considered of such general interest on the national horticultural stage that the creation of new gardens are newsworthy.

Charles Lemon's own activities become clearer in the press in other instances. In the 'Transactions of the London Horticultural Society', published in *The Gardener's Magazine*, Carclew is mentioned in fifteen out of thirty entries in a section detailing the national success rates of plants from Australia, and the gardens of 'Mr Fox', probably George Croker Fox, in nine.[86] Such prolific ownership of exotic plants, almost certainly assisted by Cornwall's industrial links with Australia at this time, and the high survival rates attributed to those under these men indicates a great deal of leisure time spent in gradually introducing species to the British climate, or 'naturalising' them. While the mild climate around Falmouth was almost certainly a contributory factor in the survival of specimens, the frequency with which Fox and Lemon are mentioned in publications such as this serves as a testament to the respect they were able to command in this field, and to the dedication of their leisure time.

---

[85] *The Gardener's Magazine, and Register of Rural & Domestic Improvement*, ed. by John Claudius Loudon (London: Longman, Orme, Brown, Green, and Longmans, 1837), XIII, p. 87.
[86] *The Gardener's Magazine, and Register of Rural & Domestic Improvement*, ed. by John Claudius Loudon (London: Longman, Brown, Green, and Longmans, 1840), VI, pp. 484-485.

This recognition also highlights the national interest and importance of the Falmouth gardens. Rare plants nurtured and grown successfully in Britain could potentially be acclimatised and shared around the nation.

Upper class leisure and 'cottager' gardens

The Royal Horticultural Society of Cornwall can be viewed as a means for the display of leisure time in addition to functioning as a space for sharing and discussing exotic and indigenous plants. Certainly, the RHSC must have considered itself to be fulfilling real needs in society, which will be discussed in more detail shortly, but the display of leisure time was a consequence – whether deliberate or inadvertent – of the way the group was organised. Its upper class members, such as Sir Charles Lemon, George Croker Fox and John Vivian, from Pencalenick House in Truro, used meetings and exhibitions to physically display their plants – many exotic but some indigenous – to the rest of the society, and to the public in general.[87] The first exhibition, held on 29 June 1832, was reported to have seen the showroom 'besieged by crowds' keen to view the displays.[88] At this time, Britain was – argues Margaret Willes – 'addicted to flower shows in all forms and sizes' as horticulture became a national obsession.[89] In some ways, exhibitions of exotic imports were even seen to justify imperial expansion and bolster the beauty of the empire.[90] In this instance the display element within the work of men such as Lemon is undeniable. By becoming a part of the exhibition, in the case of Lemon contributing a large amount of plants to decorate the hall in addition to showcasing other specimens, the extent of his leisure time becomes clear, as does the vast property that he must own in order to grow such quantities of beautiful plants for donation. The RHSC did not simply serve as a means of display, however. Indeed, this assumption is immediately complicated when attention is drawn to the fact that the lower classes, the 'cottagers', also displayed items from their own gardens at the exhibitions.[91] The

---

[87] 'The Royal Horticultural Society of Cornwall', *Royal Cornwall Gazette, Falmouth Packet & Plymouth Journal*, 7 July 1832.
[88] Ibid.
[89] Margaret Willes, *The Gardens of the British Working Class* (London: Yale University Press, 2014), p. 224.
[90] MacKenzie, *Museums and Empire*, p. 7.
[91] Willes, p. 224.

social structures and hierarchy of power within the institution are more complex than this.

The RHSC appears to have identified two main aims or areas of focus upon its formation, and these aims clearly mark a class divide. It was stated in 1832 that the society was formed 'for promoting the study and practice of Botany and Horticulture, and for improving the condition of the poor by the distribution of prizes to Cottagers'.[92] The *Royal Cornwall Gazette* observed in a discussion of the first exhibition that the society would lead to 'many important benefits, to the community at large'.[93] Nevertheless, it was very much positioned publically as of interest to the upper classes, which organised its formation and management, and the lower classes, which were seen to benefit from this. Commenting on similar institutions within the country, the newspaper continued: 'Their good effects are not exclusively confined to the rich; they pervade all classes of society, and tend more to add to the comfort and happiness of the Industrious Cottager, than to the possessor of the most splendid mansion.' In this atmosphere of apparent harmony between all strata of society, divisions and distinctions can be discerned which show how horticulture supported unequal power relations between the upper and the lower classes, which in supported the ideology of 'rulers' and 'ruled' that was so important for empire.

An initial divide can be seen in the areas of interest within horticulture that were pursued by the upper and lower classes. Reports of early exhibitions note that upper class men such as George Croker Fox exhibited 'rare and valuable plants' from Latin America and Australia, and expensive or exotic fruits such as melons and grapes, while in the designated cottagers' section, prizes were awarded for common or inexpensive items such as apples, geraniums, currants, and peas.[94] This is not in itself surprising, as the lower classes would naturally not be in a financial position to grow rare or expensive items. However, as the years passed, the categories into which the cottagers could enter became restricted to exclude ornamental plants and focus activities on edible crops. This decision, made in 1841, was barely explained to the public, the *Royal Cornwall Gazette* observing only that 'for substantial reasons

---

[92] Ibid.
[93] Ibid.
[94] 'Royal Horticultural Society of Cornwall', *Royal Cornwall Gazette, Falmouth Packet & Plymouth Journal*, 20 July 1833.

[the society had] discouraged this part of the exhibition', with greater attention given to 'the more useful articles' such as leeks, potatoes, onions and lettuces.[95] Compared to the first exhibition, in which there were a number of categories in which the upper classes could enter fruit and vegetables for judging, by 1841 the 'Flowers' category contains an extensive list of sub-categories and entrants, while there are very few edible items entered by the upper classes.[96] At this point, a divide becomes obvious between the affluent and their ornamental plants and the lower classes and their edible produce. In the newspaper report, which could of course represent the event in a light contrary to the wishes of the society itself – this cannot now be known – it appears that the ornamental category is far larger than the cottagers' categories, in which were awarded far fewer prizes. The 'substantial reasons' for these changes can only be surmised, but the decision was almost certainly linked to the view of proper employment for the working classes, tied in with ideas of the moral education afforded by horticulture. The direct assertion that cottagers should not concern themselves with flowers went against centuries of tradition. As early as the mid-seventeenth century, the lower orders had combined gardening for pleasure, through the cultivation of flowers, with productive gardening for the kitchen table.[97]

It was believed, and indeed regularly stated, that the cultivation of vegetables by cottagers would lead to improved morals among the class, and to a higher level of cleanliness and care in and around the home. In 1833, John Vivian explained that the 'principal object' of the society was to 'better the condition and improve the moral habits and moral feelings of the laborer [sic]'.[98] Almost a year later, in a speech at the opening of a society exhibition, William Carne, former Mayor of Falmouth,[99] stated that where the ground outside houses was cultivated, 'a correspondent degree of cleanliness will be found to prevail within the cottage.'[100] Concern with the morals of the working classes was common at this time. Towards the end of the

---

[95] 'Royal Horticultural Society of Cornwall', *The Royal Cornwall Gazette, Falmouth Packet and Plymouth Journal*, 21 May 1841.
[96] Ibid.
[97] Willes, p. 5.
[98] 'Royal Horticultural Society of Cornwall', *Royal Cornwall Gazette, Falmouth Packet & Plymouth Journal*, 20 July 1833.
[99] 'Mayors of Falmouth, 1800-1899', Falmouth Town Council, <http://www.falmouthtowncouncil.co.uk/web/the-mayor/mayors-of-falmouth-1800-1899/> [accessed 3 September 2013].
[100] 'Royal Horticultural Society of Cornwall', *Royal Cornwall Gazette, Falmouth Packet & Plymouth Journal*, 31 May 1834.

eighteenth century, there rose a view that the nation was in decline, with, Philip Connell argues, a focus on the corrupting power of commerce and luxury.[101] As the lower classes were viewed as corrupt and immoral, there was a drive to educate and improve that continued into the nineteenth century. Societies were formed that saw the working classes carrying out activities alongside their social superiors; the intention being that they could be educated and their morals improved by this proximity.[102] It was generally thought that with the working classes more dedicated to improvement than raucous behaviour, the classes might coexist more congenially, and the threat posed by unruly masses be diffused.[103] The education of children became more of a priority around Falmouth due to the Foxes, and in 1839 Anna Maria Fox established a children's horticultural society with an exhibition at Penjerrick, in order that the process begin earlier in life.[104] It was seen as important to raise the morals of the lower classes and to direct their efforts towards disciplined, practical work to break away from social problems such as unrest and overpopulation.[105] Knowledge and science became linked to moral, rational thought.[106] Although much of what we may consider 'science' on a national scale, such as industrialisation and botany, had strong links to the economy,[107] even everyday working class science such as vegetable growing can be viewed as economic science, as the cottagers could grow their own food and provide for themselves.

Aside from any financial gain, it appears from the newspaper reports recently discussed that the moral benefit to the cottagers of participation in the horticultural society lay in the proper use of leisure time. The RHSC was, states Naylor, 'the first to mark out moral advancement as an aim in itself rather than as a fortune by-product of industrial innovation.'[108] In an 1835 speech to the RHSC, its Chairman, Dr Carlyon, appealed to the upper classes for encouragement 'to the utmost' of

---

[101] Philip Connell, *Romanticism, Economics and the Question of 'Culture'*, Oxford: Oxford University Press, 2001), p. 64.
[102] Andrew August, *The British Working Class 1832-1940* (Harlow: Pearson Education, 2007), p. 58.
[103] Ibid.
[104] Barclay Fox, p. 154.
[105] Connell, p. 65.
[106] Drayton, 'Knowledge and Empire', p. 236.
[107] Connell, p. 77.
[108] Naylor, 'The Field, the Museum and the Lecture Hall: The Spaces of Natural History in Victorian Cornwall', p. 498.

gardening among the cottagers, 'as the most likely way of enabling them to resist successfully the allurements of that many headed monster the Beer-shop'.[109] The raucous and violent leisure activities of the working classes were at this time viewed as immoral and dangerous, especially in a population so geared towards discontent and poverty.[110] For the upper classes, during this time of class anxiety, the 'mass' was a terrifying body.[111] Suitable recreation for the working classes was a topic expounded by notable Flushing[112] resident and Sheffield MP James Silk Buckingham, who put forward in 1835 his ideas for 'Promoting the Sobriety, Recreation and Instruction of the Labouring Classes'.[113] In his view, 'Healthy Recreation and Instruction' were blessings to be bestowed upon the working population, while drunkenness was to blame for increases in disease, poverty, crime, and extinction of moral feeling.[114] Among his suggestions for curing the evils of intemperance, aside from restricting the sale and consumption of alcohol, was a greater amount of time spent outdoors for 'athletic and healthy exercises'.[115]

Buckingham's comments represent a general move in attitudes towards moral improvement of the working classes, certainly in Falmouth, where societies such as the RHSC and the Royal Cornwall Polytechnic Society made special attempts to engage the poorer strata in education and industry. This change also took place nationally, with their 'betters' leading the way in defining and creating appropriate leisure for the working classes.[116] Leisure could be organised around many themes, including music, libraries and parks,[117] but in Cornwall the obvious choice, given the local interest in plants, was horticulture. The education and improvement of the cottagers fell to the higher classes. In a speech on behalf of the horticultural society, John Vivian addressed his upper class audience, his 'fair friends', and beseeched them to 'co-operate with us in pointing out to the cottagers in your respective

---

[109] 'Royal Horticultural Society of Cornwall', *Royal Cornwall Gazette, Falmouth Packet & Plymouth Journal*, 30 May 1835.
[110] August, p. 52.
[111] August, p. 9.
[112] Flushing is situated near to Falmouth, and was the upmarket location of residence for the Falmouth Packet captains and senior staff.
[113] James Silk Buckingham, 'Mr. Buckingham's Bills for promoting the sobriety, recreation and instruction of the labouring classes', *Hume Tracts* (1835)
[114] Ibid.
[115] Ibid.
[116] August, p. 58.
[117] Ibid.

neighbourhoods, the inducements which are offered to them for employing their leisure hours in their gardens, after the ordinary labours of the day are over.'[118] In this address, the distinction between upper and lower classes, rulers and ruled, educated and uneducated, is very clear.

Discussions of the RHSC revolve around the recurring themes of work, leisure, waste and money. These themes similarly recur in Veblen's theories of conspicuous leisure and conspicuous consumption. The working classes are defined by the fact that they work and do not own large amounts of property, frequently being referred to in exhibition reports as labourers and cottagers.[119] Among the superior pecuniary classes, Veblen observes, 'Vulgar surroundings, mean (that is to say, inexpensive) habitations, and vulgarly productive occupations are unhesitatingly condemned and avoided. They are incompatible with life on a satisfactory spiritual plane – with "high thinking".'[120] The upper classes, as already noted, are defined by their abstention from productive work for subsistence,[121] and the financial abundance that allows them to visibly spend money on the 'unproductive consumption of goods'.[122] In this instance money was spent on rare exotic plants that, while interesting for study by serious botanists such as Lemon, were nevertheless largely ornamental. For the working classes, however, any 'waste'[123] of time in conspicuous leisure or money in conspicuous consumption, is seen as wrong by those above them. This can be interpreted as an attempt to prevent the trickle-down effect: the observance of the standards of the leisure classes, in some way, by those lower in the social hierarchy.[124] While the lower classes could not emulate the upper classes in importing and growing exotic ornamentals, they could – and initially did – attempt an emulation of this conspicuous leisure by growing native ornamentals for exhibition. As already noted, this practice was later discouraged and the cottagers were pushed to grow only fruit and vegetables, which cannot be perceived as

---

[118] 'Royal Horticultural Society of Cornwall', *Royal Cornwall Gazette, Falmouth Packet & Plymouth Journal*, 20 July 1833.
[119] See for instance 'The Royal Horticultural Society of Cornwall', *Royal Cornwall Gazette, Falmouth Packet & Plymouth Journal*, 7 July 1832 and 'Royal Horticultural Society of Cornwall', *Royal Cornwall Gazette, Falmouth Packet & Plymouth Journal*, 20 July 1833.
[120] Veblen, p. 37.
[121] Veblen, p. 36.
[122] Veblen, p. 69.
[123] Veblen, p. 97.
[124] Veblen, pp. 83-84.

conspicuous leisure due to the usefulness and productivity of the labour: leisure time spent in a vegetable garden is not time wasted. This conspicuous labour was made publicly clear through cottagers' displays. Likewise, emulation of the upper classes was again thwarted by a refusal to allow cottagers into the literal or metaphorical discussion – the 'high thinking' which is so incompatible with their lifestyles – about ornamentals within the society. After the RHSC exhibition in 1832, a special dinner was held for the 'Gentlemen' of the society, with a 'fashionably attended' ball later in the evening.[125] Clearly, neither of these events was open to the lower orders. Excluded from the possibility of emulation, for many years the cottagers showed little interest in the society exhibitions, and in 1834 it was observed by the exhibition speaker William Carne that regretfully there was little competition among the cottagers, and the products displayed were 'small and inferior'.[126] This mirrors a general national disinterest among the working classes in so-called 'moral' leisure activities that had been organised by their class superiors.[127] Only in 1850 was there an upturn in numbers entering for the cottagers categories, with eighteen people winning prizes, although this pales in comparison with the vast number of prizes given in the general categories.[128]

This fiercely defended social divide, and the prevention of the trickle-down effect, mirrors in some ways one of the original motivations behind the creation of royal exotic gardens. In early modern times, as social status became complicated by new sources of pecuniary and political power, gardens came to be a means by which rank could be policed.[129] Culture, as Mukerji argues, was 'essential both to mobility and its restriction.'[130] In these times, gardens helped to support the rank of the aristocracy. By the mid-nineteenth century, after ornamental horticulture had trickled down to become the domain of the upper classes, the protection level had also shifted downwards. Instead of separating royalty and aristocracy from the *nouveau riche*, the gardens separated the upper classes, including men of new wealth such as

---

[125] 'Royal Horticultural Society of Cornwall', *Royal Cornwall Gazette, Falmouth Packet & Plymouth Journal*, 13 October 1832.
[126] 'Royal Horticultural Society of Cornwall', *Royal Cornwall Gazette, Falmouth Packet & Plymouth Journal*, 31 May 1834.
[127] August, p. 58.
[128] 'Royal Horticultural Society of Cornwall', *The Royal Cornwall Gazette, Falmouth Packet and Plymouth Journal*, 13 September 1850.
[129] Mukerji, p. 655.
[130] Ibid.

the Foxes, from the classes beneath them. For this distinction to work, it was important that the lower classes be educated to the limit defined by the upper classes, but prevented from entirely emulating their "betters": if this were to happen the exotic garden could lose its symbolic value entirely.

If the cottagers were defined by their display of functional, productive horticulture, the upper classes expressed themselves in opposition to this utilitarianism via their interest in exotics. While these exotics could span several continents, with each exhibition report referring to a different species, there was one type of plant that became associated with the rich in Cornwall. Orchids were a Victorian status symbol: beautiful, exotic, expensive and delicate.[131] During the first half of the nineteenth century, the growing demand for orchids, combined with the fact that they were difficult to transport successfully, made them costly and so they became an exclusive, upper class plant.[132] They were kept in hot-houses or glass houses, often possessed only by serious botanists or those with wealth and land, such as Sir Charles Lemon. Around 1833 and 1834, Kew began to significantly expand its collection with shipments from Demerara and Surinam.[133] By the end of the 1840s, the number of species in Britain had increased and there was a large national community of orchid enthusiasts: the plant became so popular that the craze became known as 'orchidelirium'.[134] Even in 1886, when Lewis Castle's history of the orchid family was published, it was still historically considered a plant for 'the wealthy patrons of horticulture', even if the wealth required for purchase was, by then, smaller.[135] Catherine Ziegler notes that the costliness of orchids, in addition to the difficult growing environment required and complicated hybridisation process, ensured that after its growth in popularity in the 1830s, orchid owning would remain 'a mark of wealth, refinement and status for another century.'[136]

---

[131] Joan West, 'A Study of the Cornish Plant Hunters, William and Thomas Lobb' in *History around the Fal: Part Five* (Exeter: Fal Local History Group/University of Exeter, 1990), pp. 55-77 (p. 66).
[132] Brian Milligan, 'Frederick Sander, the Orchid King', *Orchid Societies Council of Victoria* <http://www.oscov.asn.au/articles2/sander.htm> [accessed 5 September 2013]
[133] Lewis Castle, *Orchids: Their Structure, History & Culture* (London: Journal of Horticulture, 1886), p. 42.
[134] Catherine Ziegler, *Favored Flowers: Culture and Economy in a Global System* (Durham, North Carolina: Duke University Press, 2007), p. 22.
[135] Castle, p. 6.
[136] Ziegler, p. 22.

During the 1830s, when orchids were hard to obtain, the wealthy members of society in and around Falmouth were uniquely positioned for pursuing this status symbol. In March 1833, Sir Charles Lemon and George Croker Fox received a 'choice collection' of living orchids from the Packet Service's Captain Sutton, obtained on a journey to Rio de Janeiro.[137] In the same year, the Duke of Devonshire saw *Oncidium* orchids at an exhibition; an encounter that sparked his own interest in the plant, and – Ziegler argues – can be seen as instigating the popularity of orchids in high society.[138] Thus, men such as Fox and Lemon, and indeed Falmouth as a location, were present at the early pinnacle of fashionable horticulture. In this context, the living species that arrived in Falmouth, from which others could potentially be bred, become highly important and extremely valuable. In a report on the RHSC in 1841, the *Royal Cornwall Gazette* observed that the region was becoming known for its orchidaceous plants, adding: 'Through the port of Falmouth, means are afforded and it seems readily adopted, for obtaining [...] curious and interesting plants in great abundance and variety.'[139] By displaying orchids alongside the cottagers' vegetables, Lemon and Fox were able, whether intentionally or not, to show their status, wealth and global connections to the assembled crowd.

Inequalities of power and social status were reinforced by the RHSC in many ways, several of which have already been discussed, while others, such as the careful layout of exhibitions, cannot be detailed fully here. Nevertheless, in the prominence given to exotic displays within exhibitions, and the class division inherent in society talks, luncheons and balls, the upper classes were placed at the forefront of an institution supposedly created for the promotion and exhibition of horticulture among the lower classes.[140] Despite the society's apparent focus on appropriate leisure for labourers, it is undeniable that its very existence was dependent on the interest in exotic plants among the upper classes, which collected and cultivated them, and the middle and lower classes, which flocked to view them. An interest in horticulture in Cornwall owed its origins to Falmouth and the exotics obtained through the port. Society activities primarily took place in the fashionable, wealthier

---

[137] *The Floricultural Cabinet, and Florist's Magazine* (London: Whittaker & Co., 1834), II, p. 18.
[138] Ziegler, p. 23.
[139] 'Royal Horticultural Society of Cornwall', *The Royal Cornwall Gazette, Falmouth Packet and Plymouth Journal*, 21 May 1841.
[140] See for instance Barclay Fox, p. 55 and 'Royal Horticultural Society of Cornwall', *Royal Cornwall Gazette, Falmouth Packet & Plymouth Journal*, 13 October 1832.

portions of Cornwall around Falmouth and Truro, rather than in the poorer industrial regions of the working classes. While the reinforcement of class hierarchy and power structures are important in the context of empire, it must be borne in mind before moving on to a discussion of this, that any effects within local communities felt as a consequence of the society were, in fact, effects of the plant hunting craze in Falmouth.

As discussed, through the establishment of the RHSC, and the personal horticultural activities of men such as Sir Charles Lemon, a social hierarchy determined by power, wealth, and leisure time was reinforced in Cornwall. Social relations between the upper and lower classes were clear, with appropriate recreations established by the former with regard to the latter. This was not simply an arbitrary effect; rather, it was a desired outcome in a country, and a region, where the unruly working classes had posed a serious threat to social order for some time. Having created a local class identity for themselves based on exotic plants, the upper classes sought to influence class consciousness among the lower classes; to move the collective identity away from alcohol, gambling and rough games[141] to gentle productivity. With Britain's ever-expanding population, and the growing density of working class people in industrial areas, there was a real anxiety that the masses could become dangerous.[142] In Cornwall, as in so many other areas, riots were instigated by the working classes due to poverty and frustration with a hierarchical system that they saw as unfair and detrimental to themselves.[143] The miners as a body became known for drunkenness and rough behaviour, to the extent that the first working day after a Saturday pay-day was traditionally called 'Maze Monday' or 'Bad Monday' due to the effects of the alcohol.[144] Providing recreation other than drinking was therefore seen, both nationally and locally, as a step towards curbing unruliness.[145] The violence and unruly behaviour that seemed to accompany drinking and working class leisure came under great criticism at this time from the middle classes and radicals.[146]

---

[141] August, p. 51.
[142] August, p. 9.
[143] London, National Archives, HO 45/1801
[144] Tony Deane and Tony Shaw, *Folklore of Cornwall* (Gloucestershire: The History Press, 2009), 44.
[145] Buckingham, 'Mr. Buckingham's Bills for promoting the sobriety, recreation and instruction of the labouring classes', p. 1
[146] August, p. 52.

It is hard to ascertain exactly how influential the horticultural society was in taming the working classes. Certainly, it was believed at the time that it was instrumental,[147] though the rise of Methodism among mining families could be the real instigator.[148] It was stated in 1839 that the pursuit of horticulture had been the most effective in promoting 'morals and manners' in Redruth, an industrial heartland with a high population of working class people, and 'formerly very dissolute'.[149] Whether or not this is the case, the popular belief was that the working classes had, in some way, been shown a correct and moral path through horticulture, and this belief led to the promotion of this system nationally.[150] Hugh Seymour Tremenheere, a man employed – among other duties – to investigate the conditions among mining populations nationally, concluded that cottage gardens had led to an improvement in 'good order', 'steadiness' and 'the pecuniary interests' of the poor.[151] The inference is certainly that the cultivation of produce led to a reduction in dissatisfaction and rioting, and that with an increase in money, poverty-induced riots could be reduced. It was also believed by W. M. Tweedy, Treasurer of the RHSC, that engagement with the ideals of the society, notably proper recreation and productivity among the poor, lead to an increase in national pride and loyalty to the state.[152] Cultivation of ground and productive leisure would lead, he said, to the lower classes feeling as interested as the upper classes in 'the maintenance of good order' and promotion of the peace and prosperity of the country.[153] These effects were said to be enjoyed further afield than Cornwall. At a society meeting in 1839, it was proudly stated that 'the greatest merit of this society was that it had led to the formation of a great many others called Cottage Societies'.[154]

---

[147] 'Royal Horticultural Society of Cornwall', *The Royal Cornwall Gazette, Falmouth Packet and Plymouth Journal*, 13 September 1850.
[148] The Methodist religion had spread throughout mining communities by this time, and is today credited with teaching poor families the principles of thrift and pride in the home, which led the miners to self-improvement.
[149] 'Cornwall Horticultural Society', *The Royal Cornwall Gazette, Falmouth Packet and Plymouth Journal*, 31 May 1839.
[150] 'Cornwall Horticultural Society', *The Royal Cornwall Gazette, Falmouth Packet and Plymouth Journal*, 31 May 1839.
[151] Ibid.
[152] 'Royal Horticultural Society of Cornwall', *The Royal Cornwall Gazette, Falmouth Packet and Plymouth Journal*, 13 September 1850.
[153] Ibid.
[154] 'Cornwall Horticultural Society', *The Royal Cornwall Gazette, Falmouth Packet and Plymouth Journal*, 31 May 1839.

The subduing effects apparently caused by the formation of so-called cottage societies had real implications for empire in the first half of the nineteenth century. The RHSC may have led to a national reinforcement of social structure and hierarchical power, but the people targeted by these activities were nevertheless subjects of the British empire as much as those living overseas in colonies. A core principle of horticultural societies was the taming, under the guise of improvement, of the potentially hostile, volatile, and dangerous strata of society. Certainly, not all white British people enjoyed the same standing in the empire, and the poor cannot be seen as representing 'the colonisers' purely due to nationality. Rather, they were subjects who needed to be guided by their rulers into the correct way of life for promoting health, wealth, peace, and loyalty. This view is shown in the journals of James Williamson, a surgeon with the Packet Service in Falmouth, who in 1832 considered the British working classes as comparable with the natives of Bermuda. Having commented on the lack of morals among the black Bermudans, Williamson nevertheless observed after witnessing a 'black funeral' that 'I never witnessed anything so orderly and decent among our lower classes at home.'[155] This sentiment was echoed by John Fairbairn, editor of the *South African Commercial Advertiser*, and by the editor of the *Nelson's Examiner* in 1843. In discussing the Xhosa of South Africa, Fairbairn warned that the threat posed by 'uncivilised barbarians' such as these could also be found in lower British society.[156] The *Nelson's Examiner* argued that the minds of the British working classes and 'savages' had much in common, with confined views and low artifice.[157] The taming of white working class people can thus be seen as a sort of proving ground for ideologies of empire. The education and moral improvement of the poor in Britain was referred to by the Bishop of Exeter in 1848 as an example of what could be achieved in the colonies: as an ideal to aspire to in locations such as New Brunswick, in Canada.[158]

The ideals that guided the RHSC, and a desire to maintain distinctions between classes, can be seen in existence in colonial locations such as Canada. In 1834, the Toronto Horticultural Society was formed to cater to both lower and upper class

---

[155] James Williamson, '2nd Voyage to Halifax & Bermuda', *Maritime Views* <http://www.nmmc.co.uk/index.php?/packet_surgeons_journals/voyage_9/bermuda/> [accessed 9 September 2013].
[156] Lester, p. 43.
[157] Ibid.
[158] 'England', *The Royal Cornwall Gazette, Falmouth Packet and Plymouth Journal*, 21 July 1848.

needs, aiming to 'ameliorate the wants of the humble, and [to contribute] to the gratification of the exalted.'[159] Though the society sought to encourage the introduction of improved crops,[160] thereby being guided by motivations of economic horticulture, it was also influenced by ideals of the moral improvement of the poor.[161] Though ideas of horticulture for the working classes changed over time to prioritise neatness and beauty in gardens, rather than the growing of fruit and vegetables, the act of gardening itself remained intrinsically linked to the notion of morality and a sense of belonging and loyalty to one's area or, if interpreting this more broadly, the empire as a whole.[162] This example demonstrates that regardless of location, whether in Britain or one of her colonies, the same ideals were distributed and all people were viewed as subjects. Thus, Falmouth and the RHSC can be seen to be interacting to a great extent with a wider, colonial dialogue.

The introduction of exotic plants to Falmouth had many repercussions for the local population. Gentlemen of leisure, such as Sir Charles Lemon, and even those who earned their own money, like the Foxes, were able to use these plants as a demonstration of their superior rank in society. Through the formation of the RHSC in 1832, Lemon, the Foxes, and other upper class associates found a space to share both plants and ideas, and to contribute to the formation of other discourses surrounding class, recreation and morality. In a time of great social change and anxiety, plants were a channel through which grand estates such as Carclew could be made yet more impressive, while simultaneously serving as a means of control over the potentially unruly masses existing at the base level of wealth production. The differences between people that these plants, as expensive, exotic, colonial products, could highlight was significant in forming class consciousness, and became a part of the upper class identity for those living around Falmouth. This strong identity was pitched against that of the lower class masses, seen as unruly both in Cornwall and elsewhere, and used as an attempted means of social improvement. If the assertions of the RHSC are true, the society also led to the formation of others like it, thus

---

[159] Leslie Jermyn, 'Lawn and Order: The Politics of Horti-Culture in Toronto', *vis-à-vis: Explorations in Anthropology,* 9 (2009), 158–169 (p. 162).
[160] 'Toronto Horticulture Society', <http://www.waymarking.com/gallery/image.aspx?f=1&guid=9541b1b8-92ac-49a1-a4be-b50443682915&gid=3> [accessed 9 September 2013].
[161] Jermyn, p. 162.
[162] Jermyn, p. 163.

spreading these ideals nationally.[163] This is not relevant simply to a study of Falmouth or Britain; these power relations had implications for the way that colonial subjects were approached. While the RHSC was not categorically the inspiration for colonial social improvement, it was at the very heart of a wider narrative that influenced how the lower-ranking subjects of empire, white or black, at home or abroad, should behave. An interest in horticulture, awakened among the upper classes in Falmouth, ultimately led to the town, and surrounding towns, becoming part of a global dialogue about class and leisure that informed an understanding of the obligations and duties of society's rulers, or educators, and the ruled. The British domestic sphere, here typified in the form of a private garden, was not a realm removed from the ideologies of empire, but rather a silent force at the heart of it. The following chapter will explore in more detail the ideological effects of contact between these two worlds – the home and the empire – as Falmouth became a gateway through which the domestic and the foreign could interact.

---

[163] 'Royal Horticultural Society of Cornwall', *The Royal Cornwall Gazette, Falmouth Packet and Plymouth Journal*, 13 September 1850.

Chapter 4: Bringing the empire home: identity and the Other

> We called at [Pearce's] Hotel on the Begum of Oude, who is leaving England [...] on a pilgrimage to Mecca. [...] Her dress was an immense pair of trousers of striped Indian silk, a Cashmere shawl laid over her head [...] a great deal of jewelry, and a large blue cloak over all. She was very conversable, showed us her ornaments, wrote her name and title in English and Arabic in my book, and offered to make an egg curry.[1]

The Begum of Oudh[2] emerges from the pages of Caroline Fox's diary as a genial but exotic, even alien, character. Aunt to the King of Oudh, in India, and daughter of his predecessor, she enjoyed a privileged position and was able to travel. In December 1836, the Begum visited Falmouth as part of a pilgrimage to Mecca, staying there in a hotel while socialising with the local upper classes, such as the Fox family.[3] To Caroline Fox, the Begum was completely different to the British society she generally mixed with: in dress, speech, religion, morals, and even cuisine.[4] Likewise, Caroline's brother Barclay, present at the same occasion, found her to be 'an oddity if human being ever deserved to be called so.'[5] Nevertheless, her extreme difference appears to have fascinated them both. Barclay referred to her as 'her brown Excellency' and spoke at length of her appearance: '[h]er person dark olive, broad nosed, black jaguar-like eyes [...] dress inexplicable'.[6] In language and speech the two nationalities were noticeably estranged, as the Begum wrote in Arabic and spoke in mispronounced and 'misplaced' English.[7] Social and religious practices varied wildly between the two: Caroline was shocked to discover that an additional motivation for the Begum's visit to England was to procure wives for the King of Oudh.[8] At the end of December, Barclay also met the Begum's husband, an Oudh ambassador, who was travelling from Falmouth to Bombay by steamer.[9] Like his wife, the ambassador was a character that Barclay found entirely foreign; 'a very odd

---

[1] Caroline Fox, p. 11.
[2] Sometimes spelled Oude, as by Caroline Fox, or known as Awadh.
[3] Caroline Fox, p.11.
[4] Ibid.
[5] Barclay Fox, p. 100.
[6] Ibid.
[7] Ibid.
[8] Caroline Fox, p. 15.
[9] Barclay Fox, p. 100.

fellow with tiger-like eyes'.[10] The Foxes appear to have found very little in common with the husband and wife: their journal entries focus almost exclusively on the differences between their cultures. This is not surprising; by this period in time the ambiguously named 'Orient' had become what Edward Said describes as 'one of [Europe's] deepest and most recurring images of the Other.'[11] As this chapter will demonstrate, the Fox family's reactions to the Begum operated within a context of difference and familiarity that was becoming increasingly common in Britain's wider maritime empire, as well as in Falmouth.

This example highlights the meetings between entirely different cultures, and those from geographically distant areas, that were brought about through Falmouth. Elsewhere in Cornwall, it would have been far more unlikely for Indian royalty and the British upper classes to meet. Only in Falmouth did such an occurrence resemble the commonplace: Fox's diary, and those of her brother Barclay and uncle Alfred, make repeated reference to meetings with royal or noble travellers from countries such as Turkey, Ashantee,[12] Portugal, Saxony, and Brazil.[13] As wealthy foreign travellers came into Britain through Falmouth, so too did the wealthy British leave the country via the port. In June 1809, Lord Byron arrived in the town to depart for Lisbon and the beginning of his Grand Tour. For ten days he waited restlessly, unimpressed by his busy, provincial surroundings and keen to be away from England, but frustrated by a lack of wind that prevented sailing.[14] To pass the time, he wrote letters to his mother and friends, explored the nearby castle of St Mawes, and observed the unruly behaviour of the locals.[15] Almost a decade earlier, in 1800, his fellow poet Robert Southey travelled from Falmouth for Lisbon, finding nothing in the town but 'Dirt, noise, restlessness, expectation, impatience'.[16]

Falmouth in the first half of the nineteenth century was neither provincial town nor cosmopolitan centre, instead functioning as a busy, noisy thoroughfare through

---

[10] Ibid.
[11] Edward Said, *Orientalism* (London: Penguin Books, 2003), p. 1.
[12] In what is now Ghana.
[13] As shown in Caroline Fox, p. 57 and p. 99, Barclay Fox, p. 47, and Alfred Fox, p. 27 and p. 7.
[14] George Gordon, Lord Byron, 'Falmouth Roads, June 30th, 1809' in *Letters and Journals of Lord Byron: Complete in One Volume*, ed. by Thomas Moore (Frankfurt: H. L. Brönner, 1830), p. 83.
[15] Ibid.
[16] Joseph Cottle, *Reminiscences of Samuel Taylor Coleridge and Robert Southey* (London: Houlston and Stoneman, 1847), p. 220.

which the world's travellers passed. Here was an active town of industry, and its primary industry was passage. People, information, cultures: all moved in and out of the port, occasionally colliding as they did so and producing sparks of understanding or antagonism; sometimes ideological. This chapter will examine these collisions, or moments of contact, through the eyes of the people who experienced or instigated them. It will argue that Falmouth was instrumental in the creation of both inclusive and exclusive systems of dialogue that were important to the British empire, most particularly the 'placing', in terms of identity and hierarchy, of those who could be considered foreign. Through this, there were created exclusive notions of British national identity, based on superiority, that were informed by interaction with the Other. Through careful and complicated negotiation, the opportunity for encounters offered by Falmouth led to renegotiations of what it meant to be British; or not. Far from being a provincial town away from the heart of Britain and its empire, Falmouth became deeply entrenched in a global dialogue concerned with Britishness and power.

The town occupied a strange space in terms of connectivity and regionality, being well-connected to the world, particularly the British empire, by sea, but by land remaining a town on the south coast of Cornwall, at the far end of England. The working classes living in Falmouth were probably more likely to come into contact with people travelling from overseas, than with people travelling from elsewhere in Cornwall. In her memoirs, Caroline Fox recalls talking to a Falmouth woman who had never travelled further than Redruth, around ten miles away.[17] Yet this woman was quite likely to have seen a great number of foreigners in Falmouth. Even for the wealthy, like the Foxes, more frequent contact was made with travellers than with those living elsewhere in Cornwall. Caroline Fox lamented the removal of her friend Dr Calvert to Penzance, almost thirty miles away, with the words: 'We shall miss him much.'[18] Interaction, however brief and basic, between the inhabitants of Falmouth and the travellers that passed through the port was therefore significant. This marked the difference between Falmouth and the rest of Cornwall, as it became part of a separate world: the sea that provided its income made it unique as a point of contact with the world of empire. The majority of travellers would not penetrate

---

[17] Caroline Fox, p. 130.
[18] Ibid.

much further into the rest of Cornwall, besides travelling along the roads that led to and from London. The time-space compression that occurred by sea therefore confused the notion of Otherness in Falmouth. Though the Other was often constructed on the basis of race and nationality, it was also influenced by geographic distance, and this is certainly complicated by the fact that for people living in Falmouth, towns within Britain may have been temporally as distant as spatially distant countries such as Portugal. In 1830, the Packet Service surgeon James Williamson noted a journey of six days from Falmouth to Portugal.[19] Aboard a mail coach, with between four and six horses galloping constantly and being regularly changed, a journey from Falmouth to London would have taken between two and three days.[20] However, undertaken by a domestic horse or carriage, the pace must have been far slower with more stops, and if travelling further than London, the travel time would have increased dramatically. Some sense of temporal and spatial proportion was restored by the fact that, for those with money, journeys within Britain were often taken by sea rather than land, as maritime travel remained superior to overland travel.[21] For those restricted by their financial means, however, Falmouth remained better connected to the nation and the empire by sea than it did to the farther reaches of Cornwall or Britain by land. Due to this, the town became an enclave within the region, where notions of Britishness and Otherness could be explored in a way that was remarkable for a provincial town. It thus stands as a unique and deeply interesting site in a narrative of identity linked to empire.

The notion of the Other – who or what is British, or not – was complex and ever-changing, as cultural and geographic distance was constantly redefined. Catherine Hall, a prolific writer on the cultural impact of empire, argues that the colonies had a profound effect on the national identity of Britain, providing a means of definition by comparison: the foreign served as a benchmark against which Britishness could be measured.[22] Though this may be true in a general sense, a contemporary view of

---

[19] James Williamson, 'Journal of a Voyage from Falmouth to the Mediterranean', *Maritime Views* <http://www.nmmc.co.uk/index.php?/packet_surgeons_journals/voyage_5/> [accessed 16 October 2013]
[20] Gay, Susan, *Old Falmouth* (London: Headley Brothers, 1903), p. 143.
[21] Barclay Fox, p. 108.
[22] Catherine Hall, 'The nation within and without' in Catherine Hall, Keith McClelland and Jane Rendall, *Defining the Victorian Nation: Class, Race, Gender and the Reform Act of 1867* (Cambridge: Cambridge University Press, 2000), pp. 179-233 (pp. 180-181).

national identity is best gleaned using individuals as specific examples, in recognition of the fact that identity was, and shall always remain, personal and subjective. It is not possible to speak for the entire population of Falmouth, and as such this thesis will not attempt to do so. The study of individuals as a means of exploring identity is a method of which Hall approves: 'Letters and diaries that record personal feelings and reactions are particularly valuable in telling us about what people thought and felt.'[23] In this chapter, the journals of British subjects – both those who stayed at home, and those who travelled to the colonies from Falmouth – will be utilised to determine how identity was constructed, reinforced, and altered according to contact with the empire.

Encountering difference

Travellers visiting Falmouth – passing through on their way to or from Europe and the empire – often spent several days in the port, whether by choice, in preparation for a journey, or while waiting for correct sailing conditions. Some were British, travelling via the Packet ships for business or pleasure,[24] while others were foreigners travelling to or from their native countries.[25] As such, there was ample opportunity for contact to be made with the residents of Falmouth. The 1815 publication *A Falmouth Guide*, designed to be 'a complete directory to strangers, going abroad in the Packets', acknowledged the amount of time passengers spent in port with directions to the town's accommodation and social areas, such as the inns.[26] Visitors, whose aim might well be to explore landscapes far from Cornwall, were encouraged to fully explore and engage with Falmouth as a destination in its own right, and in doing so to create a tourist spectacle of their own. The guide boasted as an attraction 'the variety of human countenances to be met with, whose commercial concerns bring them from different parts of the world.'[27] Here, interaction between the people of disparate nations is brought to the forefront as a

---

[23] Catherine Hall, 'Culture and Identity in Imperial Britain' in *The British Empire: Themes and Perspectives*, ed. by Sarah Stockwell (Oxford: Blackwell Publishing, 2008), pp. 199-217 (p. 205).
[24] James Williamson, in his '2nd Voyage to Halifax & Bermuda', notes that among the ship's passengers is one Major Henderson, travelling to join his regiment in Bermuda.
[25] For instance, in 'Journal of a Voyage from Falmouth to the Mediterranean', Williamson notes the presence on board of a Spanish gentleman named Senor Capdeviello, travelling from Falmouth to Spain after a business trip to England and Scotland.
[26] R Thomas, *A Falmouth Guide*.
[27] R Thomas, *A Falmouth Guide*, p. 34.

novel form of entertainment. The constant contact, however brief, between Britons and foreigners led to the exchange and formation of ideas concerned with race and national identity. This could be as simple as a glance at a foreigner informing views on differences in appearance and dress, or could be a more extensive experience such as the hours spent by Caroline Fox in the company of the Begum of Oudh. In either case, Falmouth became a site of 'culture contact': a location where the empire and the British were able to meet, and where ideas of national identity could be formed and altered because of this contact.[28]

When discussing the British empire and its colonies, notions of the British and Other are deeply complicated by the fact that there was, at this time, no official distinction between white British subjects living in Britain and subjects of other races living in the colonies.[29] It was only in 1981 that the British Nationality Act made any formal differences in citizenship, and until this time the extent to which people did or did not qualify as British was highly negotiable.[30] Perceptions of the British and the foreign were therefore apt to change, and were constantly informed by contact between the two, the type of contact that took place in and around Falmouth. The town was arguably a node within a network of travel and communications that informed identity as ideas and people passed constantly through. In using the analogy of a network, it should not be implied that more traditional ideas of network, such as a geographic centre and periphery, are to be followed. Instead, the importance of the local should be highlighted, as Miles Ogborn argues: 'the specific "local" geographies of imperial sites, territories, and networks are understood as a vital part of the exertion of imperial power'[31] Though this may be intended by Ogborn as a comment on the local within the colonies, away from Britain, the importance of local sites in the empire should include the empire at home. Similarly, Kathleen Wilson argues that 'empire as a unit was a phantasm of the metropole: all empire is local.'[32] In a study of Falmouth it will become clear that this location, physically small and far from the geographic centre of London, was nevertheless

---

[28] Gascoigne, p. 580.
[29] Catherine Hall, 'The nation within and without', p. 180.
[30] Ibid.
[31] Miles Ogborn, *Indian Ink: Script and Print in the Making of the English East India Company* (Chicago: University of Chicago Press, 2007), p. 3.
[32] Kathleen Wilson, *The Island Race: Englishness, Empire and Gender in the Eighteenth Century* (London: Routledge, 2003), p. 213.

influenced to a great extent by the empire, and was in turn influential. In this place, the impact of global communications on local ideas of national identity and race can be discerned. As Lester argues, 'ideas of legitimate behaviour towards others and corresponding notions of Britishness itself moved through, and were contested within, circuits connecting Britain with each of its colonies.'[33] Falmouth was certainly one such point of connection and led to definition or redefinition of ideas of the British.

Catherine Hall defines othering as a process by which distinctions between self and Other, included and excluded, are made.[34] Othering is inextricably linked to culture, Hall viewing this as the way in which meanings are produced and exchanged, and how these meanings influence social and institutional worlds.[35] In the context of the empire, othering was vital to the constitution of British identity, as differences between races were used to identify what the Briton was not: '[t]he "fullness of identity depends on what it lacks.'[36] When viewing a particular race as barbaric, for instance, a Briton naturally distances himself or herself from this trait, in so doing defining his or her own race as civilised. Effeminacy and passivity in another race marked out the British as masculine and in control.[37] Constructions such as these are dependent on contact, or at least information, about other nations and races, and port towns such as Falmouth were well-positioned to offer this. By the first half of the nineteenth century, the empire came to have a real impact on perceptions of British national identity, though in some ways this may have become normalised to the extent of unconsciousness. Hall and Sonya Rose describe the effect of the imperial as 'infusing' everyday life.[38] The average citizen of Britain was neither strongly pro- nor anti-imperialist, simply existing in a state of passive influence.[39] The process of othering and the construction of national identity were not exclusively state-led, but instead carried out in some way by most subjects of the empire. Hall refers to the differences highlighted during othering as 'grammars of difference': the marking of

---

[33] Lester, p. 25.
[34] Catherine Hall, 'Culture and Identity in Imperial Britain', p. 203.
[35] Catherine Hall, 'Culture and Identity in Imperial Britain', p. 202.
[36] Catherine Hall, 'Culture and Identity in Imperial Britain', p. 203.
[37] Ibid.
[38] Catherine Hall and Sonya Rose, 'Introduction: being at home with the empire' in *At Home with the Empire*, ed. by Catherine Hall and Sonya Rose (Cambridge: Cambridge University Press, 2007), pp. 1-31 (p. 2).
[39] Ibid.

distinctions as part of a never-ending and constantly contested fixing of binaries between coloniser and colonised, or sometimes between men and women, and rich and poor.[40] Grammars of difference changed according to contemporary events. For instance, during the Napoleonic Wars France was othered, whereas during the abolition of slavery both slaves and colonisers living away from Britain were marked as different.[41]

The Orient in Falmouth

The encounters between the Begum and ambassador of Oudh and Caroline and Barclay Fox, represent the global reach of Falmouth in terms of connecting people, and provide an interesting insight into the effects of these encounters. The interactions between the Begum and the Foxes were in many ways typical of the contact between the Orient and Britain at this time. Oudh was not at this point a formal part of the British empire but certainly felt the effects of it: several areas of the kingdom had been annexed by the British East India Company in 1801[42] and it was in the process of gradually becoming subordinate to the British.[43] It would go on to be formally annexed to the empire in February 1856. The Begum and her family therefore had an ambiguous, uneasy relationship with the British, being neither colonial subjects nor truly independent. Nevertheless, the way in which British people viewed those from the Orient was heavily influenced by colonial attitudes, for reasons which will be elaborated upon shortly. In this encounter, Barclay and Caroline place themselves in the role of the West, while the Begum and her husband the ambassador represent the East. This simple divide, between self and Other, was a key aspect of what Said terms Orientalism: an 'intellectual power' held by Europeans in dealing with the Orient.[44] One definition put forward by Said, and the most compelling in the context of colonialism, is that Orientalism can be viewed as 'a Western style for dominating, restructuring, and having authority over the Orient.'[45] This can be accomplished through study, representation and control; the

---

[40] Catherine Hall, 'Culture and Identity in Imperial Britain', p. 204.
[41] Ibid.
[42] Rudrangshu Mukherjee, *Awadh in Revolt, 1857-1858: A Study of Popular Resistance* (New Delhi: Permanent Black, 2002), p. 1.
[43] Mukherjee, p. 32.
[44] Said, *Orientalism*, p. 41.
[45] Said, *Orientalism*, p. 3.

Europeans – which Said sees as primarily Britain and France at this time – taking control over the representation and ruling of the Orient. The Orient as it was viewed within Europe was thus created by those living within Europe.[46] General knowledge of places such as India was informed by the production of texts and representations made by those who encountered it in many capacities, as scientists, travellers, traders, and so on.[47] Within this dialogue, East and West were clearly demarcated.[48] India, where Oudh was situated, had at this time a historic tradition of being dominated by the West.[49] It did not occupy a threatening role in relation to Britain, but was instead characterised by a history of passivity.[50] This history, and the enforcement of ideas of Western dominance and Eastern weakness, found an outlet in texts and representations. The Orient was typically described, or represented, as weak, childlike, irrational and immoral, while Europe was strong, mature, rational and virtuous.[51] This tradition of binary representation can be discerned in the accounts of the Begum and her husband that were put forward by Barclay and Caroline Fox.

A brief digression from this material must be made in order to address the use of Said in this context. While Said's theory of Orientalism is now well-known, it has not been without criticism in the years since its original publication in 1978. Writers such as K. Humayun Ansari and Dennis Porter have disputed Said's somewhat simplistic view of discourse, in which he does not allow for the existence of dissonant voices.[52] Ansari points out that from the mid-nineteenth century, there was a far greater plurality of voices within Western discourse than Said acknowledges.[53] In the latter half of that century, greater interaction between Oriental and European cultures (a distinction problematic in itself, and one that will be explored later) led to the production of texts which challenged imperial rule and Christianity.[54] Twentieth

---

[46] Said, *Orientalism*, p. 40.
[47] Said, *Orientalism*, pp. 39-40.
[48] Said, *Orientalism*, p. 39.
[49] Said, *Orientalism*, p. 73.
[50] Said, *Orientalism*, p. 74.
[51] Said, *Orientalism*, p. 40.
[52] K Humayan Ansari, 'The Muslim world in British historical imaginations' in *Orientalism Revisited: Art, Land and Voyage*, ed. by Ian Richard Netton (London: Routledge, 2013), pp. 3-32 (p. 8) and Dennis Porter in Bill Ashcroft and Pal Ahluwalia, *Edward Said*, 2nd edn (London: Routledge, 2001), p. 74.
[53] Ansari, p. 9.
[54] Ansari, pp. 10-11.

century and present-day scholars concerned with the Orient also dispute the social and political motivations that Said would attribute to their work, claiming, as Bernard Lewis did, that it is 'pure scholarship' without influence.[55] While acknowledging these concerns and debates, this chapter will selectively draw upon Said's work due to its relevance to the first half of the nineteenth century. This time period is accepted by critics such as Ansari to be one in which Said's appraisal of the situation was most – though not exclusively – accurate.[56] While there were undoubtedly some challenging discourses the prevailing attitude at time in which the sources for this chapter were produced, was colonialist.[57] One important distinction that must be made, however, is that while knowledge produced in a time of imperial authority was affected by it – and while, as Ansari argues, 'those who produced histories of the Orient did indeed legitimise political ideologies *of their time*' – the knowledge itself may not have been produced with this intent.[58] 'The prejudices of their culture and age', as Lewis stated, render them 'captive of their own times', even if this captivity is unconscious.[59] It is interesting to study texts such as those produced by the Foxes as products of the society and culture in which they lived, rather than intentionally political messages. Their value lies in interpreting how empire pervaded everyday life and affected the population on an unconscious as well as a conscious level.

The influence of Orientalism is certainly evident in the diary descriptions of the Begum of Oudh. In Caroline Fox's account of their meeting, the Begum appears to be childlike in her actions, which are unrestrained and impulsive. Caroline observes with irony that on a second meeting she 'graciously' gave a 'shriek of pleasure' at their arrival.[60] On sitting with another acquaintance, known as Mrs Clavel, the Begum, according to Caroline, patted and stroked the woman before declaring 'Love I you'.[61] Here, the role of the British as mature and cultured is contrasted with the Orient's childlike, impulsive qualities. A sense of disorder also prevails in the narratives of the Foxes; a disorder that contrasts with the order and organisation of

---

[55] Bernard Lewis in Ansari, p. 3.
[56] Ansari, p. 8.
[57] Ansari, p. 9.
[58] Ansari, p. 16.
[59] Lewis in Ansari, p. 16.
[60] Caroline Fox, p. 12.
[61] Caroline Fox, p. 11.

the British and once again reinforces the divide between the weak, childlike, erratic East and the strong, rational, ordered West. The Begum's clothing is said by Barclay to be 'an uncouth jumble', while she has 'messes [...] scattered about within her arm's length.'[62] Caroline's representation of her speech is erratic and jumbled also, as typified in one passage regarding shawls: 'She promised her and Leonora a Cashmere shawl apiece, adding, "I get them very cheap, five shillings, seven shillings, ten shillings, very good, for I daughter king, duty take I, tell merchants my, make shawls, and I send you and miss."'[63] Though there is a clear language divide here, the representation of her speech creates a sense of disorder that serves to expose the apparent dichotomy of East and West.

In documenting the appearance and culture of the visitors, Caroline and Barclay consolidated their differences and marked them firmly as Other; belonging to the dark and foreign Orient. The Begum and her husband[64] are both repeatedly referred to in terms of colour and race: Barclay uses the words 'brown' and 'black' in description, while highlighting the differences in culture characterised by the Begum's 'gaudy' dress.[65] The animal terms, 'jaguar-like' and 'tiger-like', employed by Barclay, again hint at difference, this time constructing the foreigners as animalistic and thus primitive and uncultured, in opposition to the civilisation and culture of the West.[66] The notion of strength and weakness that is at play in these examples is one that, Said argues, is 'instrinsic to Orientalism.'[67] A yet more obvious display of dividing 'us' from 'them', West from East, can be found in direct references to oddity or strangeness in people from the Orient. The whole Orient, as it was popularly viewed in Britain at this time – indeed, since the late eighteenth century – was viewed as 'an illustration of a particular form of eccentricity.'[68] Oddness was, Said states, 'enjoyed for its own sake'.[69] Practices that were considered bizarre or grotesque were found to be amusing to Europeans, as they

---

[62] Ibid.
[63] Caroline Fox, p. 11.
[64] Whom Caroline names as Molvè Mohammed Ishmael and Barclay names as Moolree Mohammed Ishmael Khan.
[65] Barclay Fox, p. 100.
[66] Ibid.
[67] Said, *Orientalism*, p. 45.
[68] Said, *Orientalism*, p. 102.
[69] Ibid.

celebrated the extreme difference of the Oriental people.[70] The oddity of the Begum of Oudh and her husband is stated by Barclay Fox three times in two separate journal entries.[71] The Begum's unrestrained behaviour appears to have been viewed as strange to the extent of amusement; Barclay noted: 'She stretched out a brown leg and & pulled up her trowsers [sic] to show the material. It was altogether great fun.'[72] In this bizarre scene, within the encounters of the foursome as a whole, the difference between East and West is striking; as indeed, Caroline and Barclay must have seen it to be. Evidently, this oddness was ultimately felt by the ambassador, who dressed 'in the English costume' when meeting Caroline and Barclay at the end of December.[73] In this attempt to fit with British society, the Oudh native appears, unlike his wife, to accept that society's dominance and cast off, however temporarily, his own culture. Caroline's description of it as a 'costume', however, emphasises that this change in dress does not allow him to become somehow British. To them, it will always be a costume, and he will always be a representative of the dark Orient.

Though Oudh would not become a formal part of the British empire for another twenty years after this meeting, the representation of the Begum and the Ambassador nevertheless fitted into a framework of Orientalism serving the purposes of colonialism. The marking of East and West and, vitally, weak and strong, incapable and capable, was a necessary process that occurred in advance of colonialism. '[C]olonial rule was', Said argues, 'justified in advance by Orientalism, rather than after the fact.'[74] The process of othering, which took place over several decades, ultimately assisted in legitimising empire: if the natives of Oudh were figured as weak and incapable of ruling their own country, the strength and civilisation of Britain could become a reasonable interjection. Said argues that even minor works, those not overtly concerned with politics, could play a role in Orientalism: 'it always rose from the specifically human detail to the general transhuman one.'[75] Observations on human nature might well be used twenty years later to justify

---

[70] Said, *Orientalism*, p. 103.
[71] Barclay Fox, p. 100.
[72] Ibid.
[73] Caroline Fox, p. 14.
[74] Said, *Orientalism*, p. 39.
[75] Said, *Orientalism*, p. 96.

political policy.[76] Though much of the truly influential literature in this process was produced by popular writers or official bodies, under the banner of science, politics and travel, accounts such as the Foxes' serve as examples of how Orientalism was acted out on a smaller, more local, scale. In representing the Orient in this way, whether intentionally or not, Caroline and Barclay Fox worked towards assimilating the foreign, in this case Oudh, and justifying British rule there. The examples show how even in Falmouth, in the extreme south-west of Britain, the laying of foundations for colonial rule permeated both real-life encounter and the texts that resulted from it. Here, the Orient and Britain had their identities reinforced and the British were made dominant.

Though Said's theory of Orientalism can certainly be applied to this example, it should not be accepted wholeheartedly. Said has been criticised by other theorists for oversimplifying the relationship between East and West, and for implying that the coloniser always held power over the colonised.[77] In the instance of the Begum and her husband, the former is granted some rights of representation in the journal of Caroline Fox. Though she is largely viewed as strange, her own view of the British and their social order – which she holds to be equally strange – is also recorded. Fox notes the Begum's comments that the King was a 'very good man, but he no power. – Parliament all power. [...] For public charity King give one Sovereign [...] King Oude, he give one thousand rupees, palanquin mans with gold stick, elephants, camels; no ask Parliament.'[78] Though the representation of the Begum remains one of strangeness, she does nevertheless have a voice. The interaction between the Foxes and those from Oudh is therefore not as rigid as Said might have it; rather it is an interaction in the true sense of the word, involving – though arguably to a minimal extent – both sides, despite remaining a dialogue in which Orientalism has a key role to play.

We see, then, that meetings between Britain and the Orient were not always dependent upon entirely simple power relations between a coloniser and its future subjects. Another more problematic encounter, in terms of power structures, took

---

[76] Ibid.
[77] Robert J.C. Young, *White Mythologies*, 2nd edn (London: Routledge, 2004), p. 182.
[78] Caroline Fox, p. 12.

place on 4 October 1834, when Barclay Fox was aged seventeen. Thrown into frequent contact with foreigners of many nationalities due to his family's shipping interests and consulships, Barclay had a greater level of interaction with the empire than many people in Falmouth. On 3 October, Barclay notes in his diary: 'took a row with Cavendish to the Turkish brig, boarded & inspected her & her crew, a queer group of Turks and Greeks.'[79] This brig was almost certainly the *Aslang*, which arrived in Falmouth from Smyrna on 20 September,[80] and departed for Exeter on 4 October, the day after Barclay's inspection.[81] On the day of the ship's departure, accompanied by a friend, Barclay enacted a comedic and highly mischievous scene:

> In the evening [G. Thompson] & I dressed up like Turks with turbans, sword, beard & moustache, &c., &c. We first came to the house & having alarmed the servants, applied to Papa for passports.[82] He referred us to Uncle Alfred, where we went, & on his refusal threatened to stab him. We then went to the Tregelleses, who unfortunately were out, but the servants & children being in, we asked them in broken English if the Turkish Consul lived there. They all assured us with the greatest anxiety that he did not & were extremely earnest in explaining where he did. This we pretended not to believe & the whole household being collected, I stalked in, laying my hand upon the hilt of my sword, at which two screaming rushed upstairs, and one into the parlour & slammed the door. I pushed it open, but finding only a little girl there screaming her lungs out, I marched out & the door was immediately barred & bolted behind. In about an hour a message came to our house from the Tregelleses to know if G.T. & I were or were not the perpetrators of all the alarm. I went over to know the meaning of the message & heard as exaggerated accounts of ourselves as possible. The servants would not be persuaded it was us but said that either was twice as big as me, that we swore dreadfully, that I drew my sword & the other a knife from his bosom (probably the pipe that G.T. was smoking), that we had black legs & that our feet looked very suspicious of being cloven.[83]

Around eight months later, Barclay again dressed up as Turk. This time he was accompanied by a different friend, who in turn assumed the character and dress of a

---

[79] Barclay Fox, p. 71.
[80] 'Ship News', *Royal Cornwall Gazette, Falmouth Packet & Plymouth Journal*, 20 September 1834.
[81] 'Ship News', *Royal Cornwall Gazette, Falmouth Packet & Plymouth Journal*, 11 October 1834.
[82] Robert Were Fox served as consul to the US at this point, but could not have helped Turkish men with passports.
[83] Barclay Fox, p. 71.

Turkish woman. He later commented: 'My wife flirted with Uncle G.,[84] whilst I carried off Prissy by force as a substitute.'[85] These incidents, though greatly exaggerated for comedic effect, shed light on contemporary views of the Turks, and through examining the characteristics ascribed to them can also provide a commentary on notions of Britishness. The first instance of role play was almost certainly informed or inspired by Barclay's visit to the Turkish brig only the day before. If, as Hall argues, 'what is seen as outside an identity, different, other to it, is in fact constitutive of it',[86] it is useful to first examine the construction of Turkish identity in this example, in order to discern the inference of British identity and the power relations implicit in this.

The primary physical characteristics of the Turk, as played by Barclay, are the turban, facial hair and aggressive stance, seen in the description of how he 'stalked in' and 'marched out'.[87] The carrying of a sword, though part of the dress, also hints – at least to the audience witnessing this incident – at an aggressive or violent nature. In character, he is also aggressive, threatening to stab Alfred Fox. Not only would an act of violence such as this be remarkable in a polite English home, it is made more so by the lack of provocation to any attack: Alfred Fox has simply refused to provide the unknown Turk with a passport. Barclay Fox therefore characterises the Turkish as unreasonable and quick to anger, with aggression and threatened violence becoming the first course of action in a negative situation. The Turk as viewed by Barclay is also suspicious and disbelieving; refusing to accept the word of the Tregelles servants as to the location of the Turkish Consul. By the servants confronted with the figures of Barclay and Mr Thompson, the character of the Turk is viewed as even more violent, actually drawing a sword and knife, instead of simply touching a sword and not carrying a knife. The violence of a Turk is so expected by these people that it is assumed, even in the absence of actual violence. There was, at this time, a tradition of the Turk being seen as a villain in Britain. Mummers plays, performed at Christmas or during other celebrations in Cornwall, as they were in many other places, typically cast the 'Turkish Knight' as the villain,

---

[84] George Croker Fox, living at Grove Hill in Falmouth.
[85] Barclay Fox, p. 77.
[86] Catherine Hall, 'Culture and Identity in Imperial Britain', p. 203.
[87] Barclay Fox, p. 71.

often in opposition to St George as the hero.[88] These plays, featuring the knight, were performed in Cornwall for many years; certainly up to 1855.[89] In the story recounted by Fox, the Turk is physically viewed as large and dark, and implausibly devil-like in the body. Thus, here the differences in the Turk's appearance, compared to a British man, are socially informed, rather than intrinsic. The process by which the so-called Turk is understood by the servants has its basis in relations of power, rather than biology: difference is, as Himani Bannerji argues, understood not in terms of what people actually *are*, but how they are defined in a context of domination.[90]

In contrast to the Turks, the British characters in this story – excepting, of course, Barclay Fox and his friend – emerge as reasonable and civilised, keen to avoid confrontation. At the Tregelles house, the word 'earnest' is used in reference to the inhabitants' honesty and pacifying temperament. Though the servants and children may be prone to screaming and hysterics, the upper class men remain calm. Robert Were Fox simply refers the Turks to the correct contact, despite the fact that they have alarmed his servants and were, presumably, acting in an exaggeratedly 'foreign' manner for amusement. The perceived civilisation and pacification of the British is not only evident in the description of their behaviour here, but also implied in the behaviour of the "Turk". The basis of the comedy for Barclay and his friend is that the characters they have taken on are markedly different to anything expected of themselves as British men. Barclay's carrying off of a young girl by force is clearly the opposite of his behaviour in real life; a fact illustrated by perusal of his journal, which refers to several exchanges between himself and young women which are marked in their politeness and civility.[91] The identities of the Turkish and the British are therefore, as Hall explains, 'constructed in a process of mutual constitution'[92] whereby the making of the Turkish Other leads to the making of the British. If the Turk is violent and barbarous, the British are civilised.

---

[88] 'Guise-Dance Play, Saint Keverne [Cornwall, 1855]'
<http://www.folkplay.info/Texts/85sw72mw.htm> [accessed 6 December 2013]
[89] Ibid.
[90] Himani Bannerji, 'Politics and the Writing of History', p. 287.
[91] For instance, p. 74, p. 76, p. 268 and particularly pp. 283-284.
[92] Catherine Hall, 'Culture and Identity in Imperial Britain', p. 203.

Undoubtedly, Barclay Fox's rendering of the Turk as a character has its basis in received stereotypes from this period. The Orient, particularly hostile or problematic areas of it such as Turkey, had no great history of being explored and analysed by Europeans, although as Ansari argues, Muslim and Christian peoples *did* interact through trade and the exchange of ideas; neither were 'hermetically sealed, separate entities'.[93] Nevertheless, at this time the majority of British people – though certainly not all – primarily dealt with the Orient as an imagined geographic location formed through assumption and design: Tim Fulford, like Said, sees the Orient as a location whose primary function was to be the opposite of the West.[94] Despite any possible evidence to the contrary, the way alternative religions and cultures were represented in Oriental works such as Robert Southey's *Curse of Kehama* in 1810 led to a general apprehension regarding an alien East that the public could not come to terms with.[95] Fulford discusses what he calls 'moveable Easts': the result of a process by which unfamiliar cultures were characterised by writers in terms of what they believed the East was like, after which these assumptions were imposed back on to the East.[96] Essentially, the East became an 'imagined culture' whose characteristics, such as religious fanaticism, could stand-in for any previously alien or incomprehensible locations and people.[97] In the example of Barclay Fox and the Turk, it is clear that Fox is engaging not with facts about Turkey, based on dealings with its natives in the port, but with a general British expectation of what a Turk might be like.

One strong reason for this almost exclusive reliance on stereotype is that Fox's encounter with the Turks in port on 3 October 1834 was his first. According to public reports of ship arrivals and departures, found in the *Royal Cornwall Gazette*, the *Aslang* was the first Turkish ship to land in Falmouth, though there are a small number of sailings by British ships to Constantinople and Smyrna during 1833.[98] The arrival is therefore significant in showing the improved relations between the

---

[93] Ansari, pp. 15-16.
[94] Tim Fulford, 'Plants, Pagodas and Penises: Southey's Oriental Imports' in *Robert Southey and the contexts of English Romanticism*, ed. by Lynda Pratt (Aldershot: Ashgate Publishing, 2006), pp. 187-201 (p. 187).
[95] Fulford, 'Plants, Pagodas and Penises: Southey's Oriental Imports', p. 196.
[96] Fulford, 'Plants, Pagodas and Penises: Southey's Oriental Imports', p. 200.
[97] Ibid.
[98] 'Ship News', *Royal Cornwall Gazette, Falmouth Packet & Plymouth Journal*, 2 February 1833 and 'Ship News', *Royal Cornwall Gazette, Falmouth Packet & Plymouth Journal*, 16 March 1833.

British and the Turks after the latter's defeat in the Greek War of Independence; a weaker race was thus allowed access to Britain. Despite this new opportunity for contact, Fox's attitude mirrors the prevailing approach of the time: Orientalism as 'a political vision of reality' that constrained more realistic accounts.[99] This vision blended with reality to produce a privileged dialogue about the East that situated power with the British, or Europeans.[100] The vision that resulted was limited by a certain vocabulary associated with this privileged position.[101] Ultimately, in literature a truly accurate rendering was not encouraged or desirable.[102] Even the use of the word 'Turk' had a basis in stereotype and ideology. As Daniel Martin Varisco explains, from the sixteenth century the term 'Turk' had had negative connotations in the West.[103] Historically, Varisco says, Turk was used as an alternative to 'Muslim'; to 'turn Turk' meant to convert to Islam.[104] However, from the end of the sixteenth century the designation Turk was used to imply a renegade or, as time passed, a cruel or hard-hearted man.[105] Though Fox's characterisation of the Turk was initially performative and designed for a relatively small audience, rather than popular consumption, it nevertheless appears to have conformed to these literary and historic expectations. Though he had the means to paint a more accurate rendering of the Turks due to his recent meeting with them, this does not appear to have been his aim. In a decision that supported the status quo, Fox took the ideological view of the aggressive Orient and promoted it to friends, family and servants.

Othering or Orientalising the Turks was a process that was far more nuanced and problematic than Said acknowledges. His construction of the Orient depends on cultural and geographic distance between the East and West; to be, in some cases, adjacent to Europe but not part of it.[106] Said's theory of Orientalism requires that the West be separate from the East, that the Orient be externalised away from Europe.[107] Writers such as Derek Bryce criticise Said for failing to explore in any great detail

---

[99] Said, *Orientalism*, p. 43.
[100] Said, *Orientalism*, p. 44.
[101] Ibid.
[102] Ibid.
[103] Daniel Martin Varisco, *Reading Orientalism* (Seattle: University of Washington Press, 2007), p. 72.
[104] Ibid.
[105] Ibid.
[106] Derek Bryce, 'The Absence of Ottoman, Islamic Europe in Edward W. Said's *Orientalism*', *Theory, Culture & Society*, 30 (2013), 99-121 (pp.100-101)
[107] Bryce, p. 104.

the problematic presence of the Ottomans within (or without) *Orientalism*. A major issue with the East/West binary is that far from being temporally and spatially distant, the Ottoman Empire was, in fact, a part of Europe.[108] For centuries, it had encompassed territory in southeast Europe as well as Anatolia and Arab lands.[109] Regardless, it was important to a sense of Western identity that the Ottomans be seen as different, an enemy of Europe.[110] The Ottoman Empire's initial expansion was west, which was viewed as an Islam attack on Christianity, an invasion of the Other, though this was not necessarily the case: Bryce sees the empire's expansion west as a natural, more mediated course of action.[111] The Ottomans, not located far away but embedded as they were within Europe from the sixteenth century onwards, were a power that it was hard to dismiss.[112] Representations within Christian Europe were of a despotic, alien power, despite the fact that by the eighteenth century this view was at odds with the reality of Ottoman rule in Europe, which Bryce views as far more moderate.[113] He argues that far beyond any evidence to the contrary, the discursive rendering of the 'Turk' as despotic lingered on as a convenient European fantasy.[114] In fact, the nineteenth century marked the beginning of a period of serious anti-Ottoman feeling.[115] It is this discourse, attempting to place artificial distance between so-called Christian 'Europe' and the Ottomans, that Barclay Fox's encounter feeds into. The Ottomans, and the 'Turks', were not Oriental in the sense that Said might use the term; they were not historically weak like peoples from India,[116] nor were they representatives of Islam living separately to the West.[117] Rather, they were a competing power from within the heartland of Christendom, and such a problematic presence had to be dealt with through ideology and stereotype.

Another point to consider when discussing the Turks in a context of Otherness, is that the Turkish sailors themselves must also have viewed Fox, and Britain, as alien to some degree. As already noted, British ships had visited Ottoman lands before,

---

[108] Ibid.
[109] Bryce, p. 100.
[110] Bryce, p. 105.
[111] Ibid.
[112] Bryce, p. 107.
[113] Bryce, pp. 110-111.
[114] Bryce, p. 111.
[115] Bryce, p. 113.
[116] Said, *Orientalism*, p. 74.
[117] Ibid.

but this encounter appears to have been the first time – at least in many years – that a Turkish ship had visited Falmouth, meaning that it would have seemed stranger to these sailors than Turkey did to British ones. Whereas for the Ottomans empire was a traditional part of life and identity, stretching back to the thirteenth century, for the British an extensive empire was something that developed comparatively quickly and generated great change in the country. To the Turks, it may well have seemed as if theirs was the solid identity, whereas that of the British was Other. This is an alternate view that neither Fox nor Said appear to have explored.

As an opposing imperial power, the Ottoman Empire had, for many centuries, been a threat to the British empire. However, during the 1830s the former was seen to be in decline, to be defeated and weak. Whether this was truly the case is debatable, though it was perceived this way.[118] The Ottoman Empire was in losing power and under threat from Russia,[119] and as such was forced to accept help from the British in order to keep its enemies at bay.[120] The violence and opposition to Christianity and civilisation displayed by the Turks was therefore seen by Europe to have caused their failure as a race: their weight as rulers was weakened and it was the British who, in their own view, emerged as a growing power with greater influence. Histories from the 1830s and 1840s, such as that written by John Reid in 1840, focused on the many historical failures of the Turks, from the death of its rulers to defeat in battle.[121] Though written after Fox's characterisation of the Turk, the attitude in this work nevertheless represents the prevailing one at this time;[122] as a potential opposing power, the Turks were seen to have failed.[123] John Cam Hobhouse, who published an account of his travels in Albania in 1813[124], criticised the Turks for their 'savage appearance' and detailed an unprovoked attack by a Turkish man on a British

---

[118] Archibald Alison, 'The Fall of Turkey' in *Alison's Miscellaneous Essays* (Philadelphia: Carey & Hart, 1845), pp. 266-279 (p. 266)
[119] Edward Upham, *History of the Ottoman Empire: From Its Establishment, Till the Year 1828*, 2 vols (Edinburgh: Constable & Co., 1829) II, p. 390.
[120] Jon Parry, 'The British and the Middle East, c. 1830-c.1865', *University of Cambridge* <http://www.hist.cam.ac.uk/undergraduate/tripos-papers/part-ii-papers-for-2012-2013/paper-j> [accessed 30 October 2013] (p. 1)
[121] John Reid, *Turkey and the Turks: Being the Present State of the Ottoman Empire* (London: Robert Tyas, 1840), pp. 20-
[122] The Turks were also portrayed as having failed as a nation by Archibald Alison in his essay, mentioned above, which was originally written in 1833.
[123] Bryce, p. 113.
[124] The text was published in London in 1813 by James Cawthorn, and in America in 1817 by M. Carey and Son.

seaman.[125] Works such as this contributed to a general view of the Turk as savage and violent, and ultimately uncivilised. Hall argues that during this period race, which she defines as being 'understood in terms of climate, culture, or biology', was seen to mark out the Anglo-Saxons, who were 'the most civilized people in the world', from other races who 'must serve them and in time some would learn to live like them.'[126] Unlike India, which was viewed as historically weak by Britain,[127] Turkey was instead a potential aggressor that had *become* weak, or was at least viewed as such.

An area in which the Ottomans might be considered threatening, or at the very least provocative, during this period was religion. Christianity was viewed as a key part of British civilisation; it was seen to mark moral superiority and a disciplined nation.[128] In the 1880s, it was described in a survey of the empire as 'the religion of the dominant race', despite Christians comprising only one seventh of the empire's subjects.[129] Here, Christianity marks out the British as dominant; as natural leaders and rulers. In contemporary texts, the religion of the 'Mussulman'[130] was specified in relation to the barbarous behaviour of the Turks. Likewise, as already stated, the term 'Turk' was historically synonymous with Islam.[131] Barclay Fox's own depiction hints at religious difference; the turban he dons marking the Islam religion sits in contrast to the Christianity of the British.[132] A description of the Ottoman Empire notes how, in Greece, Christians 'were everywhere sacrificed to the sword of the furious and fanatical Mussulman.'[133] Islamic provinces – those away from Europe – were dangerous for the British to cross as they journeyed to the valuable areas of India, and historically the religion had been linked with a strength that stood in contrast to the passivity of the rest of the Orient.[134] Difference in religion was what

---

[125] J. C. Hobhouse, *A Journey Through Albania, and Other Provinces of Turkey in Europe and Asia, to Constantinople, During the Years 1809 and 1810*, 2 vols (Philadelphia: M. Carey and Son, 1817), I, p. 25.
[126] Hall, 'Culture and Identity in Imperial Britain', p. 204.
[127] Said, *Orientalism*, p. 74.
[128] C A Bayly, *Imperial Meridian: The British Empire and the World 1780-1830* (Harlow: Pearson Education Limited, 1989), p. 115.
[129] Richard Temple, 'The General Statistics of the British Empire', *Science*, 4 (1884), 214-215 (p.214).
[130] A Muslim
[131] Varisco, p. 72.
[132] Though Fox was a Quaker: a Christian but nevertheless a nonconformist.
[133] John Reid, p. 28.
[134] Said, *Orientalism*, pp. 74-76.

marked out the Ottomans as separate to the rest of Europe, and one of the factors that was originally seen as threatening to it, rendering it necessary to create distance through discourse.[135] Fox's mocking of the stereotypical violence and aggression of Islam, and the Turks in general, can therefore be interpreted as an attempt to neutralise this threat, and to capitalise on recent failures and weaknesses to promote Britain as the ultimate power.

Race and difference, constantly renegotiated, were therefore at the heart of ideologies concerning the British empire, regardless of whether the Other was a member of the empire or not. The Turks were not subjects of Britain but were nevertheless useful for comparison as failed rulers, and as a comparative assertion of British civilisation. The comedic performance of Barclay Fox, characterised as it is with aggression and extreme difference, therefore becomes interesting in this context. A young man's mischievous behaviour thus signifies, whether consciously or not, the perceived weaknesses and pitfalls in the Turkish identity and the counterpoints in the British that make them natural rulers of empires. The Orientalised Turk, as a character created by the British, became a repository for the fears and desires of the latter. In Fox's display, we can discern the sense of performance and artifice associated with British views of the Orient. The example also highlights a British fascination with the barbarous, dangerous 'East' – even when it was closer to home – that captured the imagination. Barclay's handling of the Turk as a character, when combined with the attitude shown towards the Begum of Oudh, demonstrates that there was no fast rule for approaching the Orient. Each instance encapsulates a different set of fears and social relations. In the case of the Begum, the Foxes were meeting with a future colonial subject that was perceived to be, in many ways, less powerful and capable than themselves, as British people. Their representations of her are therefore written from the perspective of affirming this general weakness and lack of suitability to rule. The British, in this example, perceive themselves as rational, civilised, powerful rulers. Turkey, as a somewhat declining power but former aggressor and political actor in Europe, is instead made to appear weak through an excess of force that borders on the ludicrous and irrational. Again, though by different contrasts, Britain's superior nature emerges as

---

[135] Bryce, p. 108.

one that is rational and civilised, and therefore infinitely more powerful. In both cases, a real-life encounter is taken as the basis for promoting a politicised, Orientalised, dialogue concerned with otherness. Falmouth's function as a port with connections to the empire and beyond therefore validated Orientalism, which in turn had a real impact on future colonial relations.

'Britishness' and civilisation

The examples of othering the Orient already given have demonstrated a firm yet playful, even humorous, means of marking identity and difference. Though the Ottoman Empire was a competing power it was often perceived, as already argued, as a power in decline and was popularly seen as posing little threat as a military force.[136] Indeed, the arrival of the Turkish brig in Falmouth was itself indicative of more cordial relations between Britain and Turkey. Likewise, Oudh was a location deferential to Britain after the 1801 treaty which annexed the country to the East India Company.[137] The Orient at this time therefore posed little challenge to the British empire and could be treated with levity as it was put in its place. Far greater threat could be found in the figure of the slave, or ex-slave. The 'negro' threatened change to the British empire and British identity in differing ways. As time passed, from the turn of the nineteenth century to the 1830s, the question of black identity and the abolition of slavery was one that divided British subjects and confused notions of what it meant to be British, and conversely, what it meant to be Other.

The perception and definition of British identity was complicated by the ambiguous space occupied by subjects of the empire who had become, or may become, 'civilised'. Civilisation is in itself a problematic notion. The term is here used to refer to conformity to a British way of life in religion, etiquette, manners, and education. During the 1820s and 1830s, there were lively debates about the character of so-called 'blacks' or negroes, and the treatment of slaves. Ultimately, this involved discussions of the potential for slave emancipation, and what this meant for

---

[136] 'Saturday, September 22, 1832', *Royal Cornwall Gazette, Falmouth Packet and Plymouth Journal*, 22 September 1832.
[137] Philip Lawson, *The East India Company: A History* (London: Routledge, 2013), p.112.

identity.[138] As a location with strong maritime links to the West Indies, with regular Packet sailings for mail delivery and a trade in imports and exports,[139] Falmouth came to be a part of this ongoing dialogue about black identity and emancipation. The issue was one that was entirely relevant and important to the port. People with business interests in the plantations travelled to the West Indies through Falmouth, and returned this way.[140] The *Royal Cornwall Gazette* printed numerous articles about the treatment of slaves, emancipation, and the effects of freedom, which indicates that alongside a popular interest in the topic, it held real relevance to the travellers and businessmen that lived and stayed in the area.[141] Empire was not something that simply happened away from Falmouth. As Hall notes, 'a significant number of Britons had some kind of direct economic connection to empire – through trade, commerce, or investments',[142] and many people in Falmouth would have been directly or indirectly involved in events overseas. With Packet ships and trade ships arriving regularly in port from colonies such as Jamaica, the town became a location where changing ideas of race and nationality could be negotiated. This negotiation allowed for the creation of new ways through which the figure of the 'negro' could be controlled and assimilated.

In discussing black identity and perceptions of civilisation, it seems prudent to begin with Falmouth's most well-known figure in this area. The story of Joseph Emidy has already captured the public imagination[143] and is more thoroughly researched than many of the other examples used in this chapter. Richard McGrady, and Emidy's contemporary James Silk Buckingham, have recounted most of the few facts that can be gleaned from his life.[144] Nevertheless, his is a fascinating tale in the context of

---

[138] For instance, 'Negro Slavery', *Royal Cornwall Gazette, Falmouth Packet & Plymouth Journal*, 21 June 1823.
[139] Lysons, p. 101.
[140] James Williamson, 'Journal of a Voyage from Falmouth to Jamaica & Carthagena and back', *Maritime Views*, <http://www.nmmc.co.uk/images/uploads/Packet%20Voyage%201-4.pdf> [accessed 20 February 2014], pp. 12-15.
[141] Such as 'Slavery and Slave Trade', *Royal Cornwall Gazette, Falmouth Packet & Plymouth Journal*, 3 May 1823, 'Negro Slavery', *Royal Cornwall Gazette, Falmouth Packet & Plymouth Journal*, 5 July 1823, 'Slavery', *Royal Cornwall Gazette, Falmouth Packet & Plymouth Journal*, 17 March 1832, and 'Saturday, October 11, 1834', *Royal Cornwall Gazette, Falmouth Packet & Plymouth Journal*, 11 October 1834.
[142] Hall, 'Culture and Identity in Imperial Britain', p. 201.
[143] 'The Bicentenary Concert', <http://www.emidy.com/bicentenary> [accessed 20 February 2014]
[144] Richard McGrady, *Music and Musicians in Early Nineteenth-Century Cornwall: The world of Joseph Emidy – slave, violinist and composer* (Exeter: University of Exeter Press, 1991) and James

Falmouth, and one that cannot be ignored. Indeed, the story of Emidy serves as a first step to a more thorough examination of perceptions of slaves and the slave trade as they relate to Falmouth; a subject previously unexplored. Emidy, a native of Africa, was taken into the Portuguese slave trade as a young man, at some time between 1780 and 1790.[145] It is possible that he was baptised by Portuguese slavers during the early stages of his time with them, as this was a practice that was seen as humane and allowed the slaves greater interaction with white people.[146] In 1795, Captain Sir Edward Pellew of the Royal Navy's HMS *Indefatigable*, based in Falmouth, was in Lisbon awaiting repairs to his ship when he came across Emidy at an opera.[147] Emidy was a proficient violinist[148] and Pellew contrived to 'impress' him into the Navy as his ship's violin player.[149] According to James Silk Buckingham, who later met Emidy, the latter was kidnapped upon leaving the theatre.[150] He appears on the ship's muster list as a Lisbon volunteer, though the appointment was clearly far from voluntary.[151] Emidy served as a ship's musician for several years,[152] and according to Buckingham his distaste and desire for escape were so evident to the captain and officers that he was never allowed on land during this time.[153] After his service, Pellew allowed him to be released in Falmouth, where he settled into society and began working as a violin teacher and musician.[154] In September 1802, he married a respectable local woman named Jenefer Hutchins in Falmouth's church of King Charles the Martyr.[155]

It appears from records that Emidy behaved in every way that might be expected of a civilised British man. He and his wife had children, who regularly attended church; in fact, his son Richard became a Sunday school teacher.[156] Conformity to religion had been, for the previous thirty years or more, a popular route through which

---

Silk Buckingham, *Autobiography of James Silk Buckingham*, 2 vols (London: Longman, Brown, Green, and Longmans, 1855) I
[145] McGrady, p. 16.
[146] McGrady, p. 15.
[147] McGrady, p. 25.
[148] Though it is not known how he came to be so skilled in the instrument while a slave.
[149] Buckingham, *Autobiography of James Silk Buckingham*, p. 167.
[150] Ibid.
[151] McGrady, p. 25.
[152] Buckingham claims he served for seven years, but McGrady estimates around five.
[153] Buckingham, *Autobiography of James Silk Buckingham*, p. 169.
[154] McGrady, pp. 39-40.
[155] McGrady, p. 41.
[156] Ibid.

Africans in Britain could aspire to British subject status.[157] Though his faith may well have been genuine, it must also have been acknowledged as a means by which acceptance could be earned. Emidy mixed successfully with the local community, giving violin lessons and staging musical events.[158] From studying the sparse known facts of his life, it would appear that Emidy was able to integrate into the communities of Falmouth and Truro, where he later lived, well. One compelling reason for this is that Falmouth, where he was able to first build his reputation and career as a musician, was a culturally diverse location in comparison to the majority of Cornwall. Far more foreigners were seen here, and Emidy would have been less incongruous than he might have been elsewhere. Settling and marrying, becoming part of the fashionable social scenes of Falmouth and Truro,[159] he was able to demonstrate to the local people that he was a civilised ex-slave, rather than a barbarous foreigner. Buckingham comments on his 'rapid progress in reputation and means.'[160]

Emidy's public support from Buckingham, and the largely warm reception he appears to have received within Falmouth, is illustrative of the town's nuanced, and in places abolitionist, attitude towards slavery. Both Buckingham and the extended Fox family were public in their opposition, with Buckingham noting in his autobiography the affinity he felt with the Quakers on this topic.[161] Anti-slavery sympathies are evident in the histories of several of the Fox family: an entry in Alfred Fox's journal, dated 1 August 1838, notes 'Negroes in our Colonies free – glorious thought, awakening gratitude.'[162] As early as 1788, George Croker Fox toured Cornwall sharing his opposition to the practice.[163] In the same year, Thomas Clarkson, a man responsible for the founding of several anti-slavery committees, visited Falmouth, noting in his memoirs: 'From Plymouth I journeyed to Falmouth,

---

[157] Kathleen Wilson, 'Citizenship, empire, and modernity in the English provinces, c. 1720-90', in *Cultures of Empire: A reader*, ed. by Catherine Hall (Manchester: Manchester University Press, 2000), pp. 157-186 (p. 170).
[158] McGrady, pp. 41-42.
[159] McGrady, pp. 40-42.
[160] Buckingham, *Autobiography of James Silk Buckingham*, p. 169.
[161] Buckingham, *Autobiography of James Silk Buckingham*, p. 20.
[162] Alfred Fox, p. 18.
[163] Clare Midgley, *Women Against Slavery: The British Campaigns, 1780-1870* (London: Routledge, 1992), p. 17.

and from thence to Exeter'.[164] This conscious decision to visit the town, by no means on the way between Plymouth and Exeter, demonstrates a clear desire to involve its residents in the abolitionist cause, and a belief in the value of doing so. George Croker Fox was later recorded as being a member of Clarkson's committee, which campaigned for abolitionism and frequently corresponded with other societies based in America.[165] Most likely, it was on his behalf that he had protested throughout Cornwall. Contact with prominent abolitionists seems to have continued through later generations. Interestingly, in 1838, Barclay Fox met, on disembarkation, a group of abolitionists from a West Indies Packet ship, the latter having arrived in Falmouth after travelling to oversee the emancipation of slaves.[166] The town's Packet links to colonies such as these must have had a direct impact on how residents viewed the slavery debate, with both pro- and anti-slavery representatives travelling back and forth. Later, in 1839, an unrelated meeting was held during which 'diabolical' accounts of American slavery were presented, along with a display of iron chains, anklets, and other brutal paraphernalia.[167]

Despite this, and their frequent attendance at anti-slavery lectures,[168] the Foxes did entertain and engage with those involved in the trade, with Caroline noting the visit in 1837 of an American, 'a very intelligent young man' with interests in the slave trade, with a discussion taking place about the 'damage' done to both masters and slaves by abolitionism.[169] They were also friends with Henry de la Beche, a slave owner – albeit one with an opposition to excessive violence[170] – who was a popular and well-liked guest at their house in Falmouth.[171] Due to the close sea links with the West Indies, the town must therefore have been a location rife for debate on the subject.

In any case, Emidy's acceptance into wider British society was not as complete as it might have seemed in Falmouth. Though this appears to have been a welcoming and

---

[164] Thomas Clarkson, *The History of the Rise, Progress and Accomplishment of the Abolition of the African Slave Trade by the British Parliament* (London: John W Parker, 1839), p. 326.
[165] Clarkson, p. 337.
[166] Barclay Fox, p. 135.
[167] Barclay Fox, p. 145.
[168] For instance, Caroline Fox, p. 117 and Barclay Fox, p. 37 and p. 199.
[169] Caroline Fox, p. 36.
[170] Caroline Fox, pp. 17-18.
[171] For instance, Caroline Fox, p. 4 and pp. 15-16.

diverse community, Emidy nevertheless found himself restricted by his race elsewhere. A talented composer, he entrusted Buckingham with several musical compositions when the latter travelled from Falmouth to London in 1807, in the hope that a professional opinion might be given on the pieces.[172] The reception was initially favourable: a group of professional musicians performed the music and liked it.[173] Mr Salomans, leader of the fashionable Hanover Square Rooms, suggested to Buckingham that Emidy travel to London to perform publicly.[174] This idea was, however, disputed by the rest of the group on the grounds of Emidy's race and background: 'Mr Betts and all the others thought his colour would be so much against him, that there would be a great risk of failure; and that it would be a pity to take him from a sphere in which he was now making a handsome livelihood and enjoying a high reputation, on the risk of so uncertain a speculation.'[175] It is likely that this rebuttal was well-meaning and simply reflective of the society in which the men lived. Evidently, though Emidy was able to achieve a certain measure of success in the fashionable, diverse areas of Cornwall, minor fame in London might have been a step too far up the ladder for an ex-slave. In this example, we can see the processes of what Kathryn Woodward terms symbolic and social marking.[176] Symbolic marking refers to 'how we make sense of social relations and practices'; how we decide who is included and excluded.[177] Social marking is then how this inclusion and exclusion is lived out in society.[178] Though Emidy lived among British society, and appears to a certain extent to have been accepted as a part of it due to his religion and musical talent, he could still be socially excluded. Clearly, Emidy was symbolically marked as an outsider by his skin colour, this being the one factor specified by the group of men belonging to the Hanover Square Rooms. As a man of 'colour', Emidy could not be one of them, despite his musical ability. In Cornwall, Emidy's violin was a symbolic marker that allowed him to be included – albeit occasionally in a servile sense as a teacher – in white, middle- and upper-class society. In this instance, the violin served as a marker of inclusion. However, away

---

[172] Buckingham, *Autobiography of James Silk Buckingham*, p. 170.
[173] Ibid.
[174] Buckingham, *Autobiography of James Silk Buckingham*, p. 171.
[175] Ibid.
[176] Kathryn Woodward, 'Concepts of Identity and Difference' in *Identity and Difference*, ed. by Kathryn Woodward (Milton Keynes: The Open University, 1997), pp. 7-61 (p. 12).
[177] Woodward, p. 12.
[178] Ibid.

from Cornwall, in more privileged and fashionable circles, the violin competed with a far baser form of symbolic marking – that of skin colour – and lost.

The example of Emidy illustrates that though civilisation granted some acceptance, it was not possible for a man who was racially Other – symbolically marked with dark skin – to transcend the perceptions of his race to become 'British'. An 1808 watercolour depicting Emidy performing in Truro Fig. 9) portrays his skin colour as markedly different to the white men he stands beside. His physical difference is undeniable, and most likely exaggerated: while the rest of the group sits or stands upright, Emidy is hunched over his violin in a manner suggestive of a primate.

Fig. 9: Watercolour of Joseph Emidy

An 1808 watercolour painting, entitled *A Musical Club, Truro* (artist unknown), which shows Joseph Emidy performing in Truro and is thought to be the only known portrait of him. Reproduced with the kind permission of the Royal Institution of Cornwall.

The image is generally representative of Emidy's not-quite belonging. His story illustrates how, as Kathleen Wilson argues, 'Africans living in Britain clearly experienced the fractured and hybrid identities that in part constituted, and were constituted by, the diasporic experience and the crucibles of nation-state and colonialism.'[179] Indeed, his story is not his own. Emidy is represented only by wealthy white men such as Buckingham, the onlooker who drew him in 1808, and brief local newspaper reports, again written by white men in positions of power; in this instance, editorial power. In this case, as Edward Said argues, '[t]he power to narrate, or to block other narratives from forming and emerging',[180] is a clear sign of the link between culture and imperialism. Though Emidy was granted power enough to live as a free man and mingle with the society of Cornwall, he seems to have lacked the power to speak, or rather write or draw, for himself.

Despite these cases of othering and exclusion, acceptance and inclusion were also possible in Falmouth. In this area of frequent foreign interaction, where differences in appearance were often seen, it may have been conformity in manners and attitude that mattered most. Thus, the character traits and level of civilisation among foreigners, and indeed the British, was the prominent marker of national identity. Clearly, the attitudes of individuals within the town must have varied, as there was no homogenous view of empire and its subjects at this time.[181] However, the story of Emidy implies that here, for many people, Britishness was highly influenced by behaviour. One key way of dealing with 'negroes',[182] therefore, could be to neutralise the threat they posed by encouraging them to mimic the behaviour of the British rather than adopt their own culture that might compete with, or threaten, the existing social order. Here, it is useful to consider Bhabha's theory of mimicry, that 'elusive and effective' strategy of colonial power and knowledge, through which colonial subjects are made to mimic the coloniser, while still being marked as an outsider.[183] In Emidy's case, he mimics the British in dress and behaviour, but in the 'double articulation' of mimicry is nevertheless clearly marked out as Other by his

---

[179] Wilson, 'Citizenship, empire, and modernity in the English provinces, c. 1720-90', p. 173.
[180] Edward Said, *Culture and Imperialism* (London: Vintage, 1994), p. xiii.
[181] Wilson, 'Citizenship, empire, and modernity in the English provinces, c. 1720-90', p. 170.
[182] The word 'negro', sometimes capitalised, was used in popular literature of the time, for instance in 'Abolition of Slavery', *Royal Cornwall Gazette, Falmouth Packet & Plymouth Journal*, 26 April 1823.
[183] Homi Bhabha, *The Location of Culture* (London: Routledge, 1994; repr. 2009), p. 122.

race.[184] As Bhabha and David Spurr argue, mimicry has the potential to disrupt the authority of British discourse by highlighting its ambivalence, and by allowing space for the colonial subject, once inhabiting the identity in some way, to turn its gaze back on the coloniser or to create resistance.[185] By denying Emidy any kind of power, keeping him in a servile position, the potential threat of his 'British' identity was contained.

As a man of humble background Emidy was fairly easily excluded from gaining too much social power. However, othering on the apparent basis of 'civilisation' could also take place when the subjects were powerful social figures in their own culture. On 17 April, 1840, the Fox family met with the Princes of Ashantee,[186] William Quantamissa and John Ansah.[187] The princes were accompanied by their British tutor and travelling companion, Reverend T. Pyne. In her journal, Caroline reports that her first impression of '"these images of God cut in ebony"' was that they were 'tolerably intelligent' but 'quite disposed to be haughty if that spirit is fostered'.[188]

The princes visited Falmouth in 1840 as part of a wider tour of Britain undertaken with their tutor.[189] Their relationship with the British is a highly interesting one. From 1831, they were held as hostages by British forces in Cape Coast during a period of conflict between the British and the Ashantees. The King of Ashantee, attempting to broker peace with the British, lodged the two princes, Quantamissa being his own son and Ansah[190] being the son of a former king, along with six hundred ounces of gold, in Cape Coast Castle.[191] The deposit of the princes was made in order to secure the king's 'future good conduct', as dictated by the British.[192] It appears that while the princes were in British company, they came under the instruction of missionaries attempting to convert the natives of the Gold

---

[184] Bhabha, pp. 122-123.
[185] David Spurr, *The Rhetoric of Empire: Colonial Discourse in Journalism, Travel Writing and Imperial Administration* (London: Duke University Press, 1999), p. 186, and Bhabha, pp. 126-127.
[186] Or Ashanti. For the purposes of clarity and consistency, Caroline Fox's own spelling of the word, Ashantee, will be adopted here.
[187] Caroline Fox, p. 98.
[188] Caroline Fox, p. 98.
[189] John Beecham, *Ashanti and the Gold Coast: Being a Sketch of the History, Social State and Superstitions of the Inhabitants of those Countries* (London: John Mason, 1841), p. 311.
[190] Ansah is mistakenly referred to in Caroline Fox's journal as 'Ansale'.
[191] Beecham, pp. 82-84.
[192] Beecham, p. 84.

Coast to Christianity.[193] They were apparently among the first successes of this mission; John Beecham, in his 1841 history of Ashantee notes that they 'both became convinced of the truth and excellence of the Christian religion'.[194] The forenames, William and John, which were mentioned by Fox, were not their own by birth but were instead awarded to them on baptism into the Christian faith.[195] The princes were educated by the African Committee, a group through which the British government managed the affairs of the Gold Coast.[196] Their visit to Falmouth occurred during this time of education, after which the princes returned home with the Niger Expedition, organised by the Society for the Extinction of the Slave Trade and for the Civilisation of Africa.[197] As examples of the success of British intervention in Africa, and of the civilising mission, the princes were valuable tools in an attempt by the British to gain more power in areas such as Ashantee, while simultaneously positioning themselves as moral and liberty-loving, using 'civilisation' as an alternative to slavery. This event was part of a wider context of power struggles between the British and the Ashantees. The wars between the two which saw the princes taken hostage were the first of many struggles that occurred during the nineteenth century as the British tried to take control of the Gold Coast.[198] This was no mean feat, with wars being fought between 1823 and 1900.[199] Finally, in 1901, the Ashantee kingdom was formally annexed to the British empire as part of the Gold Coast.[200]

The princes' visit to Falmouth is therefore significant to the wider analysis of the impact of colonialism in and from the port that is attempted by this thesis. The town became an arena for the display of British power and morality, as the Ashantees – historically known for being aggressive and therefore powerful[201] – had been made to accept intervention and education, as illustrated in the form of the princes. The success was not only over the Ashantees, but members of their royalty. The

---

[193] Beecham, p. 310.
[194] Ibid.
[195] Beecham, p. 311.
[196] Ibid.
[197] Ibid.
[198] Harold E. Raugh, *The Victorians at War, 1815-1914: An Encyclopedia of British Military History* (Santa Barbara: ABC-CLIO, 2004), p. 30.
[199] Ibid.
[200] Ibid.
[201] Beecham, p. 38.

imposition of British ideals of education and religion, and the relinquishing of existing ones, therefore marked out the colonialists as powerful, and the Ashantees as weak. During their stay, the princes were introduced to many powerful people in Falmouth who could spread this message much further than the port. Caroline Fox's journal notes that she accompanied the princes on a visit to Tregothnan, home to the Earl of Falmouth, and to Glendurgan, home to her uncle Alfred Fox,[202] an influential businessman with many interests overseas.[203]

The activities undertaken by the royals during their stay were fitting with those traditionally enjoyed by the English. While at Glendurgan, they fished, played cricket and leap frog, and took part in scientific demonstrations.[204] They spoke English, and discussed the education of their fellow countrymen. Caroline described them as 'very nice intelligent lads, gentleman-like and dignified.'[205] In this description, however, Fox appears to be at odds with herself. In her narrative of the princes, there is an uncomfortable mixture of contradictions, which can be traced to the difference between the princes' race and history, and their new-found manners and education. The marriage between the body of an Ashantee prince and the civilisation of a British gentleman appears forced and unnatural: here, there are obvious instances of what Bhabha terms 'slippage' that mark their differences to the 'real' British.[206] Just after describing the princes as 'dignified', Fox notes how, on a visit to Pendennis Castle, they seized a woman in a chair and 'galloped off' up the hill with her.[207] Again in contrast with the description of dignity, she describes how, when Quantamissa is 'too much puffed up', he refuses to take his tutor's arm.[208]

More seriously, Fox appears to have doubts as to the sincerity of their transformation, observing that '[t]hey laugh in a knowing manner when slavery is alluded to'.[209] This sense of holding secrets, or laughing at the British, hints that the princes may well be using mimicry as a cover for some kind of resistance or

---

[202] Caroline Fox, p. 99.
[203] Charles Fox, p. 11.
[204] Caroline Fox, p. 99.
[205] Ibid.
[206] Bhabha, p. 122.
[207] Ibid.
[208] Ibid.
[209] Caroline Fox, pp. 99-100.

undermining. Certainly, Fox's account of them gives the impression that their Anglicization is only partial, or imitated, rather than representing any kind of genuine transformation.[210] The British empire's pride in its civilising power is undermined by this encounter, as there is an implication made by Fox that moral reform, in relation to attitudes towards slavery, has not really taken place, but that this hollow imitation is 'enough'. In this example we see how mimicry can locate the cracks in an empire's apparent dominance: the British have not successfully civilised the Ashantees.[211] Using a very similar case study Bhabha refers to European humanism thus 'ironizing itself'.[212] The princes' hollow imitation destroys the entire justification for imposing the British identity on them in the first place: so-called civilisation has not really taken place, and yet they are still being used as marketing props for the British empire. Fox appears to be a part of this discourse: though she conveys doubt, dislike or distrust is never directly stated on her part, and indeed, when the royals leave she describes their visit as 'really pleasant'.[213]

As with the case of Emidy, there appears to be a complex relationship between the British, in this case Caroline Fox, and those who in appearance are Other to them but in attitude mimic them. While Emidy was, at best, middle-class, the princes occupied an ambiguous place in terms of hierarchy and class. Technically, as royalty in their own country, they were high-ranking there, but are subservient to the British in their role as former or current hostages.[214] In addition to this, they were no longer in their own country, the land of their power, and had allowed themselves into a position of weakness by mimicking British customs and relinquishing their own. This made the princes harder for somebody like Caroline Fox to mentally position. Emidy's power was restricted so that he posed no threat, but the princes could potentially hold power and so were a more threatening Other, which might use mimicry for the purposes of resistance. Their awareness of their own position is subtly criticised and their rank reduced through descriptions of them as 'puffed up' and 'haughty',[215] which indicate

---

[210] Bhabha, p. 124.
[211] Bill Ashcroft, Gareth Griffiths and Helen Tiffin, *Post-Colonial Studies: The Key Concepts* (New York: Routledge, 2000), p. 139.
[212] Bhabha, p. 124.
[213] Caroline Fox, p. 100.
[214] It is unclear when the princes ceased to be hostages; they appear to have remained with their British tutor for some time, and so may have stayed under British control beyond their physical imprisonment in the Cape Coast castle.
[215] Caroline Fox, p. 98.

that their pride is misplaced rather than justified. Fox clearly cannot accept their own belief in their superiority over her and the other British companions. Her journal thus describes them in weak terms, with this pride becoming a fault, and highlights childlike behaviour such as their 'gallop[ing]'.[216] She doubts their ability to accurately speak for themselves, arguing that '[t]heir remembrances of their own country are, I shou'd fancy, rather brighter than the actual fact.'[217] Through this statement, Fox attempts in some way to undermine or contain the threat posed by the princes. Ultimately, however, despite their subjugation, this example serves as an instance of colonial subjects exerting resistance against the colonisers.

Fox's encounter with the princes allowed her to go some way towards a mental negotiation of their position and identity, however problematic this was. Her unease indicates that they are each firmly regarded as a 'mimic man': a 'flawed colonial mimesis' who is Anglicized but emphatically not English.[218] She cannot identify with them as like herself– or the British generally – due to the slippage of mimicry, though she is keen to commend them for the ways in which they conform to her ideal of behaviour. Her narrative therefore reiterates the importance of British 'civilisation', or at least the appearance of it, both to the perception of British identity and to the control of those who exist outside of it.

Encounters from Falmouth

While important encounters took place between the British and the Other in and around Falmouth, it was not necessarily the case that every meeting took place in the port. Significant interaction between subjects of the British empire and those living at home in Britain occurred *from* Falmouth, as well as in it, as the town's overseas connections allowed people to travel both out and in. Regular Packet ships sailings formalised travel between Britain and the empire, as crews made scheduled journeyed to colonial locations such as the West Indies. In these instances, the ships came to represent a portable version of Falmouth and Britain. As a mixture of business and domestic space, populated with white British men, they served as a

---

[216] Caroline Fox, p. 99.
[217] Ibid.
[218] Bhabha, p. 125.

stepping-stone between home and abroad, facilitating interaction from a base equipped with existing British ideas of empire, in the form of men, who also served as a means for transporting representations of new experiences back home. During the course of their business, the Packet crews and any paying travellers met with many different colonial subjects, including both white residents and natives, or slaves. The results of these encounters, such as altered views or information repeated as text, were then brought back to Falmouth, or beyond, and distributed, forming part of a wider British dialogue on the colonies and their people.

A valuable source in demonstrating how important these encounters away from Falmouth were, are the journals of the Packet Service surgeon Dr James Williamson. Williamson worked in the service between 1828 and 1835, travelling to locations such as Brazil, the Mediterranean, Halifax, and Buenos Ayres.[219] Of greatest interest to this chapter, however, are the journals of his voyages to Jamaica, undertaken between August and December 1829[220] and March and August 1832.[221] While travelling, Williamson frequently went ashore to explore his surroundings and meet various people, often those who were British but lived abroad. His experiences were collected together in his journals, which appear to be a mixture of logbook or journal entries and copies of letters home. While many of his colleagues must have passed on their observations to loved ones purely by word of mouth, Williamson created accounts that can, to this day, provide a unique insight into the effect that Falmouth's colonial travel links had on perceptions of British and foreign identity.

Within the journals, it is easy to discern the same complex and uneasy relationship between the British and those we might loosely term 'of African descent' that arose in accounts of Joseph Emidy and the Ashantee princes. The same issues of power, freedom, subservience, and civilisation recur in his accounts, particularly in relation to the question of slave control and emancipation in Jamaica. This was a live issue in Britain during the 1820s and 1830s, as abolition was discussed in the House of Commons as well as through public campaigns and meetings, and the popular press.

---

[219] 'Packet Surgeon's Journals', *Maritime Views*
<http://www.nmmc.co.uk/index.php?/packet_surgeons_journals/> [accessed 26 February 2014].
[220] Williamson, 'Journal of a Voyage from Falmouth to Jamaica & Carthagena and back'.
[221] James Williamson, 'Second Voyage to Jamaica & Mexico', *Maritime Views*
<http://www.nmmc.co.uk/images/uploads/Voyage%2010,%20Jamaica.pdf> [accessed 26 February 2014].

Williamson's second visit to Jamaica took place during one of the most turbulent periods of its colonial history. When he arrived there in May 1832, it was to find a 'prevalent discontent and sense of insecurity' in the wake of a failed slave uprising that had ended in January of that year.[222] Known as the Baptist War, Christmas Rebellion, or Great Jamaican Slave Revolt, this was a rebellion that occurred when slaves refused to return to work without wages after their Christmas holiday.[223] The planned strike turned into an armed revolt, causing damage to property, then including slaves, worth over £1,154,589.[224] Over six hundred rebels were killed, around half during the rebellion, and half through execution afterwards.[225] Williamson states that the uprising was caused by a mistaken belief, a 'most fatal error', on the part of the slaves, that the British government had ordered their release, and that their masters had become 'dependant colonists', 'bound to obey' it.[226] As the masters had not been given instructions, and thus had not lost their ability to legally control the slaves, the uprising was suppressed. This comment indicates the delicate perception of power that held slaves in place: in Williamson's view, they took advantage of a possible reduction in the power their owners enjoyed to attempt to reduce it further and gain control of their own lives. Clearly, this served as a direct threat to British colonial strength, despite the discussions taking place at home about relinquishing control of slaves on Britain's own terms.[227] After this, the white masters in Jamaica worked to display their undiminished authority through reprisals. The display was heightened as the bodies of hanged slaves were left on show in the town centre of Montego Bay for weeks afterwards; a visual symbol of their failure and ultimate powerlessness in being slain.[228] Elsewhere, slaves were decapitated and their heads placed on poles in public areas.[229] Coloured by this incident, Williamson's journal entries following his description of the uprising are concerned

---

[222] Williamson, 'Second Voyage to Jamaica & Mexico', p. 10.
[223] Verene Shepherd, 'Baptist War (1831-1832)' in *Encyclopedia of Antislavery and Abolition*, ed. by Peter Hinks, John McKivigan and R. Owen Williams, 2 vols (Westport: Greenwood Press, 2007), I, pp. 81-82 (p. 81).
[224] Ibid.
[225] Ibid.
[226] Williamson, 'Second Voyage to Jamaica & Mexico', p. 10.
[227] 'Slave Emancipation: Crown Slaves', *House of Commons Parliamentary Papers* <http://gateway.proquest.com/openurl?url_ver=Z39.88-2004&res_dat=xri:hcpp&rft_dat=xri:hcpp:fulltext:1831-013170> [accessed 28 February 2014]
[228] Robinson A. Milwood, *Western European and British Barbarity, Savagery, and Brutality in the Transatlantic Chattel Slave Trade: Homolgated by the Churches and Intellectuals in the Seventeenth-Nineteenth Century* (Bloomington: Xlibris, 2013), p. 213.
[229] Ibid.

with power and control, and seek to place these firmly with the colonists.[230] The reinforcement of power through display and discourse, especially concerned with death, was not unusual. For decades, the masters and slaves in Jamaica had existed in a state of unease amid constant struggles where means of social control and resistance were ever changing.[231] Yet his narrative shows how the idea of power that gave colonists their strength was one crafted by large numbers of Britain's populace, as well as those living in the colonies. It was a perception put forward and maintained by people on an everyday basis, but it gained the most strength at home when advanced by those who, like Williamson, had first-hand experience to lend their accounts authenticity. It was this sense of authenticity through proximity that Falmouth could offer. Discourses such as his, which appeared – however rightly – to be based in fact, played an important part in shaping the general view of events in the colonies that was held by the population of Britain.

Indeed, Williamson's observations – noted during the period between the abolition of slavery in Britain in 1807, and in the colonies in 1833 – can be viewed as part of a far larger pro- and anti-slavery print culture. During the late eighteenth and early nineteenth century, the 'war of ideas' reached fever-pitch as colonists and those with interests in the plantations and slave trade went head to head, through literature, with abolitionists.[232] Though the trade was abolished in Britain in 1807, the debate persisted as slaves continued to work in colonies overseas, with both sides appealing to issues of morality and legality in their arguments.[233] Even the *Royal Cornwall Gazette* featured articles debating the trade, observing that 'Public attention appears at length to be excited to the consideration of a subject of the deepest national importance.'[234] As becomes clear from this statement, the 'subject' of slavery was one that pervaded public culture and national consciousness, primarily due to the

---

[230] Williamson, 'Second Voyage to Jamaica & Mexico', pp. 10-15.
[231] Vincent Brown, *The Reaper's Garden: Death and Power in the World of Atlantic Slavery* (Cambridge, Massachusetts: Harvard University Press, 2008), p. 3.
[232] Brycchan Carey and Sarah Salih, 'Introduction' in *Discourses of Slavery and Abolition: Britain and its Colonies, 1760-1838*, ed. by Brycchan Carey, Markman Ellis and Sarah Salih (Basingstoke: Palgrave Macmillan, 2004), pp. 1-8 (p. 3).
[233] Srividhya Swaminathan, *Debating the Slave Trade: Rhetoric of British National Identity, 1759-1815* (Farnham: Ashgate Publishing, 2009), p. 5.
[234] 'Slavery and Slave Trade', *Royal Cornwall Gazette, Falmouth Packet & Plymouth Journal*, 3 May 1823.

increasing amounts written about it in the press, fiction and non-fiction.[235] From the 1790s onwards, the British public had proven highly receptive to debates focusing on slavery and national identity, which fed a hunger for more.[236] Followers of Wilberforce and the Clapham sect – noted evangelical Anglican activists – published vast amounts of cheap, distributable literature while also writing articles for magazines, or, in the case of the *Anti-Slavery Monthly Reporter* (1825), forming their own.[237] Articles were also republished in various different forms, with the *Royal Cornwall Gazette* reprinting from the *Cheltenham Gazette* and anti-slavery pamphlets to oppose the 'revolting institution' that rendered its masters and mistresses 'dead alike to the feelings of tenderness and delicacy'.[238]

Emphasising the humanity of the slave was a frequently used tactic in anti-slavery literature, highlighting as it did the subsequent taint of slavery on the character of 'the Briton'.[239] Indeed, as Swaminathan posits, the British national identity became a sort of battleground upon which both types of campaigner fought.[240] Though, as will become clear, Williamson's writings are too complex to be simply branded pro-slavery, they are interesting for the way that their pro-slavery elements appeal to the differences between ruler and ruled, British and non-British. Like Brycchan Carey and Sarah Salih, I choose to consider Williamson's texts not as 'source material' but as 'cultural events which took place within, and were structured by, the specific discursive formations of slavery, abolition and emancipation.'[241] Although his observations were not intended for wide distribution, his journals and letters nevertheless serve as an example of the type of discourses of slavery, focusing on the nature of national identity, that were recorded during this time, and can be viewed as significant markers of the 'war of ideas'.

---

[235] Carey and Salih, pp. 2-3.
[236] Swaminathan, p. 6.
[237] Stephen Tomkins, *The Clapham Sect: How Wilberforce's Circle Transformed Britain* (Oxford: Lion Hudson, 2010), p. 231.
[238] 'Slavery and Slave Trade', *Royal Cornwall Gazette, Falmouth Packet & Plymouth Journal*, 3 May 1823 and 'Negro Slavery', *Royal Cornwall Gazette, Falmouth Packet & Plymouth Journal*, 21 June 1823.'
[239] Swaminathan, p. 6.
[240] Ibid.
[241] Carey and Salih, pp. 3-4.

Williamson's narrative of his 1832 trip to Jamaica repeatedly attempts to deal with the threat of the slaves by figuring them as weak, in terms of self-control, morality, and intellect. Though he claims to occupy a neutral position between the slaves and their British masters, referring to himself as 'an uninterested spectator', he nevertheless describes the slaves in negative terms.[242] After relating the story of the slave rebellion, he states that 'the whites must be constantly on their guard, and should they be worsted much expect to experience the most horrible treatment which implacable revenge for imaginary ill treatment can inflict.'[243] In this statement, Williamson makes his view clear: he does not believe slavery to constitute ill treatment, and makes a clear distinction between the 'whites' who are threatened and their opposites the 'blacks', who are vengeful and unreasonable. In relating the rebellion, the slaves are described in savage terms. He notes that 'Men put to death with excruciating tortures - women deforced[244] and then murdered - and children slaughtered before the parents with the most ingenious cruelty were scenes which actually occurred.' He concludes, '[f]rom the tender mercies of the Blacks, good Lord deliver us.'[245] The entire episode is enlarged, demonstrating that Williamson's account is almost certainly based on hearsay and discussions with people in Jamaica. In contrast with this narrative of uncontrolled bloodshed, only fourteen colonists were actually killed during the Baptist War.[246] Likewise, Williamson's estimate of four thousand slaves killed[247] is almost seven times the actual amount.[248] The result of this is that the threat posed by the slaves is made to seem more urgent, and the slaves themselves to appear barbarous and out of control, thus in need of subjugation. While this apparent enemy to the empire is made villainous, by increasing the estimate of slave deaths, the British themselves emerge as a far greater and more fearsome power than they really were. Though the account is false, Williamson's testimony has a veneer of authenticity due to its basis in real life encounter.

---

[242] Williamson, 'Second Voyage to Jamaica & Mexico', p. 11.
[243] Williamson, 'Second Voyage to Jamaica & Mexico', pp. 11-12.
[244] A word based on 'deforce', and probably meant to indicate rape.
[245] Williamson, 'Second Voyage to Jamaica & Mexico', p. 10.
[246] Shepherd, p. 81.
[247] Williamson, 'Second Voyage to Jamaica & Mexico', p. 10.
[248] Ibid.

A concern with death and mortality looms over Williamson's narrative, reflecting a general preoccupation amongst both slaves and colonists at the time; a subject dealt with at length in Vincent Brown's 2008 text *The Reaper's Garden*.[249] Williamson's journals and letters relating to Jamaica frequently touch upon violence, illness, and ultimately death, as shown in part through the accounts of the rebellion.[250] The actions of both white colonists and slaves are viewed in terms of their relation to death, or the possibility of it. As Brown notes, those living and working in Jamaica were all too aware of their own mortality and death was a common occurrence, whether caused through illness or violence.[251] The population was constantly in flux, with new arrivals replacing those who had left or died, resulting in an unsettled society.[252] The display of slave bodies after the 1831/1832 rebellion was certainly a grisly show of power, but not an uncommon one. Visual reminders of mortality and the dead had become central to Jamaican politics, with the whole preoccupation resulting in what Brown terms 'mortuary politics'.[253] Mortuary politics, as he argues, mediated discussions relating to a social and moral order, property relations, local geography and history.[254] Death and power came to be intertwined, and death itself was used as a means of shaping Jamaican history.[255]

With death and power as a prevalent discourse in Jamaica, it is unsurprising that in his accounts, Williamson draws on the same themes. The threat of death, both to the white population and the black, is used in his politically influenced discussions. As we have seen, the perceived threat to the whites from the 'tender mercies of the Blacks'[256] is used by him as a justification for greater social control, and as a reason for refuting the abolition of slavery. Likewise, he perceives a threat of death to the slaves if abolition is carried out, this time through hunger, illness and want of medical care, which are needs catered to when in bondage.[257] On the grounds of death, then, Williamson attempts to argue for slavery. The subject was a tense one for the white colonists as well as the slaves. Death is the ultimate equaliser: it could

---

[249] Vincent Brown, p. 10.
[250] Williamson, 'Second Voyage to Jamaica & Mexico', pp. 8-12.
[251] Vincent Brown, p. 10.
[252] Ibid.
[253] Ibid.
[254] Vincent Brown, p. 11.
[255] Vincent Brown, pp. 11-12.
[256] Williamson, 'Second Voyage to Jamaica & Mexico', p. 11.
[257] Williamson, 'Second Voyage to Jamaica & Mexico', p. 11.

affect all races and was difficult to control.[258] Williamson's narrative attempts to deal with this issue by displaying a semblance of power in relation to death. Prior to his description of the Jamaican rebellion, he notes a visit to a British hospital in Port Royal, Kingston.[259] The hospital is described in extremely positive terms, with 'a delightful promenade', 'a wide airy piazza', and 'a perfectly free circulation of air'.[260] He concludes: 'I consider Port Royal as a model for all similar institutions in warm climates, and believe that in such an establishment the chances of recovery are as a hundred to one to what they may be anywhere else.'[261] The vision of health and cleanliness conveyed by his description gives an impression of security for those living in Jamaica, a location traditionally associated with disease and death among the whites.[262] By describing these facilities in such a way, Williamson seeks to create a discourse in which white death seems less likely. In this narrative, the likelihood of slave deaths is placed firmly in the hands of the whites. Not only do they have the power to execute, as shown in his description of the rebellion, but they also have the power to withhold medical privileges if slaves are freed, which could lead to 'sickness [...] and irremediable disease'.[263] In this narrative, the whites, more broadly representing the British empire as a whole, appear to have control of death itself, as long as they are able to remain in power politically and socially.

As in the case of Barclay and Caroline Fox and their encounters with the foreign, Williamson's narrative of slavery is a complex account based on both real encounter and politicised received stereotype. Though Said's work *Orientalism* is, rather self-evidently, focused on the oriental, it is possible to perceive similar processes of representation and othering in these accounts of the West Indies. As with the process of Orientalism, knowledge and description are here used to deal with the figure of the slave by making statements about it and placing constraints on thought and representation.[264] Though some Britons chose to represent the slave more sympathetically, Williamson adheres to a policy of mingling politicised visions of the slaves, perhaps those more commonly put forward by the plantation owners, with

---

[258] Vincent Brown, p. 17.
[259] Williamson, 'Second Voyage to Jamaica & Mexico', p. 8.
[260] Ibid.
[261] Ibid.
[262] Vincent Brown, p. 17.
[263] Williamson, 'Second Voyage to Jamaica & Mexico', p. 11.
[264] Said, *Orientalism*, p. 42.

his own experiences of them; a practice generally associated with Orientalism but equally applicable in this instance.

Having established that, in his opinion, the slaves are excessively aggressive and weak in terms of self-control, Williamson's journal goes on to cast serious doubts about their moral strength. He notes that '[t]hey look forward to leading a life of idleness and pleasure, without reflecting [that] that industry, which they hate is the only means which can prevent them from starving.'[265] Enslavement to a white master is, he claims, a morally correct choice as freedom and a lack of desire for honest work may lead former slaves to crime.[266] Ignorance, intellectual weakness, is another stereotypical characteristic of slaves that is addressed. After leaving Jamaica, the Packet ship proceeded to Belize, where a visit was paid to a 'black free school' to observe the educated boys. On speaking to the schoolmaster, Williamson found that the black children 'possess the same powers of docility and understanding as the White', and could be controlled by strict discipline.[267] Considering this to be a great success, he puts forward his own argument for the management of slaves:

> Now, my dear Jacob,[268] I cannot but say that I conceive this to be the best plan to be pursued previous to the emancipation of slaves – Let them be first enlightened, and the evils we dread from their ignorance will be averted – their freedom will then be a blessing to themselves and to society & their status in the civil, religious & moral world will be nearly if not entirely on a par with that of their White brethren.[269]

James Williamson's comments on slaves and emancipation are greatly influenced by ideas of power and control. The states of being that he indicates with the terms ignorance and enlightenment are not free of political meaning. The enlightenment he advocates, and the education undertaken at the school in Belize, are both linked to British ideals of religion, morality and culture. To him, the notion of slaves and ex-slaves being made free to pursue their own culture is dangerous, leading to 'evils'. Education is linked to docility and discipline, terms loaded with positive connotations in this instance, which equate to a tacit form of control by the British.

---

[265] Williamson, 'Second Voyage to Jamaica & Mexico', p. 11.
[266] Ibid.
[267] Williamson, 'Second Voyage to Jamaica & Mexico', pp. 12-13.
[268] James Williamson's brother, to whom this narrative was presumably addressed.
[269] Williamson, 'Second Voyage to Jamaica & Mexico', p. 14.

The level of civilisation reached by Anglo-Saxons was viewed within Europe as an ideal for the rest of the world to aspire to: those outside of this race must, as Catherine Hall argues, serve them, and in time learn to be more like them.[270] If slaves were educated and made docile before emancipation – if essentially made white in all but colour – they would pose far less of a threat to the colonial social order than they would after being simply made free. The spectre of the Baptist War, with the uncontrolled freedom that was grasped by slaves for themselves, once again looms over this narrative. Texts such as this acknowledged the probability of emancipation, however much Williamson may have disagreed with it, but sought to work towards handing power back to the British under a different guise.

An interesting recurring motif for the distinction between black and white, or uncivilised and civilised, uneducated and educated, is that of accent. Any accent unlike that of the British, which was viewed as the norm and so no accent at all,[271] served as a marker of difference. Cartoons of the time highlighted the disparity in accent between the British and Others for comedic effect, in addition to exaggerating the natural differences in appearance between the two.[272] In his narrative of Jamaica and Belize, James Williamson makes special mention of the fact that educating black children has made them lose their accents: 'I could not help remarking that in reading they had none of that negro accent which they invariably have in speaking – and their enunciation was as different as is the language of books & that of every day conversation had actually belonged to two distinct people.'[273] In this instance engagement with education, in the form of reading aloud from books, is likened to physical transformation. When the so-called 'black boys' possess the symbolic marker of a book, they lose the accents that mark them out as socially excluded and become a part of the educated, civilised group to which the British also belong. Accent, as an indicator of race, is seemingly eradicated and racial identity can be renegotiated. Any trace of an accent found in the children of colonists denoted, as Deborah Wyrick explains, a lack of 'proper' education; it was the means by which

---

[270] Hall, 'Culture and Identity in Imperial Britain', p. 204.
[271] Williamson, 'Second Voyage to Jamaica & Mexico', p. 13.
[272] A c.1830 cartoon by Robert Seymour, which appeared in *McClean's Monthly Sheet of Caricatures*, depicts two slaves talking to their child, with one observing 'A ah picanniny you eat yam yam you belly full? Him beauty Lilla', while the other replies 'Efs sambo he berry like you.'
[273] Williamson, 'Second Voyage to Jamaica & Mexico', pp. 13-14.

respectable white people could be separated from the slave domestics.[274] Wyrick encapsulates the sense of threat to social order that was felt at this time in relation to accent. The British in the West Indies feared that close proximity with their slaves might influence them into speaking like them, a fate 'very tiresome if not disgusting'.[275] There emerges, then, a sense of fear that culture contact might impact on the British, not just the slaves. Controlling the spread of an accent – in this instance under the guise of education – and attacking it at the root cause, the slaves themselves, came to be one way of controlling or protecting the perception of British identity overseas. It was also, undoubtedly, a useful tool for extending control over the body of the slave in ways that might endure beyond emancipation and the loss of ultimate physical control. By recording this, Williamson contributed to the dissemination of this ideal at a time when redrawing power structures was essential. Education was thus set to take the place of direct control through slavery.

Though Williamson's views are generally supportive of colonialism, they were not always in concert with the British government. Indeed, he goes some way towards criticising the government and abolitionists, 'whose Christian sympathies have been powerfully called into play by their fanciful ideas of the condition of slavery.'[276] While his journal entries contain a mixture of stereotype and experience, they also put in evidence an uncertainty about slavery and race that resulted from the 'war of representation' between abolitionists and pro-slavery campaigners.[277] During this time of great change, there was no one, unshakeable stance on slavery amongst the British population. British identity was constantly shifting in relation to views of the black Other. Abolitionists promoted a national identity dependent on the ideals of morality and Christianity, whereas those who were pro-slavery viewed their identity as 'an affluent, commercially savvy Briton, who understood the value of trade and would seek a more moderate solution.'[278] The importance of civilised behaviour to the perception of national identity can be found in the ambiguous space occupied by the British living and working in colonies overseas: those who could be Other in behaviour rather than race. As ideas surrounding slavery shifted during this time,

---

[274] Deborah Wyrick, 'The Madwoman in the Hut: Scandals of Hybrid Domesticity in Early Victorian Literature from the West Indies', *Pacific Coast Philology*, 33 (1998), 44-57 (p. 44).
[275] Wyrick, p. 44.
[276] Ibid.
[277] Hall, 'Culture and Identity in Imperial Britain', p. 209.
[278] Swaminathan, p. 5.

plantation owners and the white British living and working in places such as the West Indies did not always agree with the attitudes of the people and government of Britain. As the official British view of slavery in its colonies changed in favour of the slaves during the 1820s and 1830s,[279] many white people living in the West Indies, at the heart of the trade, opposed these changes.

Though the violence of slavery came to be viewed as antithetical to the British national identity, being 'an outrage on the laws of humanity',[280] this was not an accepted view in the colonies themselves. Ideas surrounding slavery evolved through time, and the British national identity was modified with them. Though some abolitionist tracts decried slavery altogether,[281] debates around the subject as it reflected upon the British were concerned with the treatment of slaves, rather than their bondage. Many of the British living in Britain championed the humane management of slaves, which included, among other things, cessation of the use of the whip.[282] In the eyes of people such as Caroline Fox and her friend Henry de la Beche, plantation owners who used the whip were brutal, whereas in the eyes of the plantation owners themselves, those who did not use the whip were wrong.[283] Falmouth, as a port frequently interacting with the West Indies through trade and the Packet Service, was well informed about events in the colonies and therefore frequently in receipt of facts that informed the opinions of its community on the subject. This example of changing attitudes illustrates that there was no one view of Britishness that was entirely comprehensive, but the behaviour of those who were racially British could render them, in the eyes of their fellow men and women, less British than others. Reprehensible behaviour, such as the extremes of violence 'which decency forbids the mention of',[284] among the so-called British, could be Other in the same way as skin colour or dress.

---

[279] Slavery was abolished in the West Indies in 1833 and replaced with an apprenticeship system, which was in turn abolished in 1838.
[280] 'Slavery and Slave Trade', *Royal Cornwall Gazette, Falmouth Packet & Plymouth Journal*, 3 May 1823.
[281] 'Literature – Negro Slavery &c.', *Royal Cornwall Gazette, Falmouth Packet & Plymouth Journal*, 16 August 1823.
[282] Ibid.
[283] Caroline Fox, pp. 17-18.
[284] 'Slavery and Slave Trade', *Royal Cornwall Gazette, Falmouth Packet & Plymouth Journal*, 3 May 1823.

Ordinary people such as Williamson drew upon these existing dialogues to inform their own views, and this merging of pro- and anti-slavery ideology is evident in his journals. During his 1829 voyage to Jamaica, Williamson discussed slavery and perceptions of it at length. [285] In his view, travel and the experience of meeting with slaves face to face, were essential in forming authentic views on slavery.[286] Though his own accounts show the influence of ideology and stereotype, as already discussed, he appears sensitive to the inaccuracies that could be promoted by engaging with literature at home. It may be expected that this distrust would be directed at pro-slavery discourse, but Williamson instead expresses doubt about the texts produced by abolitionists, which he feels take advantage of the average Briton's inability to visit the colonies for themselves: 'To us, who live far from the West Indies and know nothing of slavery but the name, the condition of a slave must be one of the utmost misery and hardship – and our sympathies, misled by our ignorance, naturally and innocently too, are granted to the unfortunate wretch.'[287]

Though Williamson went on to describe, at length, the advantages to the slave of being owned by a master, his later dialogue nevertheless displays an anxiety that he should not be considered pro-slavery by those acquainted with himself or his journals. Despite his pro-slavery comments, he insists that he is not a 'slaverite', but actually 'abhor[s] the principles of the slave trade and of slavery in general.'[288] Rather, he argues that slaves are not suitable for emancipation due to an inherent ignorance, and what he rather vaguely terms 'their opinions'.[289] Having spoken to slaves who do not desire freedom, he commends their 'common sense' in contrast with their 'ignorant brethren'.[290] He accepts that the British have done wrong, that they 'have committed the most horrible cruelties', and does not condone the actions.[291] In this, we can discern a desire to tread a middle path between pro-slavery and abolitionist ideology. Williamson thus takes up some elements of the popular views of 'gradualists' such as William Wilberforce, who lobbied for gradual

---

[285] Williamson, 'Journal of a Voyage from Falmouth to Jamaica & Carthagena and back', pp. 40-42.
[286] Williamson, 'Journal of a Voyage from Falmouth to Jamaica & Carthagena and back', p. 40.
[287] Ibid.
[288] Williamson, 'Second Voyage to Jamaica & Mexico', p. 11.
[289] Ibid.
[290] Williamson, 'Second Voyage to Jamaica & Mexico', p. 12.
[291] Williamson, 'Second Voyage to Jamaica & Mexico', p. 11.

improvements in conditions and education, ahead of emancipation.[292] In describing the vulnerability of the British to misleading texts, he infers that his own opinions, based on real encounters with the Other, are more genuine and trustworthy. Falmouth's role in the process of creating his dialogue is thus as a means of verification: those who read it will likely consider his views to be authentic, and may be influenced by them. Nevertheless, the distance he employs here, in contrast to the graphic descriptions and vehement arguments of other journal sections, suggests a defensive Othering of the entire colony of Jamaica. Though Britain's empire was seen as a part of its identity, colonies such as Jamaica were, as Vincent Brown describes, 'fundamentally alien places [...] a "Torrid Zone" beyond the boundaries of civilization.'[293] The 'nightmarish societies' created by Europeans were held at arm's-length, away from their own civilised progress.[294] Despite the Packet surgeon's attempts to argue for political and social control in Jamaica, and despite his own views on slavery, which seep through his so-called 'objective' stance, his ultimate position as narrator is as a passive observer that does not belong in the context in which he finds himself. He may empathise with his fellow whites, but in order to protect his own identity from the moral dubiousness associated with the colony,[295] he takes a step back and renders it, and its occupants – black or white – Other. In doing so, the threat to the British identity posed by the emancipation question, and any possible effects of slavery, is neutralised.

Williamson's journals thus served as a means through which 'emancipation anxiety'[296] could be dealt with. In them, he attempts to work through the confused and changeable notions of race and power that resulted from slavery and emancipation. The contemporary nature of his observations shows just how well-connected Falmouth was to the empire, and how involved its population could be in current debates around it. They illustrate the impact that this connection, and the opportunity to meet face to face with colonists and slaves that it presented, had on the notions of identity and Otherness held by the town's residents. In travelling,

---

[292] John Oldfield, 'After Emancipation: Slavery, Freedom and the Victorian Empire' in *The Victorian Empire and Britain's Maritime World, 1837-1901*, ed. by Miles Taylor (Basingstoke: Palgrave Macmillan, 2013), pp. 43-63 (p. 44).
[293] Vincent Brown, p. 17.
[294] Ibid.
[295] Ibid.
[296] Wyrick, p. 45.

seeing, thinking, writing, and sharing.[297] Williamson created a mental and literal dialogue concerned with identity that stretched from Falmouth to the West Indies.

Local and global discourse

The overseas connections of the port of Falmouth, linking both the town and the country to Britain's empire by sea, transformed it from a provincial location to a key site for interaction between Britain and foreign Others. In and around the town, important moments of contact between the two took place, and through this contact discourse concerning race, power and identity was formed. From its local setting, Falmouth became part of a global dialogue informing, and informed by, the empire. This dialogue could be both inclusive and exclusive, as the criteria for 'Britishness' and acceptability were negotiated. Those who relinquished their own cultural identity to take on that of the British, such as Joseph Emidy and the Ashantee princes, could find themselves included with limits upon their power, occupying an uneasy space in the nation. Others who embraced their differences, such as the Begum of Oudh, came to be figures of fascination to the residents of Falmouth, while their oddity could be used against them as a marker of weakness that ultimately elevated Britain to the heights of imperial rule. Observations of other nations came to be as important in defining British national identity as it did in defining them. Barclay Fox's characterisation of the Turk, inspired by real-life encounter but mired in stereotype, simultaneously set out the case for Britain being a superior ruling power as it ridiculed the failed glory of the Ottoman Empire. Similarly, the journals of James Williamson engaged with received stereotypes relating to colonial power while claiming an authenticity based on proximity to the colonies. Though this connectivity with the colonies must have inspired some interaction based in reality, what this chapter has demonstrated is that sites such as Falmouth could generate much more than factual texts. While the sources consulted – primarily journals and letters – share an appearance of objective factuality, all reflect the complex hierarchical and racial processing that occurred whenever Britain and its Others came face to face. Falmouth, being a port town connected to the colonies, gave its residents the power to narrate and to narrate on behalf of others; a

---

[297] Remembering that many of his observations are addressed to other people, primarily his mother and his brother Jacob.

vital factor in culture and imperialism.[298] The process of mutual constitution[299] that took place and the effects of these encounters between 'us' and 'them' would continue for many decades beyond Falmouth's heyday as a port town, into the period of more formal imperialism. The power relations mapped out by the British in and around Falmouth came to be a part of a much greater narrative of colonialism in which defining identity was key to determining the degrees to which subjects were rulers or ruled.

---

[298] Said, *Culture and Imperialism*, p. xiii.
[299] Hall, 'Culture and Identity in Imperial Britain', p. 203.

Conclusion

A final sailing

> The last of the Falmouth Packets has sailed, and the Establishment which has existed there for nearly 200 years has, for the present, come to an end. The Ocean Steamers and the Railroad have outweighed the local advantages and safety of the Post. [...] [T]he Brazil service alone remained; and now this also has gone, and when the *Seagull* shall return, four months hence, the last relic of an Establishment which served the Country for nearly 200 years, most efficiently and cheaply, will have vanished.[1]

As this thesis has described, during the first half of the nineteenth century the small Cornish town of Falmouth functioned as a busy, multicultural thoroughfare for the British empire's traffic in people, products, and information. To Robert Southey, it held only 'Dirt, noise, restlessness, expectation',[2] while Lord Byron found, boarding a Packet ship, 'women screaming, tars blaspheming', and a 'general noise and racket'.[3] From reminisces and records available, a picture emerges of a noisy, busy town: a place of constant activity. Louis Simond, a French gentleman visiting in 1809, noted seeing a carriage 'overladen with passengers', and hearing a 'universal clatter of iron on the pavement'.[4] It is remarkable that such a small location, geographically isolated in the south west of Britain, played host to some of the most famous and influential figures in the nation's history; men such as Southey and Byron, as well as Charles Darwin and Captain FitzRoy, and some lesser-known but equally fascinating, such as the plant hunter William Lobb, the princes of Ashantee, Lieutenant Lapenotiere of the *Pickle*, and the former slave Joseph Emidy. In this cast of players the local heroes must not be forgotten: the pioneering scientist and businessman Robert Were Fox, his children Barclay, Caroline and Anna-Maria, the avid plant collector Sir Charles Lemon, and the fearless – and sometimes foolhardy – captains and crew of the Packet Service. Each of these figures had a role to play in the empire's history, and each found in Falmouth a solution to their various needs.

---

[1] 'The Late Packet Establishment at Falmouth', *The Royal Cornwall Gazette, Falmouth Packet, and General Advertiser*, 20 December 1850.
[2] Cottle, p. 220.
[3] Byron, 'Falmouth Roads, June 30th, 1809', p. 83.
[4] *Cornwall: the Travellers' Tales*, ed. by Todd Gray (Exeter: The Mint Press, 2000), I p. 82.

For Lapenotiere, this was a safe and fast passage home with dispatches, for the Foxes and Lemon it was an opportunity to conduct overseas trade and networking, while for Emidy it was a place of freedom, however compromised this may have been. Countless others, both natives and non-natives of Britain, visited and passed through as they sought to widen their business horizons or explore the world beyond their homeland.

Such an intense period of activity, dependent as it was upon ever-evolving means of travel and expanding arenas of trade, could not last forever. Many of the traditional Packet ships, powered by sail, fell victim to the introduction of steam in the 1820s.[5] Initially, this caused no harm to the Falmouth service, as routes were simply replaced with steamers that continued to run from the town.[6] From the 1830s the Admiralty, who then ran the service, slowly transferred the Falmouth routes elsewhere.[7] The Falmouth to Lisbon service was moved to Plymouth,[8] then Southampton,[9] and in 1840 the North American mail began running from Liverpool.[10] The West India steamers likewise moved to Southampton in 1842.[11] Removal of the packets from Falmouth caused great consternation among the people of the town, with fears that 'evil and suffering' were likely to be inflicted by the change.[12] Nevertheless, by 1850, only six ships and one route – that between Falmouth and Buenos Ayres – remained in operation.[13] As the *Royal Cornwall Gazette* described, by the end of that year, the service had ended, with only one Packet, the *Seagull*, due to return from its last voyage.[14]

The impact on Falmouth was dramatic. Much of its business had relied, in one form or another, upon the Packet Service. As well as providing services and crew for the ships themselves, the town had also gained in revenue and importance from the

---

[5] M.E. Philbrick, 'The Packets Finally Depart' in *History around the Fal: Part Five* (Exeter: Fal Local History Group/University of Exeter, 1990), pp. 78-80 (p. 79).
[6] Ibid.
[7] Whetter, *The History of Falmouth*, p. 54.
[8] 'The Late Packet Establishment at Falmouth'.
[9] Ibid.
[10] Philbrick, 'The Packets Finally Depart', p. 79.
[11] Ibid.
[12] 'The Packets', *The Royal Cornwall Gazette, Falmouth Packet & Plymouth Journal*, 1 September 1843.
[13] 'Falmouth Express', *The Royal Cornwall Gazette, Falmouth Packet, and General Advertiser*, 1 February 1850.
[14] 'The Late Packet Establishment at Falmouth'.

travellers passing through who visited its shops, inns, coffee rooms and societies.[15] Tony Pawlyn, a biographer of the Service in Falmouth, estimates that for every six men employed on the ships, another two or three people would have been employed in ancillary services.[16] At its height, the service had employed over 1,200 men.[17] The economic effects of this employment, and the number of ships and people visiting the port, would have been great. A writer to the *Royal Cornwall Gazette* in 1850 lamented the decline of the town, arguing that though '[t]here are few spots in England, nay in the whole of Europe, more beautifully adapted to the development of a city than the shores of Falmouth Harbour', poverty and disease were instead rampaging.[18] The writer, known only as Armoricus, described 'the blackened and filthy back of low and irregular hovels' and 'a few patched up store houses, ever closed, ever empty'.[19] He saw, '[h]ere and there', 'a store-house, as silent as a tomb', 'standing in little danger of crumbling under the weight of goods'.[20] Without the Packet Service and with the railway in Cornwall in its infancy, there were complaints that the region had become cut off from the rest of Britain. One writer to the newspaper asked:

> Is Cornwall poor? [...] Is it destitute of enterprise, of energy, of wealth? Do its inhabitants vegetate where they were born without the desire or the necessity to move from place to place, to visit or be visited by others? Has Cornwall nothing to tempt the capitalist, the tourist, the valetudinarian, or any of the numberless pleasure seekers who float upon the surface of a wealthy and luxurious society[?][21]

Here, the negative effects of time-space compression, which has the potential to isolate and leave stranded as well as to connect,[22] are clearly felt. Faster, more convenient travel had left the Cornish disengaged, and the mobility that they had once enjoyed became a thing of the past. This rapid decline illustrates well how much of the region's success had been dependent on communications and speed.

---

[15] Whetter, *The History of Falmouth*, p. 47.
[16] Pawlyn, p. 23.
[17] Pawlyn, p. 52.
[18] 'Falmouth Improvements', *The Royal Cornwall Gazette, Falmouth Packet, and General Advertiser*, 17 May 1850.
[19] Ibid.
[20] Ibid.
[21] 'Cornwall Railway', *The Royal Cornwall Gazette, Falmouth Packet, and General Advertiser*, 20 December 1850.
[22] Massey, p. 148.

While Cornwall's isolation and poverty were not wholly caused by the loss of the Packet Service – as discussed previously, its mining industry had also declined due to overseas competition – its removal must certainly have been a factor in undermining the importance that it once enjoyed.

The introduction of the railway was doubtless a contributor to the decline of Falmouth. In the 1840s, in competition with the port of Southampton, Falmouth was felt to be the weaker of the two due to the former's rail connection with London.[23] This meant that while dispatches landed in Falmouth would have to travel by coach, those arriving in Southampton could reach the city more quickly. Ultimately, as already outlined, much of the Packet trade was relocated to Southampton. During initial meetings in 1840, it was thought that the first railway line into Cornwall would have Falmouth as its main station, due to the necessity of keeping up with technological developments that offered faster travel for the mail from Packet ships.[24] Indeed, it was argued that developing railway links between Falmouth and Exeter would actually increase the traffic of the port by making it easier and faster for passengers to travel there.[25] At this time, it was felt that if the railway did not extend into Falmouth, 'the prosperity of Cornwall was in jeopardy to a very extraordinary degree'.[26] Unfortunately, before the plan for the Cornwall Railway could be carried out, the Packets were moved to Southampton, apparently due to a belief that there would be no such line introduced to Cornwall.[27] Falmouth had once offered high-speed travel, with passages by sea from Falmouth to London being faster than those overland.[28] With the introduction of the railway and steam travel, however, it no longer afforded the best means for time-space compression.

---

[23] 'H. M. Paddle Steamers', *Falmouth Packet Archives 1688-1850*, <http://www.falmouth.packet.archives.dial.pipex.com/id28.htm> [accessed 29 April 2014]

[24] 'County Meeting on the Proposed Railway into Cornwall', *The Royal Cornwall Gazette, Falmouth Packet, and General Advertiser*, 30 October 1840.

[25] Ibid.

[26] 'Great County Meeting on the Packet Question, and on the Devon and Cornwall Railway', *The Royal Cornwall Gazette, Falmouth Packet, and General Advertiser*, 23 October 1840.

[27] 'Summary of the Packet Question', *The Royal Cornwall Gazette, Falmouth Packet & Plymouth Journal*, 2 February 1844.

[28] Beck, p. 15.

Despite meetings to discuss plans for the railway in Falmouth,[29] with estimates of when the new line might open,[30] the Cornwall Railway did not fulfil the early hopes entertained by all involved. Financial depression held up progress and investors lost both faith and money in the 'railway boom'.[31] Instead of embarking on a grand scheme to connect Falmouth with the rest of the country, there was instead put in place a smaller project to extend an existing mining railway in Hayle to connect Penzance and Redruth.[32] At this point, in 1851, it was intended that this line could then be extended to join with one from Falmouth to Plymouth.[33] Ultimately, however, the existing line was grown to instead link Truro with the rest of the country in 1859.[34] Due to further financial issues, Falmouth would not be connected by rail until over four years later, in August 1863, 'after twenty years of discouraging and heartbreaking disappointments'.[35] The Packet Service, and the potential importance of Falmouth for the mails, had been gone for over a decade, and instead of becoming the main station in Cornwall, Falmouth was a branch line. Some hope was entertained that the town might once again become a destination for the mails,[36] but this was not to be realised.

There appears to have been a certain amount of animosity between the Falmouth Packet captains and the Admiralty, which may explain the latter's reluctance to keep the Service in the town. A letter sent within the Admiralty from their base in Falmouth in May 1832, discussing the end of the Lisbon service, stated quite firmly an intention of removing it with an implication that the Falmouth commanders were excessively arrogant and possessive.[37] The author, Captain William King, argued that 'a strange opinion is entertained [...] that they possess a vested right in the

---

[29] 'Falmouth and Penryn Floating Harbour, *The Royal Cornwall Gazette, Falmouth Packet & Plymouth Journal*, 13 September 1844.
[30] 'Truro, Friday, September 20, 1844', *The Royal Cornwall Gazette, Falmouth Packet & Plymouth Journal*, 20 September 1844.
[31] Barclay Fox, p. 404.
[32] 'Cornwall Railway', *Trewman's Exeter Flying Post or Plymouth and Cornish Advertiser*, 6 March 1851.
[33] Ibid.
[34] 'Opening of the Cornwall Railway', *The Royal Cornwall Gazette, Falmouth Packet, and General Advertiser*, 6 May 1859.
[35] 'Rejoicings at Falmouth', *The Royal Cornwall Gazette, Falmouth Packet, and General Advertiser*, 28 August 1863.
[36] 'Falmouth as a Mail Station', *The Royal Cornwall Gazette, Falmouth Packet, and General Advertiser*, 20 March 1863.
[37] London, National Archives, ADM 1/4045.

Packet Service of which no power ought to dispossess them'.[38] The expectations of those in Falmouth were seen as 'unreasonable', and King disliked that many captains had stated with confidence that 'they held their situations for life'.[39] The Packet commanders' belief in their own power and job security had already caused tension within the government when the service was owned by the General Post Office. In October 1810, a mutiny had taken place in Falmouth over the banning of smuggling among Packet crews. For several decades, ships had carried contraband goods such as lemons and figs into the town to sell,[40] and taken local produce abroad. Such was the quantity of goods brought to Lisbon by the Packets that a public sale was generally opened twelve hours after a ship's arrival in the port, advertised by posters that had been printed in advance and shipped over with the products.[41] When threatened with the loss of their contraband, the crews of the *Prince Adolphus* and *Marlborough* had refused to set sail without it.[42] Ultimately, due to the consternation of the entire Falmouth Packet Service and an alleged mishandling of the case, the service was removed to Plymouth as punishment.[43] It was only by petitioning in the most penitent terms that the residents of Falmouth managed to bring about its restoration in February 1811.[44] Now, it seems, with the advent of steam the Admiralty had a reasonable excuse to rid itself of the troublesome, 'lucratively paid'[45] Falmouth crews, and took it.

With the changes that this removal brought about, the thriving multicultural society that the town enjoyed fell away. By the 1870s there were only three Jewish families remaining and no synagogue services.[46] The last burial in the Jewish cemetery, excepting one final interment in 1913, took place in 1868.[47] Residents moved out of the town to better-connected locations such as Bristol, Birmingham, Plymouth and London.[48] At the same time, as passengers no longer travelled through Falmouth

---

[38] Ibid.
[39] Ibid.
[40] Ursula Redwood, *The Story of Flushing* (Newquay: The Lithoprint Company, 1967), p. 23.
[41] Mudd, p. 25.
[42] Truro, Cornwall Records Office, X507/3.
[43] Ibid.
[44] Truro, Cornwall Records Office, CN/3216.
[45] London, National Archives, ADM 1/4045.
[46] Dunstan, p. 37.
[47] 'Falmouth Jewish Cemetery', *PastScape*
<http://www.pastscape.org.uk/hob.aspx?hob_id=1367911> [accessed 12 May 2014].
[48] Dunstan, p. 37.

from the Packets, there would have been far less foreign faces to be seen in and around the town. From 1850, Caroline Fox's journal records far less interaction with notable or foreign people, with much correspondence carried out, and news exchanged, by letter.[49]

As Falmouth's regular, formalised links to the empire disappeared with the loss of the Packet Service – though merchant ships continued to operate – its decline matched that taking place around the whole of Cornwall. The entire region slowly lost its prosperous connection with empire, most notably in the mining industry. As outlined in Chapter Two, the export of mining technology and skills ultimately contributed to the downfall of Cornish mining as overseas locations such as South America and Australia took over the trade. By 1845, Cornish mines were generating the least revenue in comparison with those in Cuba, South America, New Zealand, Ireland and South Australia.[50] As poverty began to hit the Cornish in the 1840s, many miners and their families emigrated overseas in search of better wages and living conditions.[51] With the 'gold rushes' of the late 1840s and 1850s in locations such as California, British Colombia and Victoria, yet greater numbers were tempted away from the hardship that Cornwall had to offer.[52] The Fox family's involvement in Perran Foundry ceased in 1858, whereupon it passed into the ownership of the Williams family, who closed it in 1879.[53]

Peace also had a negative impact on the prosperity of Falmouth. While much of Britain had suffered during the Napoleonic Wars, with the loss of commercial trading, Falmouth had prospered. Both the town and the crews of the Packet Service gained from the wars. Local businesses certainly profited from an increase in the number of vessels – most of them naval – visiting to collect supplies. In 1815, Falmouth was noted as having nine hotels and inns providing food and drink to those coming ashore, [54] and contained a number of other businesses relating to provisions,

---

[49] For instance, Caroline Fox, pp. 309-310.
[50] Dutton, p. 296.
[51] Sharron P. Schwartz, *Voices of the Cornish Mining Landscape* (Truro: Cornwall County Council, 2008), p. 97.
[52] Ibid.
[53] Jane Boyd-Brent and William Filmer-Sankey, 'Perran Foundry Conservation Plan', 14 December 2005, p. 6.
[54] Thomas, *A Falmouth Guide*, pp. 76-77.

including ship-repair yards, shops and lodgings.[55] Naval officers spent their time and money in the town,[56] and Packet crews enjoyed an increase in wages.[57] With most maritime traffic banned from the seas during the wars, Packets became one of the only means for people to travel into Europe and beyond.[58] The government was also known to pay out large sums in gratitude to Packet employees responsible for capturing enemy vessels, despite instructions that they should not fight unless forced to.[59] With the end of the Napoleonic Wars in 1815, Falmouth's fortunes fell.[60] When the Second World War took place over a century later, it once again heralded a surge in shipping activity in Falmouth. Fox's Arrivals Register records a major surge in ships arriving in the port, some for services or goods, and some 'for orders': to receive instructions as to where they must sail.[61] Compared to a pre-war trend of between five hundred and one thousand ships a year, the wartime year of 1941 saw a height of 2,657, with an average of 1,376 ships per year between 1939 and 1945.[62] Clearly, Falmouth's importance as a port lay partly in its value during war.

One area in which Falmouth, and indeed Cornwall, would continue to excel was horticulture. Falmouth's gardens (Fig. 10), and the rare plants that were imported into the town and surrounding areas through the Packet Service and merchant ships, provided a foundation upon which was built an entire region now known for its horticulture. By the end of the Victorian era, Cornwall had many sub-tropical gardens, including Trewidden in Penzance, Caerhays and Heligan in St Austell, and Trevarno near Helston. This passion for plant hunting continued into the twentieth century, with the creation of gardens such as Trewithen, a repository for exotic species, between 1910 and 1932.[63] This collection of gardens, along with many others, now forms a major tourist attraction for those visiting Cornwall.[64]

---

[55] Whetter, *The History of Falmouth*, p. 34.
[56] Buckingham, *Autobiography of James Silk Buckingham*, p. 9.
[57] Mudd, p. 9.
[58] Norway, p. 39.
[59] Whetter, *The History of Falmouth*, p. 34.
[60] Whetter, *The History of Falmouth*, p. 36.
[61] Jonathan Griffin, 'Fox's Arrivals', private correspondence [9 May 2014].
[62] Ibid.
[63] 'Garden history', *Trewithen* <http://www.trewithengardens.co.uk/trewithen-gardens/garden-history/> [accessed 12 May 2014].
[64] 'Gardens in Cornwall', *Visit Cornwall* <http://www.visitcornwall.com/things-to-do/attractions-and-gardens/gardens> [accessed 12 May 2014].

Fig. 10: Map of Falmouth gardens

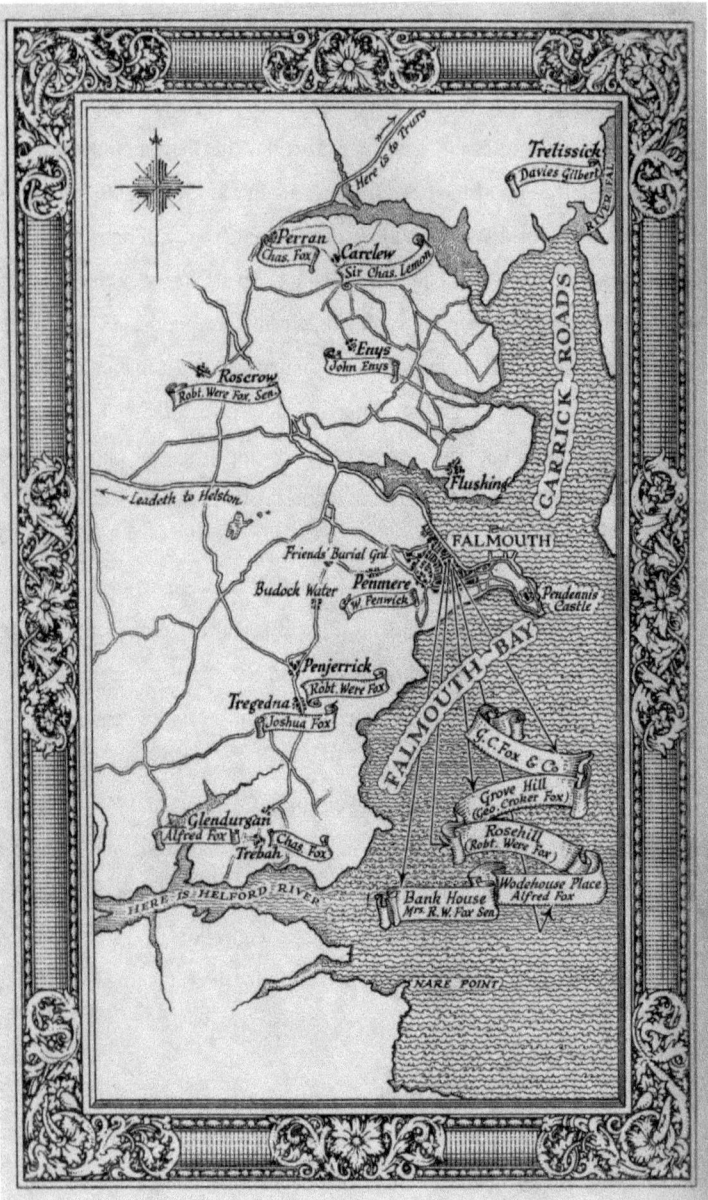

This map from Wilson Harris' 1944 biography of Caroline Fox shows the notable gardens around Falmouth and the surrounding district, indicating their owners, during the first half of the nineteenth century.

Though the majority of travellers no longer enter the region through Falmouth,[65] many are nevertheless drawn there due to this legacy of its heyday. The plants and trees, once so delicate and difficult to transport, are now a tangible legacy of Falmouth's days as a key part of the empire. Another lasting trace lies in the Moor in Falmouth, a busy thoroughfare for cars and people, which now houses a memorial erected in 1898, dedicated to 'the memory of the gallant officers and men of H.M. Post Office Packet Service sailing from Falmouth'.

A new era

It must never be forgotten that Falmouth was an invented town, built to serve certain outside interests. Initially, it was created to service Pendennis Castle in the realm of defence, as a base for ships' supplies, and a location from which troops could be quickly mustered. Later, it expanded in response to the need for shipping services due to increased overseas trade and the introduction of the Packet Service. With the dawning of peace and the removal of the Packets, the reasons for Falmouth's creation fell away, leaving a town without real purpose. Though some shipping continued, the port was not the busy thoroughfare it had once been. As already illustrated, the effect of this was poverty. For the town to succeed into the future, its benefits of natural position by the water had to be harnessed and put to a new use. The invented town was thus reinvented to serve a new set of interests, and industry was replaced with tourism. As the twentieth century dawned, a change came over Cornwall. Instead of Packet ships, Falmouth and surrounding waterways became host to the yachts of wealthy, pleasure-seeking visitors.

Among their number in the early 1900s was the London businessman Leonard Daneham Cunliffe, a man with professional connections to the Bank of England, Harrods, and the American Hudson's Bay Company.[66] Sailing in his yacht *Laranda*, Cunliffe spotted the estate of Trelissick, in Feock, at the head of the Carrick Roads. Apparently falling in love with it on sight,[67] Cunliffe took out a lease on the house

---

[65] Cruise liners of tourists do visit the port.
[66] 'Our History: People: Builders: Richard Burbidge', *HBC Heritage* <http://www.hbcheritage.ca/hbcheritage/history/people/builders/burbidge> [accessed 22 May 2014].
[67] 'The story of Trelissick House', *National Trust* <http://www.nationaltrust.org.uk/article-1355791834262/> [accessed 22 May 2014].

and gardens in 1913[68] and eventually bought it in 1927/8.[69] An article in *The Times*, noting the sale, observed particularly that the property contained yachting accommodation, and contained the heading 'Cornish Yachting'.[70] During the first half of the nineteenth century, the house had been owned by the Daniell family, who made their fortune through Cornish mining interests.[71] The loss of this industry contributed to Thomas Daniell's bankruptcy in 1831, and to the eventual passing of the house, after a period of non-occupancy, into the hands of Eastbourne landowner John Davies Gilbert in 1844.[72] The residencies of both Gilbert and Cunliffe signify a change in Trelissick from a Cornishman's display of wealth and luxury to a metropolitan gentleman's fashionable rural home; including, of course, the aforementioned 'yachting accommodation'.[73]

To nineteenth and twentieth century owners, Cornish gardens became, once again, the loci for conspicuous consumption: the display of wealth through possession of goods and lands.[74] For Cornwall, by the twentieth century an industrially depopulated region, had lost the majority of its mining concerns and instead held attraction as a provincial natural beauty spot, a reputation certainly boosted by its impressive sub-tropical gardens and mild climate. One 1919 article in *The Times*, discussing the sale of Trelissick noted 'the view over Falmouth Harbour, with the Channel in the distance' to be a major attraction to potential buyers, along with its parkland, woodland and farmland.[75] Wealth no longer circulated as freely among the natives of Cornwall, and instead flowed inwards from other locations, as evidenced by this promotion of the property in a national, London-based newspaper. The *Times* reporter observed that the value of the house, an 'admirable property', 'would not be lost upon a good many enterprising capitalists'.[76] The paper also published a brief

---

[68] Truro, Cornwall Records Office, DG/206/1.
[69] The date of purchase is unclear: 'The Estate Market', *The Times*, 9 December 1927 lists the sale as occurring in that year but names the buyer as HP Cunliffe. An English Heritage database entry for Trelissick, 'TRELISSICK', *English Heritage Register of Parks and Gardens of Special Historic Interest* <http://list.english-heritage.org.uk/resultsingle.aspx?uid=1000656 > [accessed 22 May 2014], states that Leonard Daneham Cunliffe purchased the freehold in 1928. In either case, the estate entered into the family in 1927/8.
[70] 'The Estate Market'.
[71] 'TRELISSICK'.
[72] Ibid.
[73] 'The Estate Market'.
[74] Trigg, p. 101.
[75] 'The Estate Market', *The Times*, 20 November 1919.
[76] Ibid.

history and description of Falmouth, clearly appealing to those living outside the town who would most likely be unfamiliar with these facts. While recognising Falmouth's 'importance and value' as a port, the concluding statement made was that 'it is 'agreeably situated, and has all the advantages implied by the expression "the Cornish Riviera"'.[77]

An 1898 article in the locally-produced *The Cornish Magazine*, makes plain the town's transition from industrial centre to beauty spot, beginning with a page describing in elaborate terms the 'sea-swept rocks', 'glistening sandy beaches', and 'picturesque cliffs'.[78] The writer, Charles Eyre Pascoe, states that residents of Falmouth are 'only just beginning to wake up' to the potential of the town after a 'very long sleep' in the wake of the Packet departures.[79] Lamenting the town's poverty and disconnection from London since 1850, Pacoe calls upon 'Falmouthians' to embrace its potential as a destination for visitors from outside of Cornwall, and to make it into an 'English Riviera'.[80] Falmouth's only hope of success beyond its former industry, he argued, lay in transformation into a prestigious holiday location for the wealthy.[81] In this aim, he believed, it was naturally assisted by its old-world charm of narrow streets and quaint alleys, its sea views, and picturesque castles.[82] This selling-point remains the same today: the National Trust, which presently owns the Trelissick estate, promotes its views, garden, woodland, 'amazing' natural setting, 'breathtaking walks', and coastal access to potential visitors.[83] Falmouth's industrial heritage is largely forgotten by those outside of the town. A July 2014 feature on '30 Best Places to Live by the Sea' in the *Sunday Times* included Falmouth among the thirty due to its 'original fishing-village charm'.[84]

---

[77] Ibid.
[78] Charles Eyre Pascoe, 'Falmouth: its Past, Present, and Future', *The Cornish Magazine*, 1 (1898), 210-219 (p. 210).
[79] Pascoe, pp. 210-211.
[80] Pascoe, p. 213.
[81] Pascoe, p. 215.
[82] Pacoe, p. 215 and p. 219.
[83] 'Trelissick Garden', *National Trust* <http://www.nationaltrust.org.uk/trelissick-garden/> [accessed 13 June 2014].
[84] 'Viewing Essential', *Sunday Times: Home*, 20 July 2014, pp. 25-26.

These examples represent a far wider transition in Cornwall during the nineteenth and twentieth centuries, as the region ceased to be concerned with trade and industry and came to be known for tourism, leisure, and the arts. This change was felt specifically in Falmouth, as the town's focus on science was replaced with a local interest in art. As early as 1859, the Royal Cornwall Polytechnic Society meetings were becoming dominated by art rather than science, with the observation made that '[t]he display in [the fine arts] department is more extensive than has perhaps ever been seen before', but that the display of mechanical models was 'not perhaps quite so large as at some of the previous exhibitions'.[85] A separate Cornwall Art Union was founded in connection with the RCPS in 1852.[86] Much like its parent group, the Union held shows in which amateurs could display work, with prizes given.[87] The town's new focus on art, apparent even at this time, culminated in the formation of the Falmouth School of Art, dedicated to the memory of Anna Maria Fox, sister of Caroline and Barclay, in 1902.

From the nineteenth century, well into the present day, Cornwall thus became a prime area for tourism and leisure within Britain. In particular, from the end of the Packet era, Falmouth's gardens continued to hold interest as tourist destinations. In 1850, gentlemen of the London-based Athenaeum Club, of which Sir Charles Lemon was almost certainly a member,[88] 'partook of the recreation of a cruize [sic]' to Perran Wharf to visit the gardens of Carclew, attended by a band who played music.[89] Such visits to local gardens, both by local people and tourists from outside of Cornwall, are mentioned in the papers throughout the following fifty years, and into the twentieth century.[90] Even today, the gardens of Glendurgan, Trebah, and Trelissick, all located around Falmouth, continue to draw large numbers of visitors.

---

[85] 'Royal Cornwall Polytechnic Society', *The Royal Cornwall Gazette, Falmouth Packet, and General Advertiser*, 30 September 1859.
[86] 'The Cornwall Art Union', *The Royal Cornwall Gazette, Falmouth Packet, and General Advertiser*, 11 September 1869.
[87] Ibid.
[88] He is among the listed members of the club ten years previously; the closest date achievable at present. *Rules and Regulations for the Government of the Athenaeum* (London: W. Clowes and Sons, 1840), p. 60.
[89] 'Falmouth Express', *The Royal Cornwall Gazette, Falmouth Packet, and General Advertiser*, 19 July 1850.
[90] For instance, 'Bath and West of England Exhibition at Falmouth', *The Royal Cornwall Gazette, Falmouth Packet, and General Advertiser*, 28 May 1868, 'Cook's Excursions to Cornwall', *The Royal Cornwall Gazette, Falmouth Packet, and General Advertiser*, 30 October 1875, and 'The News of the County', *The Royal Cornwall Gazette, Falmouth Packet, and General Advertiser*, 24 May 1900.

Others, perhaps less well known but also a part of the town's history, such as Penjerrick, Rosehill, and Enys, also open their gates to those seeking a peaceful or interesting environment in which to wander. And of course, there is Carclew. The house is decayed and dilapidated, the gardens both wild and restored, but nevertheless fascinating to those organised or lucky enough to visit on one of the property's few open days. Cornwall's tourist appeal now extends beyond its natural features – its gardens and, of course, its beaches – to include other reminders of its globalised past. The Cornish mining heritage draws crowds interested in history and engineering,[91] while Falmouth's own National Maritime Museum Cornwall attracts people with a desire to know more about maritime industries.[92] Art, too, though a later addition to the story, continues to appeal both as an industry or activity in itself, but also as a more recent part of Cornwall's heritage. The former fishing town of St Ives, known for its artists since the end of the nineteenth century,[93] now has a dual role as a working artists' haven[94] and as a location for art history.[95] Falmouth's own identification with art has been continued through the longevity and adaptability of the Falmouth School of Art which, after several changes of name and great expansion across two campuses, has now become Falmouth University. Specialising in arts courses, from fine art and illustration to music and theatre,[96] the university has strengthened Cornwall's reputation for having a 'dynamic art scene'.[97]

One lasting legacy of the global connections made from Cornwall in the nineteenth century was summed up in a lecture given by JH Collins at the RCPS in August 1900.[98] In the lecture, entitled 'A Century of Progress in Cornwall', Collins noted the many ways in which the horizons of the region had expanded during the previous century, including the creation of export markets for fish and mining, and the formation of newspapers and scientific societies. A generous portion of the credit for

---

[91] *Cornish Mining World Heritage* <http://www.cornish-mining.org.uk/> [accessed 28 May 2014].
[92] *National Maritime Museum Cornwall* <http://www.nmmc.co.uk> [accessed 28 May 2014].
[93] 'History', *St Ives Society of Artists* <http://www.stisa.co.uk/history/> [accessed 28 May 2014].
[94] 'Artist Gallery', *St Ives Society of Artists* <http://www.stisa.co.uk/artist-gallery/> [accessed 28 May 2014].
[95] Tourist destinations include the Tate St Ives, which displays older work as well as contemporary pieces, and the Barbara Hepworth Museum and Sculpture Garden, celebrating sculptor Barbara Hepworth, who died in 1975.
[96] *Falmouth University* <http://www.falmouth.ac.uk> [accessed 28 May 2014].
[97] 'About Cornwall', *Visit Cornwall* <http://www.visitcornwall.com/about-cornwall> [accessed 28 May 2014].
[98] 'Royal Cornwall Polytechnic Society', *The Royal Cornwall Gazette, Falmouth Packet, Cornish Weekly News, and General Advertiser*, 30 August 1900.

such achievements, as this thesis has demonstrated, was certainly attributable to the town of Falmouth. Also attributable was Collins' final closing lamentation: 'the Cornubian's[99] wider experience of the world had, perhaps, not all been gain. What had been gained in breadth had been partly, at least, lost in depth and intensity. With their many outside sympathies the old clannishness could hardly co-exist. *The Cornishman was more like his outside neighbours*'.[100] While Falmouth had allowed for the expansion of Cornish industry and the creation of a dialogue between it and the outside world – through scientific societies, products, and travel – it had also led to changes in the Cornish identity. Falmouth, and thus Cornwall, had become a part of the British empire, and as Massey would argue, retention of a sense of local place was more difficult.[101] Falmouth's 'stretching-out of social relations'[102] had changed Cornwall forever.

Beyond Falmouth

Throughout this thesis, covering many apparently disparate areas of study – military intelligence, mining, horticulture, and travel – we have seen how the town of Falmouth served as a central linking factor, which in turn fed into a far wider narrative concerned with empire, power and identity. This work offers a unique regional window onto the British empire during a short but busy period of time: the fifty years from 1800-1850. It has explored the many ways in which the empire and the town influenced and impacted upon each other. For these fifty years, Falmouth was a remarkably important location within the British empire; remarkable in the sense that it was so far away from metropolitan centres such as London, and in that it was geographically so small. The thesis has shown how the town handled a vast amount of the empire's mail and communications, both civilian and military, and how its Packet Service played a vital role in the Napoleonic Wars by gathering and transporting intelligence. Ultimately, the British success that they contributed to allowed for a significant expansion of the empire. This work has also shown how a great export of Cornish mining skills and technology to the empire took place, allowing for the creation of new sites of formal and informal empire and expanding

---

[99] Cornubia is an old Latin name for Cornwall.
[100] Emphasis added. Ibid.
[101] Massey, pp. 146-147.
[102] Massey, p. 147.

Britain's control across the globe. As mining technologies travelled out of the country, exotic plant species were travelling inwards. The port of Falmouth functioned as a networking hub and trading centre for these species, which were ultimately used to create a vision of empire at home and reinforce hierarchies of rule among those who might be considered 'white savages'. And finally, it has created a vision of what a bustling, multicultural town Falmouth became due to its colonial ties, and how interaction with other peoples had a real, discernible effect on perceptions of national identity and race.

The effects of Falmouth's role within the empire were felt on a local, national and international scale. A primary focus of this research has been to examine not only how Falmouth functioned within the empire, but also to explore how the empire affected local people. As already outlined in the introduction to this work, this reflects a general trend in colonial studies throughout the last fifteen years towards inward-looking accounts of empire, studying how empire affected the colonisers, rather than solely considering the colonised.[103] While Falmouth's maritime links may have impacted on empire on the global stage, for instance with the export of mining, they also changed the society of the town itself. James Williamson was able to negotiate his way through discourses of race and identity, forming his opinions based on contact with the empire provided through Falmouth. Those at home, such as Caroline and Barclay Fox, also shaped their own ideas of identity around both real and ideological encounters with the foreign. Falmouth, a small and rural location whose main interaction with the British empire ended in the 1850s, is nevertheless important to our understanding of that empire.

As MacKenzie argues in *The empire in one city?*, local histories can be the key to exploring more thoroughly the relationship between Britain and its empire.[104] He argues, as has this thesis, that local studies are a means of creating a wider picture of events.[105] As much as the empire created a global dialogue and an apparent global society, the effects of it would always and unavoidably be felt on a local scale, especially in those places, such as Falmouth, that played a dynamic role within it.

---

[103] For instance, Peers, pp. 452-453, Stockwell, Howe, and Wilson, *A New Imperial History*.
[104] MacKenzie, 'General Editor's Introduction' in *The empire in one city?*, p. ix.
[105] Ibid.

Studying the history of this town enriches our broader understanding of empire and its effects on the inhabitants of Britain. This work serves as a continuation of the projects carried out by writers such as MacKenzie, but extends it through shifting the focus from large towns and cities to smaller rural areas. Perhaps this investigation of Falmouth might serve as a case study for understanding the interplay between the local and global during empire, in order to prompt the same work in relation to other relevant locations. If research into other locations were to be carried out, the combined results would form a stronger image of empire as it related to the British people on a personal, cultural level. Archives across the country might be re-examined to generate an interdisciplinary account in which the people of the empire, at home as well as abroad, speak for themselves, and the global effects of smaller locations are understood more thoroughly.

www.ingramcontent.com/pod-product-compliance
Lightning Source LLC
LaVergne TN
LVHW011935070526
838202LV00054B/4657